JOHN HARVEY
KELLOGG, M.D.

ADVENTIST PIONEER SERIES

George R. Knight, Consulting Editor

Published volumes:
James White: Innovator and Overcomer,
by Gerald Wheeler

Joseph Bates: The Real Founder of Seventh-day Adventism,
by George R. Knight

W. W. Prescott: Forgotten Giant of Adventism's Second Generation,
by Gilbert Valentine

John Harvey Kellogg, M.D.,
by Richard W. Schwarz

To order, call

1-800-765-6955.

Visit us at

www.reviewandherald.com

for information on other Review and Herald® products.

JOHN HARVEY
KELLOGG, M.D.

Pioneering Health Reformer

RICHARD W. SCHWARZ

ſR

REVIEW AND HERALD® PUBLISHING ASSOCIATION
HAGERSTOWN, MD 21741-1119

The Review and Herald Publishing Association publishes biblically-based materials for spiritual, physical, and mental growth and Christian discipleship.

The author assumes full responsibility for the accuracy of all facts and quotations as cited in this book.

This book was
Edited by Gerald Wheeler
Designed by Trent Truman
Electronic makeup by Shirley M. Bolivar
Typeset: 11/14 Berkeley Book

PRINTED IN U.S.A.

10 09 08 07 06   5 4 3 2 1

R&H Cataloging Service
Schwarz, Richard W.
    John Harvey Kellogg, M.D.

    1. Kellogg, John Harvey, 1852-1943.   I. Title.

                        B

ISBN 10: 0-8280-1039-8
ISBN 13: 978-0-8280-1039-2

CONTENTS

CHAPTER   PAGE

Preface 7

Foreword 9

I   The Boy Foreshadows the Man 13

II   A Convert. 20

III   From Teacher to Doctor. 29

IV   A Man Is What He Eats 40

V   Changing American Habits 51

VI   Developing the Battle Creek Sanitarium. 62

VII   Sanitarium Ups and Downs 75

VIII   A Torrent of Words 83

IX   Variations on a Boyhood Dream. 95

X   The Unwilling Surgeon 108

XI   Products of an Active Mind 114

XII   All Work, but Little Play 134

XIII   What Manner of Man. 143

XIV   Father to 42 Children 152

CONTENTS

XV   His Brother's Keeper 162

XVI   The Ties of 50 Years Are Broken 178

XVII   Food Manufacturing and Family Quarrels 196

XVIII   New Outlets for Promoting an Old Program 207

XIX   The Last Battles 217

An Epilogue 228

Index 233

PREFACE

E ACH BOOK has a story behind it. The present one is no exception. This biography of Dr. John Harvey Kellogg really began more than a four decades when I first read Gerald Carson's *Cornflake Crusade.* Although fascinated by Carson's style and wit, I was convinced that he had related only part of the Kellogg story. Fortunately, I had in Dr. E. K. Vande Vere a teacher, colleague, and friend whose knowledge of Seventh-day Adventist history was unparalleled. When the time came to pick a Ph.D. dissertation topic, Dr. Vande Vere's enthusiastic support gave me the courage to try to unravel the Kellogg story.

As with most would-be authors, I soon found out that only the cooperation of a multitude of individuals would make my goal a reality. To name them all would tire the reader. Some, however, went so far beyond the normal call of duty in providing access to pertinent materials that I must express public thanks. In this category fell Miss Gertrude Goodwin, of the Race Betterment Foundation; Arthur White, of the Ellen G. White Estate; Dr. Dunbar Smith, of the Battle Creek Sanitarium; Eugene McKay, of the Battle Creek Food Company; and Mrs. Margaret White Thiele, of the Vernier-Radcliffe Library of Loma Linda University.

Many persons shared their memories of Dr. Kellogg with me in most generous fashion, including two former Kellogg secretaries, August F. Bloese and Roy V. Ashley, as well as Angie and Gertrude Estell, Dr. James R. Jeffrey, Dr. Emil Leffler, Dr. William S. Sadler, and Emil Storkan.

This biography is based almost entirely on the doctoral dissertation that I completed at the University of Michigan in 1964. Readers interested in the documentation for any of the events chronicled or statements made are referred to this dissertation, entitled "John Harvey Kellogg: American Health Reformer." In preparing the original dissertation I owe a heavy debt to Professor Sidney Fine, whose own excellent scholarship led him to hold up high standards for his students. He saved me from many pitfalls in both reasoning and rhetoric.

Finally, I suspect that few married authors would ever bring their books to fruition without the understanding cooperation of a long-suffering wife. At least this was certainly true in my case. The many things that she put up with in order to give me the time necessary for research, thinking, and the pain of writing, only the two of us know. In a very real sense it was Joyce Schwarz's book as well as mine. It is dedicated to her with undying affection.

—RICHARD W. SCHWARZ

FOREWORD

JOHN HARVEY KELLOGG, M.D.: Pioneering Health Reformer, follows Gerald Wheeler's *James White: Innovator and Overcomer* (2003), my own *Joseph Bates: The Real Founder of Seventh-day Adventism* (2004), and Gilbert Valentine's *W. W. Prescott: Forgotten Giant of Adventism's Second Generation* (2005), as the fourth volume in an unprecedented project in Adventist biography. Future volumes are scheduled to present such personalities as G. I. Butler as a tough-minded administrator, Dudley M. Canright as the denominations' most influential heretic, J. N. Andrews as its earliest scholar and first missionary, W. C. White as his mother's assistant and a man at the center of action, Ellen White as a woman in a man's world and Adventism's prophetic voice, Elliot J. Waggoner as a leader in the revival of righteousness by faith, and Alonzo T. Jones as the point man on the church's charismatic frontier. Each biography will focus on the individual's major contribution to the church and will be written by a person well versed in his or her topic.

John Harvey Kellogg is undoubtedly the most well-known Seventh-day Adventist ever. Not only was he larger than life during his 91 years, but people around the world are daily confronted with the Kellogg name and his products under other names as they sit down to breakfast. John Harvey did much to transform not only the Seventh-day Adventist Church but also the larger culture in his work as a pioneering health reformer. While he was not in the earliest rank of American health reformers, Kellogg still performed pioneering work in many areas that still impact the world, including preventative medicine and the development of such dietary innovations as peanut butter and cold breakfast cereals.

Schwarz's treatment of the compact (he was only five feet, four inches tall) ball of energy known to history as John Harvey Kellogg is a fast-moving read that informs not only about the man himself but also about the Seventh-day Adventist Church and the state of medical care and health service in the late nineteenth and early twentieth centuries.

The doctor's relationship with Adventism is best described as ambivalent. For much of his life he stood near the center of Adventist action from his position as chief administrator of the famous Battle Creek Sanitarium. But he spent the last third of his life outside of the church. He had come to the place where he either had to control the denomination or leave it. Meeting his match in the talented and forceful Arthur G. Daniells (president of the General Conference), Kellogg left Adventism in the early years of the twentieth century. His departure from Adventism, however, did not mean abandoning his interest in healthful living. He would remain a health reformer to the end of his days.

The publication of *John Harvey Kellogg, M.D.* is a departure in some ways from other volumes in the Adventist biography series. For one thing, Schwarz's biography lacks footnotes, whereas other volumes have been thoroughly documented. Readers who are interested in the documentation for any fact or quotation will need to go to his unpublished University of Michigan Ph. D. dissertation, entitled "John Harvey Kellogg: American Health Reformer." A second item of note about Schwarz's biography is that it is a reprint of the edition published by Southern Publishing Association in 1970. It has been selected for republication after 36 years because it not only treats the life of an important person, it is still one of the very best biographies ever published by an Adventist press.

John Harvey Kellogg, M.D.: Pioneering Health Reformer is important reading for those who have an interest in Adventist history, in biography, or in nineteenth- and early twentieth-century health reform. I trust that reading this book will be as fascinating and profitable for you as it was for me.

GEORGE R. KNIGHT,
Consulting Editor
Andrews University
December 5, 2005

John Harvey Kellogg, M.D.

CHAPTER I

THE BOY
FORESHADOWS THE MAN

THE LURE OF THE West that Europeans had felt since they first set foot on America's eastern shore infected New Englanders like a fever by the 1830s. For six generations the Kelloggs had resisted it as they developed extensive landholdings in the rich valley of the Connecticut River. But change was in the air. As the seventh son of a father burdened with debt, John Preston Kellogg realistically decided that his future would be brighter hundreds of miles to the west of Hadley, Massachusetts, the family residence for nearly 200 years.

Early one summer morning in 1834, John Preston loaded his wife, Mary, their two small sons, Merritt and Smith, and some household belongings into a wagon and headed for Albany, the eastern terminus of the Erie Canal. The young father had taken a preliminary trip as far west as Chicago, but the marshy area to the west of the lakeshore village had not impressed him. Instead, he headed for Michigan Territory and a small settlement of transplanted New Englanders begun several years earlier by an old Hadley neighbor, Lansing Dickinson. Like thousands of others, the Kelloggs traveled by canal boat from Albany to Buffalo, where they boarded a lake steamer for Detroit. Then they journeyed northwest by wagon for 60 miles or so until they reached the Dickinson farm near the present city of Flint.

With only half a dozen families and a few Indians in the neighborhood, John Kellogg quickly located a likely looking homesite. Soon he filed a claim on 320 acres of government land and established his family in an abandoned one-room log cabin about a mile south of Dickinson's home. In succeeding months he cleared sufficient space for planting patches of wheat, corn, oats, and buckwheat. In typical frontier style the neighbors rallied to help the new family "raise" a barn. The occasion may also have

Stan Hickerson Collection

raised some eyebrows, for instead of providing the hard cider that usually accompanied such events, Mary Kellogg demonstrated the family's temperance leanings by substituting a liberal supply of fresh doughnuts.

Frontier life was not easy. Comforts were rare, and even such necessities as adequate medical care were nonexistent. The latter became painfully evident three years after the move from Massachusetts when Mrs. Kellogg began to have severe coughing spells during which she frequently raised considerable amounts of blood. The doctor summoned from the little village of Flint could only suggest that she inhale the fumes of resin sprinkled over live coals, coupled with periodic "bleeding."

Somewhat later John Kellogg developed a malady that left his eyes so inflamed that for weeks he was nearly blind. When a "fly blister" to the back of the neck that the doctor had originally prescribed succeeded only in raising a "fearful sore," he had his patient dosed with huge amounts of calomel. It caused John's tongue to swell until it protruded from his mouth. Although eventually recovery came in spite of the doctor, the experiences did little to create respect for conventional medicine in the Kellogg household.

Over a four-year period Mary Kellogg's health steadily deteriorated. From time to time John secured Ann Stanley, the teenage daughter of a nearby blacksmith, to help keep the home running. Her manner and personality quickly endeared her to the sick woman. Then, following a severe lung hemorrhage in the fall of 1841, Mary Kellogg died. Shortly before her death she had advised her husband to make every effort to persuade Ann Stanley to come and care for the children for as long as possible, something the young widower almost immediately attempted to do. Eighteen-tear-old Ann, however, had contracted to teach a local school and did not feel that she could accept housekeeping duties as well. John Preston persisted. The following March the young woman joined the Kellogg family, not as housekeeper, but as wife and stepmother.

The new bride soon discovered that financial difficulties plagued the Kellogg home. Several years earlier, John had listened to a neighbor's glowing tale of the easy profits one could reap from investing in a local bank. He allowed the man to persuade him to sign a note for $500 worth of bank stock. Within a year the bank failed, and Kellogg found that as a stockholder he was liable to depositors for their losses. Quickly Ann decided that she must do her part to enable her husband to meet his obligations. She persuaded him to purchase some sheep and a loom. After teaching herself to weave, she supplied the family's clothing needs.

Ann may have also conceived the idea that a change of location would be good for the Kelloggs. The son of a neighbor had developed a 160-acre farm a number of miles to the southwest in Livingston County. Now he wanted to move back near his father. The Kelloggs agreed to trade farms, and nine months after her marriage Ann saw her new family relocated. In rural Tyrone Township the young woman soon demonstrated her vision and energy. She persuaded John to grow red clover rather than timothy for use as hay. The clover improved the quality of the soil, and the sale of its seed helped to retire the family debts. Meanwhile, the family planted apple and peach trees, currant bushes, developed a large vegetable garden, and maintained a flock of more than 100 sheep. Within 10 years the Kelloggs had one of the most prosperous farms in the neighborhood, and Ann donated her loom to a nearby widow so that the poor woman might have a source of income.

Shortly after John Kellogg moved to Michigan, he was converted and an itinerant Baptist preacher publicly immersed him in the Flint River. From then on he regularly conducted family worship in his home. In Tyrone the Kelloggs became charter members of the Hartland Center Congregational Church, in which John was later ordained an elder. To the Kelloggs it seemed only natural that they should demonstrate their religion in practical ways. They became active abolitionists and occasionally helped pass fugitive slaves on toward the Canadian border and freedom. Christian concern led them to donate their best cow to a financially hard-pressed neighboring family. With Ann's hearty approval, John even forgave another neighbor a $250 debt when it became obvious that it would be extremely difficult for the man to repay it. Vulgar language had no place in John Kellogg's conversation, and he consistently refrained from harsh, angry words in correcting his children.

Perhaps it was the family's commitment to temperance, or its unsatisfactory experience with doctors, that led the Kelloggs to subscribe to the *Water Cure Journal* several years after Dr. Joel Shew began its publication. Ann Kellogg had learned to mistrust traditional medical practitioners following the death of Emma, one of her first children. Although the child's difficulty in breathing seemed to indicate that the doctor should do something for her lungs, he insisted that she was suffering from worms and treated her accordingly. When death resulted, Ann demanded that someone perform an autopsy in her presence. It revealed no parasites, but Emma's lungs appeared badly inflamed.

The *Water Cure Journal* advocated a variety of hydropathic treatments for common ills. Shortly after her subscription began, Ann found occasion to try the new methods. One of the boys contracted measles. As soon as the other children began to give evidence of coming down with the disease, their mother wrapped them in the wet-sheet packs the *Water Cure Journal* suggested to bring out the eruptions. When they recovered much more rapidly than the first child, Ann became a firm convert to natural remedies.

The Kelloggs had lived on their Tyrone farm for nearly a decade when one summer morning in 1852, a neighbor, M. E. Cornell, stopped his buggy and climbed over the fence into a field where John was raking hay. Cornell, who had been a believer in the soon return of Jesus Christ since the days of the religious revival known as the Millerite Movement, was returning home from a series of meetings in Jackson. They had featured Joseph Bates, then on his second foray into Michigan to proclaim the distinctive doctrines characterizing the group that would become the Seventh-day Adventist Church. Cornell accepted Bates's teachings concerning the biblical doctrines of the heavenly sanctuary and the seventh-day Sabbath. He may have known that for several years John Kellogg had been dissatisfied with his religious experience, and so, with the fervor of a new convert, Cornell pressed on Kellogg the new Bible teachings that he had just found. John decided to test his neighbor's ideas through a systematic study of the Bible. Later that summer he attended a second series of lectures Bates held in Jackson. He found the messages biblical and, along with Ann and his two oldest sons, eagerly embraced them. Just six months earlier, on February 26, 1852, Ann had given birth to her second son, John Harvey. Thus from his earliest memories the future inventor of flaked cereals found himself in a Seventh-day Adventist environment.

During the year following their acceptance of Adventism, the Kelloggs sold their farm and moved to Jackson. Here they enjoyed the fellowship of a larger group sharing their religious convictions. John Preston, returning to an old family trade, began to make brooms to support his family.

The Kelloggs devoted a substantial portion of the $3,500 they had received from the sale of the farm to promoting their new faith. With three other Michigan Adventists, John advanced $1,200 to move the Review and Herald publishing plant from Rochester, New York, to the little Michigan community of Battle Creek. He also made a substantial contribution toward the purchase of the first tent secured by Adventists for public evangelism in Michigan.

When John Harvey was 4 years old, his parents moved to Battle Creek, already on its way toward becoming Adventist headquarters. The town, founded about 25 years earlier, had about 2,000 inhabitants at this time. In the "West End," where most Adventists lived, John Kellogg established a small store and broom factory and prepared to rear his growing family.

At first little distinguished young Johnny from his brothers and sisters. Although inclined to be smaller and more sickly than the average child, Johnny possessed a strong will and determination. His half-brother Merritt remembered that one day when John was about 4, the child asked to accompany him and his father on a business errand. They granted permission on the condition that the youngster keep up with the adults. "I will keep up," John said, and he dashed off ahead. Suddenly he tripped and fell flat on his stomach. Before the men could reach him, he scrambled to his feet and, fearing that they would send him home, said with a wry smile, "I did that on purpose."

Along with determination, the future doctor also possessed a vivid imagination. On many occasions he regaled his playmates with fantastic stories of near escapes from dangerous animals. It may have been such a tall tale that one day prompted his mother to ask him if he did not know that he was doing wrong.

"Yes," came the reluctant reply.

"Then why do you do it?" Ann inquired.

Quickly came the rejoinder, "Satan made me," and then after a little sober thought, "Mother, I wish God would kill Satan."

Maintaining a large family in the mid-nineteenth century involved plenty of work, and parents required children to do their share. The Kelloggs expected Johnny to keep the woodbox filled, to help prepare breakfast, to care for the cows, and to assist in the manufacture of family necessities such as soap.

One morning when he was about 10, John's parents sent him to drive the cows to water. To encourage them along, he cracked a long rawhide whip at their heels. Spotting a robin on a nearby limb, he decided to see how close he could come to it with his whip without actually hitting it. Unfortunately, he misjudged and the whip's tip struck the bird, killing it. Remorse immediately filled the boy. "I fell upon the ground," he later recalled, "and sobbed and on my knees promised God I would never kill another thing as long as I lived." As a result of the experience, John maintained that he had twinges of conscience even when called upon to swat a mosquito.

Early Seventh-day Adventists believed so strongly in the imminent return of Jesus that formal education for children seemed to many unnecessary. The belief, combined with John's poor health, delayed his first regular schooling until he was 9 years old, at which time he received six weeks of instruction in a school conducted for Adventist children by Fletcher Byington, son of the first General Conference president. It seems likely that either Ann Kellogg or his older brothers had taught John to read before he began attending school. Although he received only several more years of sporadic formal primary education from Professor Goodloe Harper Bell and Miss Theresa French, among others, John quickly became a voracious reader. After exhausting his parents' meager library, John borrowed books from the neighbors. From the first money he earned while working away from home, he used $2.50 to buy a secondhand set of Farr's four-volume *Ancient History*. Soon his private library branched out to include shorthand, botany, and astronomy texts, as well as a German grammar and a dictionary. Words fascinated John Harvey all his life. In later years he frequently carried a vest-pocket dictionary, from which he would read in spare moments.

The Kellogg household had little time for leisure, but John did learn to play the organ, piano, and violin. Throughout his life he liked to gather a group around the piano and relax in a "sing-fest." Other forms of boyhood recreation failed to interest him. He never seemed to enjoy most boys' games, and although his father taught him to play chess, John soon gave it up as a waste of time.

An early childhood experience left an indelible impression on the future doctor's mind. One of his best friends needed some minor surgery.

Adults laid the boy upon the kitchen table, and the doctor went to work while John and several other boys peered curiously through a window. The sight of blood sickened John. Several days later Ann Kellogg chanced to inquire what her son planned to be when he grew up. Immediately the reply came, "Anything except a doctor."

His mother's question set him thinking about his future career. About this time he observed a man following the repetitious movements of a machine, and suddenly the thought struck him, "That man is just like an ox." He immediately determined to avoid any vocation limited to routine acts, but rather to seek out "hard jobs that were worthwhile." Sometime later as he passed his mother's room, John overheard her praying audibly for him. He slipped inside and knelt beside her. Ann placed her hand on his head and dedicated him to God for service. From this experience he resolved to devote his life to helping others.

One morning when he was about 11 John Harvey overheard his father remark that it was nearly time for young John to become self-sustaining. The comment challenged his independent spirit, and he proposed that he would pay for room and board and buy his own clothes if in turn his father would pay him for the work he did. The senior Kellogg accepted the suggestion and arranged that John should work a regular 10-hour shift in the broom factory, sorting the broomcorn. Soon his manual dexterity enabled him to process enough corn to earn as much as $2 for a day's work, a respectable sum for the time. His financial success so bolstered his ego that when some weeks later his father gave him a watch for his birthday, the boy returned it with the remark that he could not accept anything that he had not earned.

About a year after he had begun to work in the broom factory, John sat one noon on the back steps gazing across the field and thinking of his future. Suddenly in his daydreams he saw a road winding to a little schoolhouse on top of a hill. Crowds of ragged, dirty, unkempt children streamed along the road toward the schoolhouse. Then John pictured himself standing in the doorway, beckoning the children to come in. So vivid was the boyhood impression that in later years he found himself scanning the faces of children as they passed to see if he could recognize those in his dream. Determined that his destiny lay in helping children, he began to consider a career in teaching. At 12 he was already too big for the broom shop.

CHAPTER II

A CONVERT

ONE SPRING DAY IN 1864, shortly after the close of the first full school term that John Harvey had the privilege to attend, James White called at the Kellogg home. During the visit White commented on the good reports that he had heard of John's mental abilities. He then invited the 12-year-old lad to learn the printing trade at the Review and Herald, which James White supervised as president of the Seventh-day Adventist Publishing Association. John jumped at the offer, for he saw it as an opportunity to engage in unlimited reading while learning a challenging trade. During the next four years he spent many hours working at the Review and Herald. At first he served as errand and clean-up boy, but later he learned to set type and to read proof. Eventually he even did editorial work on some of the manuscripts submitted for publication.

Young John's years at the Review and Herald proved much more significant than he could possibly realize on that spring day in 1864, for here he received his first full exposure to the health principles he spent his life in promoting.

Some early Adventist leaders such as Bates had conscientiously practiced certain principles of healthful living for years. Since 1848 Ellen White, wife of denominational leader James White, had progressively spoken out against certain unhealthful practices. The Adventists looked to Mrs. White as divinely inspired. They believed that God communicated to them through her. One such example, taking place at Otsego, Michigan, in June, 1863, directed the infant church's attention to the Christian's moral duty to study and observe basic health laws. A variety of reasons prevented Mrs. White from publishing any extensive material on healthful living until volume 4 of her series of books *Spiritual Gifts* came out in August 1864. Volume 4 contained a 32-page article entitled "Health," in which she discussed the relationship of diet and disease, pointed out the dangers of tea, coffee, drugs, and meat eating, and called attention to the importance of cleanliness, sunlight, fresh air, the rational use of water, and the value of willpower in combating poor health.

As soon as Mrs. White began to speak and write extensively on healthful living, many persons commented on the similarity of her teachings to those of earlier health reformers. Ever since the 1820s and '30s many Americans had been promoting a variety of social reforms, most prominently the abolition of slavery, but also new methods of treating the poor, handicapped, insane and criminals, and the advocacy of women's rights, world peace, popular education, and health and temperance reforms. When Ellen White began to get questions concerning the relationship of her health teachings to those of men such as Drs. J. C. Jackson and R. T. Trall, she was naturally curious, but she resolved not to read any health reform writings until she had first written out in detail the principles she had begun presenting at Otsego. When she had finished, she read the works of the earlier reformers and was astonished to note the extent to which the ideas they taught agreed with what God had communicated to her. James White also became interested in the principles of healthful living and began to collect a wide variety of health publications.

Relatively few Americans during the first part of the nineteenth century lived long enough to suffer from the degenerative organic diseases that trouble their descendants today. Tuberculosis, not heart disease, was the chief killer in their generation. They also were more likely to find their life-span endangered by pneumonia, cholera, malaria, yellow fever, typhoid, or what early Midwestern settlers called "the milk sickness," than by cancer. Although not likely to prove fatal, dyspepsia, rheumatism, catarrh, and asthma commonly afflicted people in antebellum times.

When they "felt poorly," more Americans consulted an early "doctor book" such as John Wesley's *Primitive Physic,* or dosed themselves with a favorite herb tea or Indian cure, than called a physician. The more bitter-tasting the home remedy and the more bizarre its components, the more highly it seemed they esteemed it.

As the Kellogg family's experiences had demonstrated, the people had good reason to be suspicious of early nineteenth-century American doctors. A period of apprenticeship under another physician was all the medical education that many doctors could boast of. Such medical schools as existed had virtually no laboratory or library facilities. They required no clinical training, but only attendance at a formal course of lectures. The licensing of physicians had little value, since it was generally entangled with local politics. Although by the 1830s doctors in Paris and Vienna had shown the futility of bleeding and purging and were discontinuing the heavy use of drugs, it took several decades before American physicians generally accepted their ideas.

A wide variety of drugs given in an equally wide variety of dosages represented about the only treatment most early American doctors were prepared to prescribe in times of illness. If one drug did not work, they tried another, and so on until the patient either expired, got better, or decided simply to endure his malady. Medicine had discovered most of the valuable drugs in use through simple trial-and-error methods. Calomel was such a favorite purgative that people spoke of pioneer farmers as living on bread and calomel.

With the medical profession in so poor a state, it is not too surprising that nonmedical people soon began to suggest both causes and correctives for America's physical ills. In 1827 James Hall, a prominent early historian of the West, suggested to the first meeting of the Illinois Antiquarian and Historical Society that pioneer habits were more responsible for poor health than was climate. The frontier population, he maintained, ate too much meat and not enough fresh vegetables, consumed too much hard liquor, and did not exercise sufficient care in treating simple diseases and in avoiding exposure to the elements.

In the more urban seaboard areas of the United States the habits of the average American of 1825 also contributed to poor health. Few persons prior to the great cholera outbreak of 1832-1834 recognized any relationship between filth and disease. The cities and towns had woefully inadequate systems of garbage and sewage disposal, and easily contaminated water systems. The people neglected personal cleanliness. In the East, as in the West, many ate too much that was low in quality and in nutritional value but made palatable by free use of spices and condiments. They consumed large amounts of tea, coffee, and alcoholic beverages. The diet of those having ample means included not only too much food, but too great a proportion of rich sauces and sweets of every variety. When the expected dyspepsia (indigestion) struck, Easterners swallowed large quantities of patent medicines with the same hopefulness displayed by their Western cousins who drank snake bitters and Indian remedies. It was on such a stage that a procession of American health reformers appeared, promising that improved health would be the reward of all who would follow certain basic "natural" rules of living.

Many of the reformers derived their ideas from British sources, such as the eighteenth-century Englishman, Dr. George Cheyne. His book, entitled *The Natural Method of Curing the Diseases of the Body,* stressed such remedies as water, fresh air, sunshine, exercise, and moderation in diet. The Scotch physician Andrew Combe wrote *Principles of Physiology Applied to the Preservation of Health.* Appearing in an American edition in 1834, it made suggestions similar to Cheyne's book. In 1817 a group of vegetarian Christians, led by William Metcalfe, arrived in Philadelphia from Manchester, England. Metcalfe helped organize the American Vegetarian Society in New York City in 1850.

Among the earliest of the local American promoters of natural remedies for disease was a New Hampshire farmer, Samuel Thomson. In the second and third decades of the nineteenth century he developed a wide variety of medicines from native herbs. Soon Thomsonians, or Botanics as people sometimes called them, made up a sizable segment of the American medical profession.

About the same time lecturers began presenting ideas for more healthful living on several American college campuses. In 1830 Edward Hitchcock, professor of chemistry and natural history, delivered a course of lectures at Amherst on the importance of diet, cleanliness, sleep, exercise, and mental attitudes. Hitchcock called for moderate, balanced meals, eaten slowly in a cheerful atmosphere. He cautioned sedentary individuals in particular to limit both the size of their meals and the amount of meat that they consumed, and he considered grains and fruits the most nutritious foods. In addition, he favored abstinence from tobacco, alcoholic beverages, narcotics, tea, coffee, salt pork, bacon, and foods made with large amounts of fat or grease. Professor Reuben D. Mussey promoted a similar health regimen at Dartmouth. He believed that the various bodily functions were closely connected and were all affected by the food a person ate. Mussey also taught that human beings were by nature fruit and vegetable eaters. A vegetarian diet was both superior to one relying heavily on flesh foods, and it helped to make the individual's disposition more mild and gentle.

In May 1830 another recruit joined the ranks of American health reformers when Dr. William Alcott adopted a strict regimen that included a vegetarian diet and excluded all liquids except water. A graduate of Yale University's Medical School, Alcott mixed part-time farming and years of teaching with the practice of medicine. He was one of the first health reformers to publish his ideas widely in printed form. In 1835 Alcott launched *The Moral Reformer,* a monthly journal devoted to the cause of healthful living. He also authored numerous popular books on physiology and hygiene, sex education, and character training. Alcott's major emphasis centered on cleanliness. He favored a daily bath, plenty of fresh air indoors, and the avoidance of tight clothing that restricted deep breathing. The doctor served as the first president of the American Vegetarian Society.

In order to attract substantial public attention in an era of limited communications media, the health reform movement needed an orator. Sylvester Graham, a former Presbyterian preacher and onetime general agent for the Pennsylvania Temperance Society, enthusiastically stepped into the role in the 1830s. At the start of the decade Graham spent several months in an intensive study of physiology and diet. It was probably then that he came into contact with and accepted the dietetic views of William Metcalfe's vegetarian congregation in Philadelphia. Reading the experiences of a fifteenth- and sixteenth-century Italian nobleman, Luigi Cornaro, who believed that he had regained his health by adopting a radical change in diet, also deeply impressed Graham.

As a result of his study, he broadened his former lectures on temperance to include an elaborate theory of diseases, diseases primarily caused by a disturbance of the nerves radiating from the stomach. He decided that diet was the most important factor in the maintenance of good health. Because of the great cholera epidemic of 1832, Graham secured a number of lecture engagements in New York City and won considerable acceptance for his ideas, particularly among other reformers.

During the 1830s he lectured widely throughout New England and the Middle Atlantic States. Gradually he came to modify his call for a moderate, well-masticated vegetarian diet and began to emphasize the importance of cereal foods, particularly bread made from stone-ground, unbolted, whole-wheat or rye flour. Graham's excessive emphasis on cereal foods, his enthusiastic promotion of sexual chastity, his sweeping, dogmatic generalizations, and his violent attacks on all of his opponents, particularly doctors, made him a center of controversy and threatened to bring the whole health-reform movement into disrepute. The staff doctor of a Boston lunatic asylum, after hearing Graham lecture, declared that the reformer was obviously insane.

Although Graham left his name permanently identified with types of flour and crackers, neither his strident lectures nor the more sedate writings of Alcott and Mussey produced wide support for the new health program. The public seemed to be looking for some simple new remedy. Amazingly, they found one right at hand and in endless supply—water. Soon Mrs. Mary Gove and Dr. Joel Shew began advertising its seemingly miraculous powers.

Mrs. Gove, a Quaker, started public lectures on anatomy and physiology for the women of Boston at the end of the 1830s. Although generally a Grahamite in diet, she recommended moderation rather than total abstinence from meat, spices, and condiments. Three years after she began her career as a lecturer, pulmonary tuberculosis struck her. During her recovery she began the use of water treatments and became a convert to hydropathy. Her lectures during the next few years, until her conversion to Catholicism diverted her attention from the health-reform movement, included glowing testimonials to water's curative properties.

Almost simultaneous with Mrs. Gove's adoption of hydropathy, Dr. Joel Shew, of New York City, began publishing and lecturing along similar lines. Shew had learned of the successful water treatments Vincent Priessnitz, an uneducated Silesian peasant, was giving at Graefenburg, Austria. Priessnitz, who had accidentally discovered that cold water would relieve the pain and swelling of swollen muscles, developed a whole system of baths and wet packs. Liberal draughts of water taken internally accompanied his treatments.

Dr. Shew made at least two visits to Graefenburg during the 1840s to observe Priessnitz' techniques. Returning to New York, he adopted a modified version of the Austrian's health program, to which he added friction and massage treatments. He also prescribed a program of rest, exercise, and dietary reform. In January 1846 he launched the *Water Cure Journal,* which within five years had a subscription list of 30,000. A number of health resorts featuring some adaptation of Priessnitz' and Shew's treatments opened during the next few years.

In 1849 the *Water Cure Journal* came under the editorship of Dr. Russell T. Trall, another prominent figure in the crusade to promote healthful living. Like Graham, Dr. Trall entered the health-reform movement from the ranks of the temperance reformers. An early convert to hydropathic methods, Trall blended hydropathy into a unified system of medical practice that included the prescriptions of earlier reformers on diet, fresh air, exercise, and rest.

He promoted the reform movement through both the written and spoken word. After 14 years as editor of the *Water Cure Journal,* he transformed it into the *Herald of Health.* Also he contributed regularly to a number of other short-lived health journals and wrote several books advocating reform ideas. After 1861 he undertook extensive lecture tours for several years, but his tendency to be argumentative limited his effectiveness. He would call for discussion, then deride any ideas advanced that contradicted his own.

One of the ablest mid-century synthesizers of health-reform ideas was Dr. L. B. Coles, of Boston. Coles had practiced medicine for nearly a quarter of a century when in 1848 he brought out his *Philosophy of Health,* a manual that presented simple rules for healthful living in language easily understood by the ordinary reader. Within three years he sold 26,000 copies. In addition to stressing all the major ideas of the earlier reformers, he placed special emphasis on humanity's moral duty to obey the laws governing healthful living. Failure to keep the laws of health he regarded as being as sinful as breaking the Ten Commandments. Dr. Coles also emphasized the relationship between correct habits of dress and health, the value of regularity in eating habits, and the connection between a person's mental state and their physical health. Believing all medicines to be unnatural, he suggested their use only as a last resort. Coles vehemently opposed the use of tobacco or narcotics of any kind.

Possibly the most successful of the "water-cure" institutions that blossomed in the 1850s was "Our Home on the Hillside," operated for nearly 40 years at Dansville, New York, by Dr. James Caleb Jackson. In an atmosphere approaching that of a European health spa, Jackson provided hydropathic treatments and a special diet for as many as 1,000 patients a year. He not only actively promoted health reform, but with his adopted daughter, Dr. Harriet Austin, he also played an important role in the movement for improving women's dress. In the early 1860s Dr. Jackson developed Granula, the first successful cold cereal breakfast food.

Dr. J. C. Jackson's "Our Home on the Hillside," Dansville, New York

Preoccupied with the problems of the Civil War and Reconstruction during the 1860s, Americans proved less responsive than previously to the admonitions of the health reformers. About the same time advances within the regular medical profession in antisepsis, bacteriology, and pathology began to steal the reformers' thunder. Many of their followers now shifted their attention to the gymnastic and physical culture program of Dio Lewis. As old ideas and convictions faded into the background, the collection of reform principles that had developed during a quarter of a century seemed destined to disappear as a distinctive system. At this critical moment Seventh-day Adventists added principles of healthful living to their religious tenets.

After Ellen White had written out all of the basic health principles shown her in the Otsego vision, she, her husband, and several other Adventist leaders spent three weeks observing the methods used at Dr. Jackson's establishment in Dansville. The Whites later arranged for Dr. R. T. Trall to come to Battle Creek to deliver a course of health lectures before the large number of Adventists there. They also decided to bring out a series of six pamphlets devoted entirely to the subject of healthful living. Entitled *Health, or How to Live,* they appeared in 1865. Although each contained an article written by Ellen White, the majority of the material consisted of reprints from the writings of Graham, Coles, Trall, Jackson, Dio Lewis, and others. The next year the Review office also began the publication of the *Health Reformer,* a monthly journal edited by Dr. H. S. Lay and dedicated to popularizing dietetic and sanitary reforms, not only among Adventists, but

James and Ellen White

among the general public.

As an apprentice typesetter, John Kellogg set type for both *Health, or How to Live* and the early issues of the *Health Reformer*. He became intensely interested in these publications and in the health journals the Review received on an exchange basis. In his spare moments he studied the complete works of Graham and Coles, which the Review kept for sale in its office.

Soon John began to put into practice some of the things that he had read. Although the Kellogg family had always served meat at almost every meal, and in spite of the fact that an oxtail, richly browned in the oven, was one of his favorite foods, John decided to become a vegetarian. Previously he had concluded that he was always going to be small of stature, so he now reasoned that the new diet could not hurt him much and might even prove beneficial. He also slept on the floor, with nothing but newspapers for a mattress, during an entire summer to correct a tendency toward round shoulders.

During the same time in which he was learning the printing trade and becoming a convert to health reform principles, John sometimes served as a secretary for denominational leaders. He spent several months writing out sermons dictated to him by blind minister W. H. Littlejohn and in helping him memorize them for future delivery. Sometimes he made trips with James and Ellen White. In addition, he lived for months in their home, helping Pastor White in his writing and editorial work. To the Whites, John became almost another son. In later years Ellen White wrote that her husband had acted more the father to John Kellogg than to his own sons. One day James White confided to John that in vision Ellen White had been shown that he was to fill a definite place in God's service, though just what the role was to be was not specified. But the thought humbled the young man, and his serious mind looked expectantly to the future.

CHAPTER III

FROM TEACHER TO DOCTOR

K ELLOGG HAD NOT FORGOTTEN the idea of a teaching career. In
fact, when he was about 15, John somehow obtained a book by
Margaret Fuller that favorably discussed the methods of learning that the
European pioneer of progressive education, Friedrich Froebel, was advocating for kindergarten children. John wondered if Froebel's methods
really worked. His opportunity to find out soon arrived when his father
suggested that during that summer John use his spare time to teach some
of the younger Kelloggs. The neophyte teacher began with enthusiasm,
even including some neighbor children in the class. He decided to experiment with geography. In the soft dirt of the garden, he drew huge maps
of various parts of the world. With his class in tow he then moved freely
from one country to the next, all of the time vividly describing the various places about which he had read. The experiment fascinated the children, and he found that they later remembered a surprising amount of
what he taught them.

Perhaps to give his aptitude and interest in teaching a real test, John
agreed while still only 16 to teach a district school at Hastings, Michigan.
That winter proved to be a taxing one. The young instructor found that the
school board expected him to instruct 40 pupils on a variety of levels from
first grade through some high school subjects. He had to teach from dawn
until dusk, recesses included, to get everything in. Since he had not finished high school himself, John found it something of a struggle to keep
ahead of the algebra class. As was customary in those days, the teacher
boarded around with various families in the district. In addition to free
room and board, he received $30 a month in pay. Kellogg had little dan-
ger of being lured into teaching through hopes of great financial gain.

Respiratory trouble, possibly a light touch of tuberculosis, interrupted his teaching career. For the next several years, as he was able, he completed his high school course, worked occasionally at the Review and Herald, and sometimes went to surrounding towns and farms to sell brooms from his father's shop. The spring he turned 20 found him well enough to enroll in the teachers' training course at Michigan State Normal College in Ypsilanti. Living on a limited budget, he kept a systematic record of his expenses. He was pleased to discover that with careful planning he could provide an adequate diet of vegetables, nuts, fruits, and graham bread at an average cost of six cents a day. Another encouraging experience occurred when he successfully passed an examination in methods of teaching algebra without taking the class. Practical experience, plus ideas remembered from Margaret Fuller's book read years before, had served him well.

The fall of 1872 found John back in Ypsilanti, but soon a summons to return to Battle Creek for a family council interrupted his studies. For some time denominational leaders, particularly James and Ellen White, had felt concern over the struggling condition of the denomination's Health Reform Institute, then only half a dozen years old. James White had persuaded John Preston Kellogg's oldest son, Merritt, to return from California to help out at the Institute. Merritt soon became convinced that the six-month medical course he had taken five years earlier at Dr. Russell Trall's Hygieo-Therapeutic College was not enough for his needs. As a result, he proposed repeating the course, a not uncommon thing among Trall's students. Believing that several younger Adventists should attend with him, Merritt felt certain that his half-brother, John, possessed just the qualities needed to succeed as a health reform doctor. The Whites concurred and, somewhat against his will, John agreed to accompany Merritt, the two White sons, Edson and Willie, and Jennie Trembley, an editorial assistant on the Health Reformer, to Trall's school in Florence Heights, New Jersey. John had no intentions of practicing medicine, however. He expected to use his training only in the field of health education.

Dr. Trall's medical school had seen its best days by the time the quintet from Battle Creek arrived. Founded in New York City in 1853, the Hygieo-Therapeutic College had moved to New Jersey in 1869 and continued there until Dr. Trall's death in 1877. In earlier years it had enrolled as many as 50 students for a term. The year 1872 saw fewer than 20. Dr. Trall also had a difficult time securing a satisfactory faculty. In addition to himself, he had only three other regular lecturers. On the first day of school, he approached Merritt Kellogg with an offer of an allowance of $10 a week toward the board of the Adventist group if he would give the lectures on anatomy and assist in demonstrations on cadavers. Merritt agreed and thus became teacher as well as student.

Instruction at the Hygieo-Therapeutic College emphasized the curative powers of the internal and external uses of water, a simple diet, proper exercise, and fresh air. The school placed little reliance upon drugs of any kind. John Kellogg attacked his studies with unusual vigor, generally spending six or seven hours each day in poring over his books and notes. Often he did not get to bed until two or three o'clock in the morning. His half-brother reported that he was by far the most diligent student enrolled.

A social hour that preceded the evening study period was a regular feature of life at Trall's school. The students gathered in an old dining room for conversation, stories, group singing, and an occasional dance. John provided the music for the dancing with his violin, but the departure from Adventist standards—Seventh-day Adventists and many other churches disapproved of dancing—appeared to bother his conscience. Merritt, on the other hand, was an enthusiastic participant in what he regarded as necessary exercise. None of them needed to feel conscience-stricken over the food provided. The school supplied graham mush at least once each day, but allowed no meat, sugar, salt, pepper, vinegar, or butter. Fruit was the only dessert served.

Before the winter had ended, John joined his half-brother as a part-time instructor. When the students found that Trall's school would not offer any classes in chemistry, they persuaded the younger Kellogg to give a few lectures on the subject and even purchased some apparatus for him to use in demonstrations. Fortified with one of German chemist Baron justice von Liebig's early works, John apparently did a creditable job. When he began to teach organic chemistry, however, a storm broke. Dr. Trall maintained that no chemical action had any connection with the maintenance of life, but that there was rather something called "vital action." Since John could not agree, relations between the two remained strained for the remainder of the term. In later years Dr. Kellogg minimized the importance of the 20 weeks he had spent at

Florence Heights. He claimed never to have used the unsolicited diploma that Trall mailed him.

It is understandable why John Kellogg de-emphasized the value of his education at Trall's. By the 1870s the six-month medical course, common in the first half of the nineteenth century, was definitely on the way out. With Harvard and the University of Pennsylvania taking the lead, a reorganization of medical training began. The standard course of study in reputable institutions increased to three years, with a minimum session of six months each year. Also, new laws transferred the licensing of physicians from the hands of politicians to boards controlled by members of the profession.

James White, probably more than most Adventist leaders, recognized that in the changing climate of medicine, any attempt to secure a hearing for Adventist health principles would require as a base a sound knowledge of anatomy, physiology, and chemistry. The denomination needed Adventist physicians trained in schools that paid attention to new medical discoveries. With this in mind, White recommended that John continue his medical education at the University of Michigan. His curiosity challenged by the experience at Trall's, young Kellogg readily agreed.

The University Medical School had been operating for nearly a quarter of a century when John Kellogg arrived in Ann Arbor. Although it provided almost no actual hospital experience or clinical observation and only a small amount of laboratory study in chemistry and anatomical dissection, the school had attracted a fairly reputable faculty. John almost immediately felt drawn to Professor Alonzo Palmer, a former Civil War surgeon and one of the founders of the Michigan State Medical Society. Palmer uncompromisingly opposed alcohol and was suspicious of tea and coffee. He also warned his students against heavy reliance on drugs when they could use simple methods such as bathing, regular exercise, and rest. The professor even recommended graham bread as a corrective for constipation. Other instructors, however, ridiculed Sylvester Graham and the idea of a vegetarian diet. But their remarks did not shake John's beliefs.

An amusing incident happened during John's stay at Ann Arbor that casts considerable suspicion on the abilities of some of the medical faculty. Several students reported to one of the professors that they had noted that one of the campus wells had quite a different flavor, and they wondered if water from it might have any medicinal value. In an empirical spirit several of the professors decided to use the water for a time and observe its effects. After a few days one indicated the belief that it had relieved his rheumatism, while another noted improvement in a gastric condition. To their chagrin, they soon learned that a group of campus pranksters had provided the well's peculiar flavor by dumping a variety of old shoes, tin cans, and several dead cats and dogs into it.

To secure a medical degree from the University of Michigan at that time, a student had to attend two series of lectures, each lasting 24

A young John Harvey Kellogg

weeks. Apparently little difference existed between the two series, but the university expected that attendance at the second would increase learning through repetition. Such a program did not fit in with John Kellogg's ideas of education. What undoubtedly did impress him was the repeated agitation by surgery professor Donald Maclean for a wider clinical experience for medical students. He may also have heard Dr. Edward Dunster, who had been associated with Bellevue Hospital while practicing in New York City, describe the wealth of clinical material available to medical students in the nation's largest city. In the spring of 1874 Kellogg left Ann Arbor with no apparent intention of returning to secure his medical degree there.

John spent the summer in Battle Creek, where he put his self-taught shorthand to good use by serving as secretary for the business meetings of the Adventist state conference sessions. James White, who talked with him at great length, encouraged him to continue his medical education at the best school possible. As evidence of their faith in him, the Whites lent John $1,000 to meet expenses. Kellogg soon made a decision. He would go to Bellevue Hospital Medical School in New York, which that year had graduated the largest class of any medical college in America. Although still a relatively young school, Bellevue had a wide reputation for the excellence of its progressive faculty and for its unique combination of clinical and classroom teaching.

Two of the Bellevue faculty especially shaped young Kellogg's professional career—Drs. Austin Flint, Sr., and Edward G. Janeway. Flint, the author of several textbooks, had just completed a term as president of the New York Academy of Medicine and would later serve as president of the American Medical Association. He had studied in Germany, where natural remedies for use in treating the sick had attracted his interest. Contrary to many orthodox physicians, he believed in the free use of water in treating fevers and in using hot packs to alleviate acute rheumatism. Flint first acquainted Kellogg with the extensive experiments of James Currie, a Fellow of the English Royal Society, in using hot and cold water as therapeutic agents.

Dr. Janeway had helped set up the complete hospital record system in use at Bellevue. For years he systematically checked the clinical observations he had recorded about his patients against autopsy findings. As a result he became one of America's foremost diagnosticians. Dr. Flint also earned a reputation for his expert diagnosis. Both doctors agreed to give special instruction to half a dozen students. Each noon they assembled a variety of patients with the most unusual and important medical problems. Under Flint and Janeway's supervision, the students examined the patients and reported upon them. The physicians taught the little class how to use special examining equipment and gave its members much more practice than regular students received. John paid $500, more than twice as much as it cost him for regular tuition, to join the group, but he considered the investment well worth it.

Kellogg profited from other eminent teachers at Bellevue. Professor Edmund Randolph Peaslee lectured in obstetrics and gynecology. He was so much in demand as a teacher that at one time he held lectureships in five medical colleges simultaneously. In the fields of public health and sanitation, Drs. Stephen Smith and Lewis Sayre left their marks on John. Smith first introduced Lister's methods of aseptic surgery at Bellevue and helped found the American Public Health Association. Sayre, an early advocate of compulsory vaccination, had considerable experience from serving as New York City's chief public health official. In that capacity he had been the first American health officer to treat cholera as a contagious disease. At Bellevue John Kellogg began a friendship with Dr. Smith that lasted for 40 years. In later life, Smith frequently visited the Battle Creek Sanitarium that John Harvey directed.

Partly because of a need for economy, and partly because he was already experimenting with his diet, John boarded himself while attending Bellevue. Soon after arriving in New York, he purchased a barrel of apples and another of graham crackers. From then on his regular breakfast consisted of seven crackers and two apples. Occasionally he varied his diet a little by eating oatmeal gruel or a potato baked in the fireplace in his room. Dessert consisted of fresh coconut, consumed at the rate of one per week. With only limited cooking facilities, he found it difficult to prepare cereal grains properly. It frequently occurred to him that it should be possible to purchase cereals at a grocery store in precooked, ready-to-eat form. The germ of an idea that would spawn the multimillion-dollar breakfast food industry had formed in his mind.

John had to spend only one year at Bellevue to qualify for his M.D. degree. He met the requirement that all candidates must present a certificate indicating that they had been studying at least three years under a qualified physician when Dr. O. T. Lines, of Brooklyn, who had been on Trall's faculty the winter the Kellogg brothers had spent at Florence Heights, vouched for John. Also he needed two full courses of medical lectures, but the year spent at Ann Arbor counted for one of them. In addition, he had to pass examinations in the practice of medicine, and in surgery, obstetrics, materia-medica, physiology, anatomy, and chemistry. Each candidate presented an original thesis in their own handwriting.

John entitled his graduation thesis, "What Is Disease?" After first discussing the historical explanations for disease advanced since classical times, he suggested that it was really an attempt by the body to correct some natural function that had become "dearranged." From such a viewpoint, one should consider disease a friend rather than an enemy, but a friend requiring the guidance of a physician, since nature, unable to think, might go too far and damage the body permanently. Kellogg stressed the physician's duty to seek out the cause of a particular disease, of correcting it rather than administering palliatives.

February 25, 1875, was a day to remember for the young man from Battle Creek. On it he received his M.D. during Bellevue's fourteenth Annual Commencement, held in the New York Academy of Music.

Several weeks earlier, he had purchased a new suit for the occasion, only to have it stolen the day prior to the big event. Unable to secure another garment, Kellogg appeared in his worn and frayed school suit. When he advanced to receive his degree, he let the graduate following him crowd close so that the patch on the rear of his trousers might not be too conspicuous. The ceremony, which included music by a full orchestra, impressed the new doctor from rural Michigan. It "duly licensed 193 graduates to make 'regular kills,'" he wrote to an old friend. He also commented that since getting his real sheepskin diploma, he felt "more than 50 lbs. bigger."

Instead of returning immediately to Battle Creek, Dr. Kellogg spent several weeks combing the Astor, Cooper, and Free Medical Libraries for evidence to support the health theories he had already begun promoting in the columns of the *Health Reformer.* He also took private lessons in electrotherapeutics from Dr. George M. Beard, a pioneer researcher in the use of electricity as medical therapy. Quite skeptical of most drugs, Beard believed that much of their value was simply psychological. John observed Beard treat a number of patients with placebos and the stimulus received from the brass knobs of a galvanic battery. Dr. Beard considered his results with electricity every bit as satisfactory as those obtained through the use of traditional pharmaceuticals.

Dr. Kellogg's medical education did not end in the spring of 1875. It would be a continuing process. In 1891 he wrote that he had engaged in more arduous medical study during the preceding three years than during his three years in medical school. Within the first 12 years after graduating from Bellevue, he estimated, he had spent perhaps $3,000 to improve his ability to treat eye, ear, and throat cases. Part of his continuing education took the form of regular reading of medical journals and monographs. Not only did he keep up with all the important American and British publications, but he also subscribed to and read the major French and German medical journals. By 1908 he estimated that he had invested $15,000 in a personal medical library and $50,000 in observation of and instruction by specialists at home and abroad.

Dr. Kellogg's first visit to Europe occurred in 1883. Later he made at least half a dozen more. Although one object of his first trip was to secure help for his wife's recent deafness, he spent the major part of five months in visiting leading medical institutions to observe new medical apparatus and improved medical and surgical methods. In London the doctor observed Dr. J. Mortimer Granville's techniques for the treatment of nervous disorders. Then in Paris he had an opportunity to observe the use of infant incubators for premature babies and the administering of extra oxygen for pulmonary disorders. Here, too, Kellogg attended the annual meeting of the French Société d'Hygiène, which made him an honorary member.

At the time Vienna was probably the world's chief center of medical knowledge. Dr. Kellogg spent an entire month there, following a rigorous schedule from 7:30 a.m. until midnight. A typical day might begin with instruction in throat disorders at the Vienna Polyclinic, followed by an hour of practice at treating patients. Next he might attend a clinic on skin diseases and then observe famed surgeon and cancer specialist Anton Billroth for an hour. Afterward Dr. Kellogg would go to a laboratory to study tubercular bacilli and then to instruction in ear injuries and diseases. Following a light lunch, the doctor frequently assisted Billroth's understudy in surgery, spent more time in the laboratory, studied postmortem reports, and practiced the treatment of eye disorders. During the evening he wrote the day's observations and spent perhaps an hour or so of practice in removing foreign bodies from the throat and ears of an old woman who earned her living serving as a professional "dummy" for medical students. Somewhere during the month, Kellogg also found time to examine the efforts of Dr. Wilhelm Winternitz to place Priessnitz' water treatments on a sound scientific foundation.

Before returning home, Dr. Kellogg visited a number of European "water cures" and also made a side trip to Scandinavia. In Stockholm he investigated the exercise machinery and gymnastic program begun by Dr. Gustaf Zander and T. J. Hartelius, pioneers in exercise therapy. Both men spent hours explaining their ideas and techniques to him.

Dr. Kellogg devoted his subsequent European trips to similar efforts to improve his abilities as a physician and surgeon. In 1907 he even traveled to St. Petersburg to observe the experiments of the Russian psychologist Pavlov. On one European trip he learned of the first experimental work in radium therapy. Shortly thereafter he introduced it in Battle Creek. On another occasion he discovered the electrocardiograph in use in Berlin and immediately had one sent to the Battle Creek Sanitarium, the

Adventist-affiliated medical facility he headed.

In contrast to the tactics of many of the earlier health reformers, Dr. Kellogg did not attack and discredit the medical profession. He set their conversion as his goal, something he could only accomplish if they accepted him as "regular" and in good standing. With this in mind he joined both the Michigan and American Medical Associations shortly after receiving his degree. In 1877 he helped organize a city medical society in Battle Creek. Although in the early part of his career Kellogg's unorthodox views caused many upraised eyebrows among doctors, within 20 years he had won, if not complete acceptance, at least wide respect among his colleagues.

The only professional medical organization that ever officially called Kellogg's ideas into question was the Calhoun County Medical Association. The doctor joined it in the summer of 1877, and the organization soon requested him to present scholarly or professional papers at its meetings. Eight years later, however, Dr. W. J. Fairfield formally lodged charges of unethical conduct against Kellogg, and the county society set up a committee to investigate the matter. Interestingly enough, Fairfield had previously served on Kellogg's staff at the Battle Creek Sanitarium, but the two men had quarreled. Fairfield had then resigned and made an unsuccessful attempt to start a rival institution.

The investigating committee's report proved to be highly critical of John Kellogg. It specifically charged him with violating the American Medical Association code of ethics by advertising his services; with publishing slanderous attacks on the medical profession; teaching disrespect for, and undermining confidence in, physicians; and with perverting the teachings of eminent health authorities through using fragmentary quotations from their works. The report alleged that by citing his professional society memberships in his writing, Dr. Kellogg sought to imply that such organizations approved his views. In view of the report of its committee, the Calhoun society voted that John Kellogg must stand trial before its entire membership.

The trial itself turned out to be an off-again, on-again proceeding stretching through the first six months of 1886. The investigating committee, which handled the prosecution, based its case almost entirely on the books that Kellogg had published and upon his writings in the *Health Reformer*. In defense, John Harvey contended that the Battle Creek

Sanitarium, not he, had done the advertising referred to, and hence the AMA code did not prohibit it. Many of the quotations cited as evidence against him, Kellogg stated, no longer represented his views and so should not be held against him. He also maintained that his membership in the state medical society demonstrated his "regularity" as a physician.

Twelve members of the Association, including Dr. Kellogg, attended the conclusion of the trial. The group decided that each member should cast a secret ballot as to whether or not the charges had been proved. When they counted the ballots, they found that the 12 had divided evenly, so the chairman decided that the body should drop the case against Kellogg. By the slight margin of his own vote, John Harvey had saved himself from an official condemnation that might have jeopardized his later professional career.

The following year some of Dr. Kellogg's critics preferred charges against him before the state medical society, but shortly thereafter they found it expedient to withdraw them. Before long some of the doctors who had sided with Fairfield began referring their difficult surgical cases to Kellogg. Two years after his trial, the organization before which John Kellogg had stood trial unanimously elected him its president.

Dr. Kellogg's stand in favor of high standards in medical education and his consistent opposition to secret medical cures and false remedies undoubtedly reassured many of his colleagues. His leadership in adopting significant diagnostic and therapeutic devices such as X-ray, radium, insulin, and the electrocardiograph could not but help impress them. His early membership in the American Public Health Association, the National Microscopical Congress, and the American Association for the Advancement of Science further evidenced his desire to work in harmony with his profession. On his part, John Harvey saw such memberships as a major avenue through which he might present his particular ideas on healthful living to fellow doctors. The entire 68 years of his professional life really represented a continuous crusade to teach these concepts.

CHAPTER IV

A MAN IS WHAT HE EATS

WHILE STILL A MEDICAL STUDENT at Bellevue, John Harvey Kellogg outlined in the *Health Reformer* the basic principles of healthful living that he would promote all his life. In essence his system, for which he eventually coined the phrase "biologic living," was preventive medicine at its best. It had as its goal to help people stay well, rather than just to recover from illness. Kellogg started with the premise that obedience to the natural laws of health was a moral duty and was essential to the maintenance of mental and moral as well as physical health. Biologic living demanded total abstinence from alcohol, tea, coffee, chocolate, and tobacco since each contained some factor detrimental to the body. It stressed a simple vegetarian diet as most "natural" for human beings and pointed out that one can maintain good health only if they give attention to securing proper rest, exercise, fresh air, and healthful dress. If illness struck, simple remedies were by far the safest and most productive.

Of all the factors necessary to maintain health, Kellogg believed that a proper diet was the most important. He argued that digestive disorders were the most common of human illnesses and that, in the main, an improper diet caused them. The doctor often dramatically proclaimed that a person with a "poisoned stomach" was not perfectly sane, that eating affected the character itself. In view of the central role that he assigned to diet, it is easy to understand why he so vigorously advocated eliminating foods that he considered responsible for "poisoning" the stomach.

No food came under more sustained attack by Dr. Kellogg than meat of any kind. He argued that, contrary to public opinion, its free use lessened rather than promoted physical strength. The doctor believed that eating meat was a major precipitating factor in diseases of the circulatory system and the kidneys, that it encouraged both high blood pressure and anemia, and that it was probably largely responsible for such diseases as cancer, diabetes, and apoplexy. Kellogg warned all who would listen that a meat diet would likely increase such common complaints as headaches, constipation, and dental cavities, and would also delay recovery from tuberculosis, skin disorders, and mental diseases.

To help persuade persons unaffected by fear of the physiological risks of meat-eating, Dr. Kellogg added moral and religious arguments. He contended that the taking of any kind of life tended to brutalize human instincts and, in effect, accustomed human beings to "murder and violence." A careful study of the early chapters of Genesis, he maintained, should convince sincere Christians and Jews that God had not intended originally for humanity to eat meat, but had only allowed its use after the Noachian Flood in order to shorten human life. Also, John Harvey frequently pointed out that when God granted permission to eat meat, He did so on the condition that it be free from blood (Lev.7: 26, 27; 17:14; Deut. 12:16, 23; 15:23). Thus, he would continue, a person should eat no meat until he had washed all the blood out. Since this would greatly alter the meat's flavor, he believed it would then be unpalatable to most people.

If the eating of meat had ever been expedient, Kellogg argued, the increasing incidence of disease in domestic animals meant that it was obviously no longer fit for food. To dramatize his point, the doctor on one occasion sent down to the Post Tavern, Battle Creek's most exclusive restaurant, for a prime beefsteak. He then had a sanitarium bacteriologist subject both the steak and fresh barnyard manure to microscopic examination. The results showed a higher incidence of harmful germs in the steak than in the manure. And Kellogg further demonstrated that even cooking the meat for longer than the normal period did not destroy all the germs.

Dr. Kellogg answering questions for patients at Battle Creek Sanitarium

Shortly after the turn of the century Upton Sinclair

exposed the unsanitary practices of the meat-packing industry in his novel
The Jungle. The agitation for government inspection that followed convinced many people that it would rectify the situation and make meat an
acceptable item of diet.

Dr. Kellogg believed otherwise. At about this time someone called his
attention to a little jingle that the packing industry had begun circulating
in an effort to reassure Americans about their product. Entitled "And He
Ate Meat!" it went something like this:

> "Methuselah ate what he found on his plate,
>   And never, as people do now,
>   Did he note the amounts of the calorie count;
>   He ate it because it was chow.
>
> "He wasn't disturbed as at dinner he sat,
>   Destroying a roast or a pie,
>   To think it was lacking in granular fat,
>   Or a couple of vitamins shy.
>
> "He cheerfully chewed every species of food,
>   Untroubled by worries or fears,
>   Lest his health might be hurt by some fancy dessert,
>   And he lived over nine hundred years!"

John Kellogg could not allow such misrepresentation to go unan-
swered. Since childhood he had enjoyed writing bits of poetry. Now he
dashed off a reply which, if not designed to ensure his inclusion in literature anthologies, nevertheless helped to correct the false impressions the
meat-packers had intended to leave in American minds. Entitling his com-
position "Methuselah's Meat," Kellogg wrote:

> "What Methuselah ate
>   Was not on a plate,
> For plates were not yet invented.
>   Being discreet,
>   He ate Paradise meat,
> And thus old age prevented.

For Paradise meat
Was delicious to eat,
And kept him in finest condition.
And 'twas hung on trees,
And not made to please
The deadly Live Stock Commission.
No fish was he fed,
No blood did he shed,
And he knew when he had eaten enough.
And so it is plain
He'd no cause to complain
Of steaks that were measly or tough.

"Or bearded beef grimy,
Green, moldy, and slimy,
Of cold-storage turkeys and putrid beefsteaks,
With millions of colon germs,
Hams full of trichina worms,
And sausages writhing with rheumatiz-aches.
Old Methuselah dined
On ambrosia and wined
On crystal pure water from heaven-filled springs.
Flesh foods he eschewed,
Because, being shrewd,
He chose Paradise fare and not packing-house things.
The herb-borne seed
And the tree-borne fruit
Were the foods given homo sapiens to eat.
Not eaters but eatables,
Not creatures but vegetables,
Wise old Methuselah chose for his meat."

Kellogg and the meat-packers locked horns several times over the latter's promotion of meat as a chief ingredient in the American diet. Some years later the packing industry arranged for the U.S. Department of Agriculture to prepare a large poster portraying meat as a highly desirable food and urging its wider consumption. Copies of the poster went to every post office for public display. Furious, Kellogg immediately protested what he considered to be a gross misuse of taxpayers' money. At his own expense he had a large number of the objectionable posters printed with the addition of a large note at the bottom, "See the other side." The back listed meats that he had subjected to microscopic examination in the sanitarium laboratories, together with the number of colon germs per gram observed in each. He also gave similar figures for barnyard manure, which he found to contain fewer of the germs than several kinds of meat. (The variable factors involved make it difficult to evaluate his experiment's validity.)

Now the meat industry found it their turn to be furious. They immediately lodged a complaint with the Federal Trade Commission in Washington urging that it obtain an injunction that would prohibit Dr. Kellogg from circulating his revised posters. A government attorney went to Battle Creek to investigate. He found Dr. Kellogg not at all adverse to a public hearing that would provide a perfect forum for continuing his attacks on meat as a food. After the doctor had gone over some of the evidence he would introduce in such a hearing, the attorney decided to drop the matter. Several weeks later, Kellogg chanced to meet him in a Chicago hotel lobby. "You know, Doctor," the lawyer said, "I haven't tasted meat since I saw you in Battle Creek!"

Meat was not the only food that Dr. Kellogg believed human beings should exclude from their diet. For many years he favored a complete ban on cheese. Before the pasteurization of dairy products became common, the doctor could rightfully claim that cheese contained many harmful germs. At one Adventist camp meeting, Kellogg demonstrated his disapproval of this food item by purchasing all the cheese available in the provisions tent and ceremoniously burying it. In later years he grudgingly accepted freshly made cheese as preferable to meat as a source of protein, and he became rather enthusiastic about cottage and cream cheeses.

Milk and eggs were two other foods that Kellogg long regarded with suspicion. For many years he excluded milk from his personal diet. Gradually he altered his views, however, and in 1917 he told the National Milk Congress that milk was "the choicest product of nature's laboratory." No other food product could compare with it. For years he regarded clean raw milk secured from healthy cows as superior to pasteurized because he believed the process destroyed essential natural qualities. No dairy product stirred Kellogg's enthusiasm more than yogurt. Convinced that it largely explained the longer life expectancy of the Bulgarian people, the doctor was one of the first persons in the United States to promote its use.

During his entire lifetime, Kellogg remained unenthusiastic about eggs as food. He favored their use only to supplement a diet lacking in protein, vitamins, iron, and lime. If people did eat eggs, the doctor insisted that they should take care to make sure that the eggs were fresh and well cooked.

Dr. Kellogg regarded an excessive use of sweet foods as potentially more dangerous to health than a diet that included some meat. He believed that Americans with their love of candy and sweet desserts should bring it under rigid control. The doctor objected particularly to cane sugar, since he believed that it interfered with proper digestion. Although he did not favor the total elimination of sugar from the diet, Kellogg advocated drastically reducing the amount in general use and substituting where possible such natural sweets as honey, dates, and raisins. John Harvey put salt in much the same category as he did sugar—as an unnatural addition to the human diet that, however, one could use in small quantities without bodily harm. He held that natural foods contained enough salt to meet normal body needs.

Condiments such as mustard, pepper, vinegar, cinnamon, ginger, and other spices, and foods such as pickles came under the Kellogg ban. The doctor thought that condiments stimulated the stomach's activity, while at the same time inhibiting the proper secretion of gastric juices. He frequently said that a good rule to remember was that foods which were "hot" when they were cold were not fit to eat. Since foods served extremely hot or cold in temperature would also probably interfere with digestion, he advised against their use. He favored simple meals that included a modest variety of foods accompanied by little or no liquids.

Although always referred to as a vegetarian, for many years Dr. Kellogg had little interest in making vegetables other than legumes a major part of the diet. He originally opposed the use of any that grew underground, since they did not get the benefits of direct sunlight on their edible portions. In later years he reversed his ideas and actively promoted potatoes, becoming convinced that the higher alkali content of root vegetables made them better food than most grains. Kellogg always opposed rhubarb and spinach because of their high oxalic acid content. Although the doctor originally saw little benefit in eating raw vegetables, he also modified his views on this point and came to believe that a person should eat some raw food each day.

Frequently he observed that he did not favor excluding anything from the human diet that rightfully belonged there. Humanity's natural diet, he maintained, was a combination of grains, fruits, and nuts, and he advanced many arguments in support of it. To the religious, he would refer to the early chapters of Genesis, in which the Creator provided the first human beings with a diet of fruits and seeds. If he were speaking to the nonreligious or more secular, especially those inclined to accept the Darwinist view of the human race's origin, Kellogg would stress the similarity between the digestive tract of the great apes and that of human beings. Gorillas, orangutans, and the other higher primates, he pointed out, were all natural vegetarians. Dr. Kellogg also advanced an economic argument in favor of a vegetarian diet. He pointed out that it took 100 pounds of grain to produce three pounds of beefsteak—grain that could just as well have been used as food.

Sylvester Graham, whose writings Kellogg frequently quoted, would undoubtedly have approved the doctor's emphasis on the importance of cereal grains in the diet. John Harvey insisted that the homemaker should utilize the whole seed of the grain—the rough hull and germ element as well as the more starchy bulk. He favored bread made from whole-wheat or graham flour only. His interest in grains as food prompted his later development of numerous breakfast cereals. Although he sometimes seemed to show a preference for wheat and rice as opposed to other grains, most of the time he advocated using a wide variety, since no one grain contains all the nutrients necessary for good health. Kellogg also promoted several seeds closely akin to the cereal grains, particularly sesame and psyllium, being probably the first to introduce the latter into the United States.

Fruit occupied a special place in the array of foods Dr. Kellogg recommended. People should consider having a variety of fruits in the home, be believed, as essential rather than a luxury. He maintained that well-ripened fruits were among the most nutritious and the most easily digested of foods. To his associates and patients he freely passed out apples, oranges, pears, and bananas. Fruits made up a major part of his personal diet. While traveling he often ate little more than bread and apples.

When considered pound for pound, Kellogg taught, nuts were the most nutritious food. He lamented that their limited supply kept them from occupying more than a minor place in the average diet and predicted that this would change in the future as people better understood the high quality of the protein they contained. The common belief that nuts were hard to digest he blamed on two things: the tendency to eat them at the end of a too-abundant meal, and the failure to masticate them thoroughly enough. Advocating wider cultivation of nuts, he at one time recommended enacting a law that would require the planting of a nut tree for every tree of another variety that someone cut down. On another occasion he suggested that if the nation lined all of its rural roads with a variety of nut trees, they would eventually provide as much food each year as the country could obtain from 20 million steers. Although the doctor ranked almonds as the "royalty" of the nut line, he also recommended pecans, walnuts, and chestnuts.

One of the major objections medical and nutritional experts raised against the type of diet Kellogg recommended was that it did not provide sufficient protein—the element the body uses to build and keep its tissues in repair. Meat, dairy products, and eggs have traditionally been the richest and most widely used sources of protein in the American diet. Kellogg's rejection of the usual protein sources forced him to find satisfactory substitutes. As part of his answer he recommended legumes, a category in which he included peanuts, both green and dried peas and beans, and soybeans. For easier digestibility, Kellogg advised everyone to boil rather than roast peanuts. One of the first Americans to recognize the potential of the soybean as a food, he pointed to its long history in the diet of many Orientals and stressed the high quality of its protein, the easy digestibility of its fat content, and the fact that it contained all the known vitamins with the exception of vitamin C.

Dr. Kellogg launched a counterattack against his critics by insisting that average Americans ate much more protein than they needed, something not only wasteful, but possibly harmful. Early twentieth-century

Stan Hickerson Collection

A cooking school at Battle Creek Sanitarium

physiologists did not agree on the amount of protein an individual should consume daily. Their estimates varied from one third of a gram of protein for each pound of body weight to more than a gram. Kellogg sided with individuals such as Professors R. H. Chittenden, of Yale, and H. C. Sherman, of Columbia University, who supported the smaller amount. Heavy consumption of protein, John Harvey maintained, placed too great a strain on the kidneys and liver, increased the growth of toxins in the intestines, and might contribute to an increase in dental cavities. On the other hand, he claimed that a low-protein diet increased resistance to disease, led to greater longevity, and contributed to greater physical and mental endurance. He believed that vegetarians careful enough to include two ounces of nuts or soybeans and either an egg or a half pint of milk in their daily diet would get sufficient protein for their needs.

Not only did Kellogg argue that most Americans ate too much protein, but also that they ate too much food in general. He held it to be both harmful to the individual and wasteful of the world's food resources. Intemperance in eating he considered responsible for a greater amount of evil than intemperance in drink. He believed, in fact, that overeating was a prime cause of alcoholism.

Excessive eating, according to the doctor, resulted in imperfect digestion, which in turn often caused permanent damage to the stomach.
Obesity, another consequence of overeating, came under a Kellogg warning. He pointed out that obese persons placed extra strain on their livers,
kidneys, and circulatory systems, making them vulnerable to chronic disorders. Overweight people should take themselves firmly in hand and
rigidly limit their daily caloric intake to one half of its previous amount.
They should eat mainly bulky, laxative foods, especially fresh green vegetables, and give up all sweets. Such a program, coupled with increased
exercise and sweat baths, John Harvey believed, would bring a person
back to their normal weight.

For years Kellogg advocated the consumption of only two meals a
day, with an interval of at least six or seven hours between the two. In
later years he placed less emphasis upon the number of daily meals, but
he continued to regard two as sufficient for most sedentary individuals.
For those who felt that they must eat three meals a day, the doctor recommended that they take the heaviest meal at noon and the lightest one
in the evening, since an overly full stomach interfered with restful sleep.
He also advised regular times for meals and that they never be taken late
at night or when a person was mentally or physically exhausted. Kellogg
believed firmly in a complete ban on eating between meals.

During the first decade of the twentieth century, life insurance companies shocked Horace Fletcher, a notorious gourmet, into assessing his physical condition when they refused him additional coverage as a poor risk.
Considering how he might improve his physical condition, it occurred to
him that thorough chewing might prove helpful. He began to masticate all
food until reduced to a smooth paste. Soon he lost his fondness for meat
and wine and found himself eating less than formerly. His health improved
to the extent that he found it possible to purchase all the life insurance he
wanted. Convinced that he had discovered in thorough chewing the answer
to most of humanity's physical ills, Fletcher launched a campaign to encourage Americans to masticate their food more thoroughly.

Dr. Kellogg had preceded Fletcher by a number of years in stressing
the relationship between chewing and health. Early in his medical career
he began treating dyspepsia by requiring his patients to begin each meal
by eating some hard, dry food such as zwieback or hard toast. Such food

products required more thorough mastication than other foods, and by introducing them at the start of the meal, Kellogg hoped to establish a chewing pattern that the patient would continue. Hard foods also stimulated the flow of saliva in the mouth, aiding in the proper conversion of food starches into malt sugars. The doctor had also discovered, as did Fletcher, that prolonged chewing induced a feeling of satiety earlier in the meal, helping to prevent overeating.

In the course of his crusade Fletcher visited Battle Creek, where he received Dr. Kellogg's enthusiastic encouragement. Kellogg noted that Fletcher had found that thorough mastication reduced the appeal of meat and condiments, two things the Battle Creek physician had long campaigned against.

One day when Fletcher was leaving after a visit to Battle Creek Sanitarium, he chanced to remark that he would consider his life a success if only he could attach his name to thorough mastication in the way in which Pasteur's had become connected with the purification of milk. Dr. Kellogg remarked that such a thing should not be too difficult to arrange. He would write an article on fletcherizing for his *Good Health* magazine. Since F. W. Funk, editor of Funk and Wagnall's *Dictionary,* regularly read *Good Health,* he would pick up the term and include it in the next edition of his dictionary. Much to Fletcher's gratification, John Harvey's plan worked out just as the doctor had predicted.

As time passed, however, the extremes to which Fletcher carried his doctrines increasingly embarrassed Dr. Kellogg. When Fletcher proposed that any food that could not be completely liquefied in the mouth was indigestible and should be discarded, the doctor definitely objected. He tried to convince the former gourmet that such a program would not provide adequate bulk for good digestion. Fletcher refused to be convinced and, in fact, came to make proper chewing almost a magic prescription for better health. John Kellogg could never accept such an approach. Biologic living included more than thorough mastication—it even represented much more than a proper diet. How much more, the next chapter will consider.

CHΛPTER V

CHANGING AMERICAN HABITS

FREQUENTLY DR. KELLOGG'S enthusiastic promotion of a particular aspect of healthful living led to accusations that he was a fanatic who believed that one simple remedy would cure all humanity's physical ills. He vigorously denied the charge with the picturesque reply that to use only a single natural agent to combat ill health would be like "trying to raise a great building with one jackscrew." Biologic living was really an integrated system that involved many components. It included proper diet, but also much more.

Although he did not regard water as the panacea for all ills as several of the earlier reformers seem to have done, John Harvey Kellogg did believe that it had an important use in a number of situations. Where earlier proponents of hydropathy had developed most of their treatments on a trial-and-error basis, Kellogg insisted on trying to establish the basic physiological changes the water induced at different temperatures. Eventually he developed a wide variety of baths, packs, and fomentations classified roughly according to the temperature of the water employed: cold, hot, or neutral (at body temperature).

In situations where the physician needed to lower body temperature or slow down vital functions, John Harvey recommended prolonged cold-water treatments. A cold-water spray or bath of short duration would produce a stimulant or tonic effect, since the cold initially increased blood circulation and caused deeper respiration. Kellogg recommended taking a brief cold bath or shower upon arising each morning, followed by a brisk rubdown with a rough towel. He regarded it as one of the best possible treatments for keeping the body in good condition and for building up resistance to colds.

On the other hand, Kellogg found that hot water treatments stimulated the body's vital functions and elevated its temperature. Depending upon an individual's state of health, their prolonged use might prove either invigorating or exhausting. Hot packs relaxed strained muscles and increased perspiration. The doctor discovered that he could achieve perhaps the best tonic through the alternate use of hot and cold water treatments.

Early in his career, John Kellogg learned that water could help relax a patient. Once he had to treat a large, powerfully built man, who weighed more than 200 pounds and stood more than six feet tall. The restless patient suffered from delirium tremens. After several unsuccessful attempts by Kellogg and a nurse to restrain the man through wrapping him in a sheet, the doctor decided to wet the sheet, hoping to make it more difficult for the patient to remove. Almost immediately the man became quieter. Soon he fell into a restful sleep. Kellogg used a wet sheet pack on many subsequent occasions with excellent results. He also found that a neutral bath combated insomnia. When the patient took care to avoid becoming chilled or stimulated by brisk rubbing after such a bath, the desired sleep almost invariably resulted.

One morning a young associate, whom Dr. Kellogg had just aided in securing his medical degree, approached John Harvey with a request for several weeks' vacation. Kellogg consented, but indicated that he first wanted the young man to carry out an assignment at Kankakee, Illinois. The superintendent of the state mental hospital there had recently requested that someone come from Battle Creek to instruct his nurses in the art of massage. The assignment rather startled the young doctor as he expected to get married and use the vacation as a honeymoon. Kellogg offered his congratulations when the new physician explained his plans, and then suggested that an insane asylum would certainly be a novel place for a honeymoon.

When the bride-to-be unexpectedly proved willing, the young couple took off for Kankakee. In parting, Dr. Kellogg advised them to attempt to find a way to demonstrate the relaxing influences of the neutral bath, as he believed it would prove useful in treating violent patients. Shortly after arriving at the mental hospital, the staff physicians invited the young Battle Creek physician to lunch with them. During the luncheon they discussed the case of one woman who had been violent for a number of days. Her attending physician reported that he had tried one drug after another without success. Only chloroform would quiet the patient, and the doctor had to administer it in such large amounts that he feared it might prove fatal.

Sensing a golden opportunity, Dr. Kellogg's associate confidently remarked, "I can put that woman to sleep without the use of any drug." Raucous laughter greeted his statement, but feeling the new doctor needed a lesson, the staff agreed to let him try. The young man ordered a neutral bath with the temperature of the water being constantly kept within the range of 92 to 96 degrees. Gradually the patient's shrieks diminished until she eventually fell into a sound sleep. The astonished doctors tried the neutral bath on similar patients, and their results soon convinced them that it indeed was a useful therapy. Sometime afterward the hospital superintendent read a paper on its use before a meeting of his colleagues from other institutions. Before long the neutral bath saw wide use in all parts of the country for treating mental patients.

When Dr. Kellogg began to practice medicine, most Americans considered the Saturday-night bath to be quite sufficient. Diplomatically, Kellogg suggested that a daily bath was really the most efficient of cosmetics. He pointed out that the body excreted a large amount of its waste products in perspiration, and if frequent bathing did not remove the poisons, susceptibility to skin disorders would naturally increase.

Some of the early advocates of hydropathy required their patients to drink as many as 40 glasses of water a day. Dr. Kellogg never went to such extremes. He believed that the amount of water a person needed to drink each day varied with their occupation, physical exertion, and diet. Those who perspired freely should drink more, while those who ate heavily of fruits required less. In general, John Harvey believed that a person's thirst reliably indicated the amount of water needed. But since he assumed that one of the reasons for drinking water was to provide the body with an internal bath, the doctor was unwilling to trust thirst alone. At least once a week, he asserted, an individual should make a conscious effort to drink a glass of water each hour in order to help flush out the system. The purity of drinking water always concerned Kellogg. He constantly warned against the danger of contaminating water through careless location of wells too close to barns, outhouses, or garbage dumps.

Nearly a century before the *Reader's Digest* gave wide publicity to the

U.S. Air Force's exercise program called Aerobics, Dr. Kellogg made the same claims about the therapeutic values of exercise. He promoted a systematic program of daily exercise carried on vigorously enough to induce free perspiration and long enough to produce fatigue. Like the Air Force doctors in the 1960's, John Harvey asserted that such a program would improve blood circulation, strengthen the heart, and induce deeper respiration. In addition, he saw his program as a valuable aid to digestion, the control of obesity, and as a tonic for the mind and nervous system. Again as in the Aerobics system, Kellogg suggested walking, cycling, and swimming as the most satisfying types of exercise.

Recognizing that many persons either could not or would not engage in natural exercises for a sufficient length of time each day, he became increasingly interested in mechanical exercisers and gymnastics. Throughout his career, Kellogg adapted and developed a wide variety of mechanical exercisers for use at the Battle Creek Sanitarium. He also created several series of gymnastic exercises designed both to promote general health and to correct specific physiological problems. Early in the 1920s, the Columbia Gramaphone Company produced a set of recorded physical fitness exercises that John had prepared. During the lengthy process of determining the exact number of each exercise to be prescribed, Dr. Kellogg exhausted his secretary, who performed the routines as his boss counted them out. Observing the difficulty, the doctor reversed the roles. He kept up a good pace for the remainder of the session, even though he was then 70 years old.

Dr. Kellogg was adept at presenting his ideas on healthful living with a dramatic flair not easily forgotten. At the age of 37, Yale economist Irving Fisher consulted the Battle Creek doctor in an attempt to find a remedy for the chronic exhaustion that had plagued him for several years. Hardly

Swedish treatment room, Battle Creek Sanitarium, circa 1900

had Fisher completed describing his problem before Dr. Kellogg said, "I think I can tell you at least one of the chief causes for your feebleness."

Professor Fisher expressed astonishment that the doctor would offer a snap diagnosis without even the benefit of a physical examination. "You haven't even felt my pulse or looked at my tongue," he exclaimed.

Unperturbed by the remark, Kellogg repeated that he could identify the chief cause of Professor Fisher's trouble. "It is because," he said, "you have a wrinkle in your stomach!"

Not knowing whether he was facing a prankster or being made the object of ridicule, Fisher retorted, "You can't see through my clothing. How dare you make such a reckless statement? Anyway, it isn't true. I have no such wrinkle!"

When Kellogg persisted, Mr. Fisher decided to prove him wrong. He loosened his clothing and to his amazement discovered a deep wrinkle running across his entire body just below his bottom rib. How had Dr. Kellogg known about it? The physician explained that he had observed a crease in Professor Fisher's vest that did not disappear even when he stood up. From it the doctor deduced that Fisher habitually sat in a slumped position, violating one of John Harvey's basic rules for good health: the maintenance of correct posture.

Although Dr. Kellogg did not discount the possible damage to the chest and spine because of incorrect posture, the effect on the stomach, intestines, and other internal organs chiefly concerned him. He theorized that when they dropped below their normal position, the major blood vessels of the abdomen became dilated and an unusual amount of blood tended to stagnate in the abdominal cavity, depriving the brain and muscles of needed blood and causing mental and physical exhaustion. Kellogg convinced Professor Fisher that incorrect posture was a major part of his problem and prescribed corrective exercises and a vegetarian diet. Within months the professor's condition improved markedly. He became a firm convert to biologic living and a lifelong friend of Dr. Kellogg's.

Convinced that posture problems were traceable to bad habits begun in youth, particularly in the schoolroom, Kellogg believed that teachers should make it their constant business to correct poor sitting or walking posture in their students. He frequently stopped sanitarium employees as well as patients to lecture them on their posture and to show them how

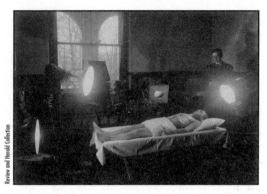

Light therapy, Battle Creek Sanitarium

he thought they should sit, walk, and stand.

Occasionally some of Kellogg's associates expressed the belief that he failed to place sufficient emphasis on the human body's need for adequate sleep and rest. John Harvey certainly recognized the necessity for sufficient sleep to restore both physical and mental energy. He always had too much to do, however, so that he frequently failed to live up to the ideal. This may have made him a little more reluctant to dramatize the point, lest someone rebuke him for not practicing what he preached. Most people, Dr. Kellogg knew, required at least eight hours of sleep each night. Some might need more and even profit from a brief midday nap. He maintained that a person could only secure the maximum benefits from sleep in a quiet, well-ventilated room, equipped with light but warm bedclothes and a thin, firm pillow. The individual should also have a fairly empty stomach and have had sufficient exercise to induce muscular fatigue.

Considering an adequate supply of sunlight as important as proper food and pure water, John Harvey began prescribing sunbaths for patients during his earliest years of medical practice. He suggested that, at first, they expose only a small amount of the body to direct sunlight for a short period of time. Gradually they could increase both the amount of skin area and the time of exposure. At the start of the twentieth century Dr. Kellogg predicted that soon the public would so widely recognize the value of sunlight that newly constructed houses would make a much larger use of glass to permit the sun's rays free entry. Since windows would not help in areas where the weather was cloudy much of the time, he suggested extensive use of electric arc lights for artificial sunbaths. He introduced such equipment at the Battle Creek Sanitarium in 1891, firmly convinced that regular use of electric light baths increased a person's resistance to colds, influenza, and other respiratory diseases.

Part of Dr. Kellogg's purpose in getting people out into the sunshine was to expose them to plenty of fresh air. The average city dweller got too little of it, and he postulated that its lack was a basic cause of many chronic diseases. John Harvey believed in rural living, but he realized that many persons had no choice about dwelling in the city. As a result, he urged them to spend as much time as possible out of doors and also to learn to ventilate their homes properly. According to the doctor, winter was one of the best times to be outdoors. Cold air, he claimed, had a tonic effect resulting from the natural tendency to breathe more deeply in cold weather, thus providing the body with a larger supply of oxygen.

The time would come, Kellogg concluded, when all new homes would automatically provide a continuous supply of fresh air. (Today's air-conditioned homes would surely have pleased him.) Until then, however, the doctor insisted that all intelligent persons should study proper ventilating techniques. He favored warming and humidifying fresh air during its introduction into a building in winter. Rooms should stay at a relatively cool 70-degree maximum temperature.

Almost all aspects of Kellogg's biologic living appear in one form or another in the teachings of earlier health reformers and in the writings of Ellen White. In the area he termed "colon hygiene," however, the doctor developed a distinctive tenet that he actively promoted during his later years. During the first decade of the twentieth century he became fascinated with the ideas being advocated at the Pasteur Institute in Paris by the famous émigré Russian chemist, Elie Metchnikoff. Metchnikoff theorized that the body absorbed toxic waste products from decomposing food residues in the lower intestine. Labeling the process "autointoxication," he declared that the body was literally poisoning itself. That many people did not understand the term "autointoxication" Dr. Kellogg demonstrated when he suggested that William Jennings Bryan might be suffering from the malady. The silver-tongued orator innocently replied, "Is that something one gets from driving too rapidly in an automobile?"

For several years Metchnikoff's theory won wide acceptance in medical circles. In England the famous surgeon Sir Arbuthnot Lane, an old friend of Kellogg's, developed a special operation in which he endeavored to cure autointoxication by removing a large section of the offending colon. Kellogg, too, first tried surgery as a remedy, but he soon became convinced that a reformed diet and the cultivation of "natural" bowel habits provided the problem's real solution.

On the basis of extensive correspondence with missionaries working among primitive tribes and from observing the habits of the great apes, John Harvey became convinced that a bowel movement following each meal was nature's way of removing poisonous decay matter from the intestinal tract before it could cause harm. Kellogg believed that the inhibitions of civilization had destroyed humanity's natural habit, and that now Americans must train themselves to evacuate the colon at least three times a day and preferably upon arising and before retiring as well.

Long after the vast majority of the medical profession had satisfied themselves that Metchnikoff's theories were wrong, Dr. Kellogg continued to regard the retention of food residues in the colon as a chief source of chronic disease, malignancy, senility, and a host of minor ills running the gamut from headache to dental decay. Vigorously opposing the use of laxatives, he argued that proper diet and habit would normally encourage elimination. If a person did need some stimulus, it should be of the natural type, such as increasing the intake of bran, leafy vegetables, and water.

Metchnikoff originally theorized that one could combat autointoxication by introducing a new strain of bacteria into the intestinal tract. To do so, he advocated eating yogurt, and for several years Kellogg enthusiastically followed his example. Although John Harvey subsequently altered his reliance upon yogurt alone, he continued to believe that the type of bacteria present in the intestinal tract had a vital importance in preventing the absorption of food residue poisons in the colon. Relying heavily upon the research of the French bacteriologist Tissier, Kellogg taught that nature started infants off with a liberal supply of helpful bacteria in the colon, but that through a wrong diet harmful strains largely replaced them. It then became necessary to "change the intestinal flora" by encouraging the free growth of acidophilus bacteria, a task he recommended accomplishing through special fruit and milk diets accompanied by substantial amounts of lactose and dextrin.

At the beginning of his medical career, John Kellogg took a firm stand against the free use of drugs in treating illness. Throughout his lifetime he remained skeptical of all but the simplest antiseptics and disinfectants. The drugs in use in the late nineteenth century, of course, differed widely from today's antibiotics, and Kellogg was not far wrong in regarding the medications available to him as falling into two major categories: stimulants and pain-killers. He believed it wrong to look upon pain as an enemy—one should consider it a divine warning to the sufferer to stop violating the natural laws of health. Hence the doctor opposed the use of even simple remedies such as aspirin on the grounds that their effects kept sufferers from discovering and correcting the true cause of their illnesses.

Kellogg's position on vaccination was similar to his attitude toward drugs. At first completely opposed to vaccination because he believed it lowered a person's vitality and resistance to disease, he later conceded that it might have value for those who refused to follow correct health habits. Believing that a strict adherence to biologic living would provide sufficient protection against smallpox, he refused to let himself be vaccinated.

When John Kellogg began medical practice, the profession widely used alcoholic beverages as a stimulant. Even many Adventist leaders on rare occasions drank a little homemade wine when feeling ill. Dr. Kellogg, however, took a firm and unvarying stand against the use of alcohol in any form. He maintained that it was not a proper stimulant, but rather a narcotic that interfered with proper digestion and caused damage to most of the vital organs. Because of their caffeine content, he also opposed coffee, tea, and cola drinks. The theobromine in cocoa and chocolate he regarded as almost equally harmful to health. Recognizing their habit-forming qualities, Kellogg suggested that by continually taking them into the body, people not only prevented themselves from getting the most restful sleep, but also ran increased danger of high blood pressure and damage to the heart and liver.

Dr. Kellogg aimed some of his most violent denunciations at tobacco and the industry that promoted it. Although lung cancer was not yet prevalent in his day, he correctly saw tobacco as a major cause for much of the heart disease that had already emerged as an American health problem. He also argued that tobacco interfered with proper growth and muscle development, caused gastric ulcer, unduly taxed the liver and kidneys, injured the brain and nervous system, and impaired judgment and moral sensibility. In fact, Kellogg wrote an entire book dealing with tobacco's effects and appealing for the discontinuance of its use.

Although he looked upon pain as serving a useful purpose, he did not regard it as something to simply endure. As one might expect, he favored natural treatments for it. Although experience convinced John Harvey that heat was an effective pain-killer, he was not sure just why, though he conjectured that it was because it relieved blood vessel congestion. Originally the doctor favored the use of moist heat—either hot water itself or hot damp cloths applied to the affected parts. In 1891 Kellogg accidentally discovered the deep penetrating power of electrically produced heat, and from then on he extensively employed various types of electric-light cabinets, and later of diathermy equipment.

During his early career, probably as a result of his study with Dr. George Beard, John Harvey became excited over electricity's therapeutic possibilities. Its stimulating effects, he hoped, would relieve a host of disorders, ranging from nervous diseases and anemia to hysteria, paralysis, and dyspepsia. Extensive experimentation with electrical currents led to a lessening of his early enthusiasm, but he continued to regard it as valuable for stimulating muscular activity. He developed numerous treatments that combined the use of electricity with hydrotherapy.

Throughout his lifetime John Harvey Kellogg insisted that optimum health had a close association with habits of dress. In the nineteenth century he was a leading proponent of dress reform for women, taking particular exception to the female corset, which he maintained displaced the internal organs and interfered with their proper functioning. Some nineteenth-century physiologists, observing that men breathed with their entire chest while women employed only the upper portion, suggested that it was an inherent sexual difference. Dr. Kellogg disagreed violently. The female corset, he maintained, prevented natural breathing.

John Harvey persuaded many women patients to disregard fashion and abandon their restricting corsets. One warm summer evening the doctor decided to carry out a little experiment that he expected would demonstrate the garment's harmful results. Selecting a new pink corset that he had recently convinced its owner to discard, he laced it tightly around the chest of Mrs. Kellogg's beautiful male collie, who had come to the office to walk home with him. Just as the doctor was settling down to observe the effect on the animal's breathing, a knock on the door disturbed him. Not wishing to have his visitor see the dog in his new garb, John Harvey stepped into the outer office. When he returned, the collie had vanished, jumping out an open window. The doctor quickly mounted his bicycle and headed for home, where a reproachful Mrs. Kellogg met him. He soon decided it was the better part of wisdom to abandon the experiment.

When women gave up tightly laced garments, Kellogg turned his attention to improving male habits of dress. Among other things he advocated a daily change of undergarments, the use of porous fabrics to allow better penetration of light and air, and the wearing of white clothing. Although he considered it essential to keep the body warm at all times, Dr. Kellogg felt that many people had a tendency to overdress. He regarded it as harmful because it induced perspiration under the wrong conditions and contributed to subsequent chilling. Also the doctor opposed the use of high-heeled, pointed, tight, or thin-soled shoes.

While recognizing that many physical ailments are imaginary and curable by the power of suggestion, he had no use for the early twentieth-century mind-cure artists or hypnotists, believing that the domination of their subjects by such practitioners weakened the patient's will at the exact time good health required its strengthening. Kellogg likewise vigorously rejected the tenets of Christian Science. He believed that Mary Baker Eddy's ideas on pain and disease were not only completely false, but harmful since they tended to destroy faith in natural remedies for human maladies. But he did realize that worry and pessimism might have a definite adverse effect on health. Thus he recommended the cultivation of a cheerful, optimistic attitude and a firm Christian faith. "Belief in God," he wrote on one occasion, "is the basis of all health. Belief gives rise to hope, and hope is one of the most powerful stimulants to which the body can be subjected."

Habits are difficult things to change. John Harvey had set himself a large task in determining to revise the way Americans ate, breathed, dressed, walked, and eliminated body wastes, but for nearly 70 years he never let himself get diverted from his goal. During those years the Battle Creek Sanitarium served as the command post from which he operated. It was also a powerful agent for propagating his message to thousands.

CHAPTER VI

DEVELOPING THE
BATTLE CREEK SANITARIUM

IN THE COURSE OF his long campaign to convert Americans to a more healthful way of living, John Harvey Kellogg used a wide variety of means to promote his ideas. One of the most effective was the Battle Creek Sanitarium. In 1876 Kellogg hesitantly agreed to serve a single one-year term as the sanitarium's physician-in-chief—he remained intimately connected with the institution for 67 years. Several years before his death, Dr. Kellogg estimated that his work at the sanitarium alone had brought him into contact with a quarter of a million persons.

The Battle Creek Sanitarium began in 1866 as the Health Reform Institute in response to the urgings of Ellen White. As the true pattern of healthful living opened to Mrs. White, she saw that Adventists should establish an institution that could care for the sick in harmony with its newly accepted principles. With James White in poor health, John Norton Loughborough led the fund-raising campaign for the proposed Institute. Major initial support came from John Preston Kellogg, who became the largest original stockholder when he subscribed $500 to the venture. Although the Institute's articles of incorporation did not designate it as an official denominational enterprise, they did limit the holding of stock to those who kept "the commandments of God and the faith of Jesus Christ." From the start the Institute's directors established the principle of operating under the counsel received from Ellen White. They were also determined that the Institute would be a center for instruction in healthful living and religious principles as well as a place to care for the sick.

When the Health Reform Institute first opened its doors under the medical supervision of Dr. H. S. Lay, it had only one patient on hand. Four months later they occupied every room in the three buildings on the original property. At the end of the first year of operation the directors could declare a 10-percent dividend on all stock certificates, and Dr. Lay called for a large building program. The directors would have followed his advice, but Mrs. White cautioned against too rapid expansion.

Largely through the influence of James and Ellen White, the Institute soon modified its financial base. In the spring of 1868 almost all of the stockholders

Early photo of Health Reform Institute

agreed to transfer their share of any future profits to the Institute's directors, who would use such funds for charitable purposes. In effect, the Institute thus became a nonprofit organization. During the next several years a policy of accepting needy church members as patients at half rates brought a severe financial setback to the Health Reform Institute. By the fall of 1869 it had only eight patients paying regular prices, and the Institute had fallen $13,000 in debt. The bad financial situation led to a reorganization of the board of directors, which resulted in placing James White and several Adventist businesspeople in control of the institution. They appointed John Preston Kellogg treasurer of the Institute, and John Harvey began his first formal connection with the Institute by occasionally serving as his father's assistant.

After four or five years of improved financial operation during which the Institute gained a considerable local reputation, difficulties developed between the lay and medical personnel. Losing faith in both groups, the directors seriously considered closing the Institute and selling its property to pay its debts. At this critical point, in the fall of 1876, leading church members persuaded John Kellogg, then only 24 years of age, to take over as physician-in-chief.

Ever since he had returned to Battle Creek from his first medical studies at Trall's college, young Kellogg had frequently received invitations to sit in on the meetings of the Health Institute's directors. After his year at

Ann Arbor, the Institute's leaders made John a director and the secretary of its board. When finished at Bellevue, they elected him to the medical staff as well. Also he worked closely with James White in editing the *Health Reformer.*

It may be that some of the older Adventists in Battle Creek resented the young doctor's influence with James White, for John soon found himself accused of criticizing and undercutting White's policies. White himself apparently retained his high estimate of Kellogg's potential, for in midsummer 1875 he persuaded the other trustees to offer John the position of chief physician at the Institute. Kellogg refused the original offer for a variety of reasons: he desired to engage primarily in research and writing; he realized that his small stature and youthful appearance led most of the Institute staff to consider him a mere lad; and Ellen White advised him that, contrary to her husband's wishes, it was not yet the time for him to assume the direction of the Health Institute.

Conditions at the Health Reform Institute deteriorated further during the winter of 1875-1876. At the same time the 24-year-old Kellogg found himself drawn into an ever closer relationship with four major Adventist leaders: James and Ellen White; Uriah Smith, editor of the church's main publication, the *Advent Review and Sabbath Herald;* and Professor Sidney Brownsberger, president of Battle Creek College. The quintet solemnly pledged to God and each other that they would work together to bring "discipline and order" to the Adventist institutions in Battle Creek. John Harvey evidently knew that the others expected him to be the one who would lead the reorganization of the Health Institute. He still hesitated, however, and in the spring of 1876 left Battle Creek to arrange an exhibit of health and temperance publications at the Centennial Exhibition in Philadelphia. From there he traveled to Wilmington, Delaware, where he spent the summer preparing several health tracts and books.

In mid-July James White and Professor Brownsberger persuaded the Institute board to renew their invitation to Dr. Kellogg to become physician-in-chief. The board assigned White the job of convincing his protégé of the urgency of the situation. Kellogg reluctantly agreed to assume leadership of the Institute for a year, provided they allowed him a free hand in restructuring the institution so that it might have what he considered to be both a rational and scientific basis.

When Dr. Kellogg officially took over the leadership of the Institute on October 1, 1876, it contained only 20 patients. Six departed with the former chief physician, Dr. William Russell, who proceeded to open a rival establishment in Ann Arbor. Soon afterward two other patients departed, leaving Kellogg with only 12 patients, housed in several small two-story frame buildings. In spite of the inauspicious beginning, James White announced that he believed the Institute's prospects for success had never been brighter. Seven months later he reported that the Institute had treated more than twice the customary number of patients during the past winter. In later years, Dr. Kellogg remembered that, before his agreed-upon year had expired, increased patronage made an expansion of the physical plant mandatory. He felt obligated to remain until the medical facility had paid for the new additions. By that time the Institute needed more space, and he gradually became so entangled in its operation that any thought of leaving the institution vanished.

Within a year after he had assumed charge of the Health Reform Institute, John Kellogg decided that a change of name would improve the institution's public image. Consequently, apparently acting entirely on his own initiative, he renamed it the Battle Creek Sanitarium. The doctor explained that the new name that he had coined, a variant of "sanatorium," would come to mean a "place where people learn to stay well." He consistently maintained that the sanitarium's teaching function distinguished it from the average medical institution.

During the first four years that Kellogg served the sanitarium as chief physician, James White remained the dominating influence on the board of directors and put his considerable prestige squarely behind Kellogg's program. John Harvey frequently testified that only James White's influence and support had enabled him to establish his program at the sanitarium. Toward the end of White's life, however, the doctor came to fear the church leader's powerful personality. Through the cooperation of Stephen N. Haskell and George I. Butler, Kellogg succeeded in forcing White off the sanitarium board and making Haskell chairman in his place. Less than a year later James White died. In his final illness friends took him to the Battle Creek Sanitarium, where Dr. Kellogg, completely reconciled to his old mentor by the emergency, tried in vain to save the denominational leader's life.

During the 1880s the Battle Creek Sanitarium gradually came under John Kellogg's complete dominance. For the first years of the decade he served as vice-chairman of the board of directors as well as medical superintendent, and in 1885 he became the first board chairman who was not also an Adventist minister. When Kellogg went away on his extended European trip in 1883, some of his medical associates tried to challenge his leadership. Even after his return, covert opposition continued for several years. But John Harvey soon found a way to consolidate his position: he simply threatened to resign. By then the directors had become so convinced that the sanitarium's growing prosperity depended upon Kellogg's continued presence that they refused to face the prospect of losing him. Instead, those who opposed Kellogg had to go.

From the beginning of his tenure, Dr. Kellogg worked to expand the sanitarium's influence. He invited local area residents to attend the concerts and entertainments provided for sanitarium patients and persuaded the sanitarium directors to launch an extensive advertising campaign. At first they considered the idea of starting a small monthly magazine, but eventually made arrangements for the sanitarium to take over the former *Health Reformer,* recently renamed Good Health, with which Kellogg had long been connected. At his suggestion the SDA Publishing Association readily relinquished the journal so that it might promote sanitarium interests as well as health-reform principles.

Kellogg's years at the sanitarium were, from the start, intensely busy ones. Almost immediately be began a program aimed at improving and expanding the institution's physical facilities. During the early years he also made it a point to examine each incoming patient and to see the patients at regular intervals throughout their stay. In addition, he prepared the advertising material, trained the lay staff in methods of hydrotherapy and massage, sometimes entertained the patients by playing his violin, and actively managed the institution's business affairs.

It occasionally took considerable ingenuity to keep the sanitarium financially solvent. Early in his tenure, John Harvey confronted a patient who had run up a considerable bill and was planning to leave without any payment. A visit to the man's room convinced Kellogg that the patient had no possessions worth attaching except a large gold watch, of which he was extremely proud and which he always carefully kept on his person.

Undaunted, early the next morning Kellogg sent word for the sheriff to come out to the sanitarium to fill out attachment papers. When he had signed the papers, the sheriff looked at John Harvey and said, "Now, Doctor, how do you expect me to get that watch? I can't pick a man's pocket!"

"Never mind," the physician replied. He then asked the sheriff to step out of sight, for he observed the delinquent patient approaching. Kellogg greeted the man cordially and inquired if he was ready for a treatment. The man expressed surprise that John Harvey should offer him one when he was just on the verge of leaving without paying his bill. "As long as you are a guest here, we want to do everything possible for you," the doctor replied. He then invited the man to go to the treatment rooms.

Without thinking, the patient complied. Once the man had removed his clothing, Kellogg summoned the sheriff, who held the watch for the sanitarium in lieu of other compensation. Finding himself outsmarted, the patient called for Dr. Kellogg and agreed to wire home for money to pay his account. When he had done so, he received the watch back and departed without apparent rancor.

In another move designed at least partially to cut sanitarium labor expenses, Dr. Kellogg lectured on the great benefits one could derive from sawing wood. He then prescribed the exercise for enough patients to guarantee the sanitarium a continuous supply of wood for its furnaces.

After several years, John Harvey decided to relieve himself of some of the financial pressures and hired his younger brother, Will Keith, to be a combination bookkeeper, business manager, and financial agent.

Although Seventh-day Adventists had founded the Battle Creek Sanitarium to promote their entire health-reform program, the financial and managerial difficulties experienced in the early days had resulted in only a partial utilization of the principles at the institution. When Dr. Kellogg assumed charge, the sanitarium gave the reform diet little more than lip service, and the facility was well on the way to becoming just another faltering "water cure." John Harvey immediately decided to place the institution on a program that would include every part of the health doctrine. His initiation of a special table in the dining room serving only a strict reform menu emphasized the diet aspect. To set the proper example, he always ate at it and required the other staff physicians to do likewise. He found it impossible, however, to enforce the strict observance of all the reform diet throughout the entire institution at one time—old ways of doing things had become too strongly entrenched. It took 20 years before Dr. Kellogg could completely eliminate meat, tea, and coffee from the sanitarium dining room.

Although Kellogg did not offer an original health regimen, the atmosphere in which he presented it was. The sanitarium became something of a combination nineteenth-century European health spa and a twentieth-century Mayo Clinic. A patient could enjoy hotel comfort while a group of highly trained medical specialists devoted their energies first to the scientific diagnosis of his ills, and then to correcting them through natural means.

The inadequacy of the original Health Reform Institute facilities became apparent to Dr. Lay within a short time after the Institute opened, but not until the spring of 1877, six months after Kellogg became chief physician, did James White propose launching a drive to raise $25,000 for a new building. By then Kellogg had wiped out the sanitarium's debts and had accumulated $3,000 in a local bank. When a stroke of apoplexy prevented White from completing his fund-raising campaign, it proved necessary to borrow a major portion of the new building's cost from commercial sources. In spite of such difficulties, the sanitarium put a new five-story building in service during the spring of 1878. It spent $10,000 on the most modern heating and ventilating equipment, which Dr. Kellogg had specially planned after a careful study of some of the leading hospitals in the United States.

Liquidating the debt incurred in constructing the new main building proved more difficult than anyone expected. Before they finished, however, Dr. Kellogg became convinced that the medical facility needed a $50,000 addition to care for the increased patronage. The sanitarium directors agreed to the proposed expansion upon the condition that Kellogg not increase the existing institutional indebtedness. In an effort to conform to the board's requirement, Kellogg organized a separate stock company to raise the needed funds. When it proved inadequate, the sanitarium again had to borrow money to complete the building project. Ellen White, skeptical about the wisdom of continually increasing the sanitarium's size, publicly labeled the addition a mistake. The "financial embarrassment" that resulted, she announced, "called into active exercise all of Dr. Kellogg's scheming and planning to gather means to lessen the heavy debt. This has caused him great care and labor, and has nearly cost his life." She also condemned what she referred to as the "grand hotel" atmosphere of the expanded sanitarium.

Apparently not worried by its indebtedness, Dr. Kellogg soon began dreaming of adding a charity wing to the main building. When the directors proved unwilling to vote a further expansion, Kellogg persuaded them to sell him several acres of land, upon which he began to construct a separate charity hospital as a private venture. The charity aspect of his new project appealed to Ellen White, and she gave her support to the doctor's plan. Upon finding that Mrs. White approved, the sanitarium directors decided to accept responsibility for completing and operating the new facility.

As the result of a program of almost continual expansion, by the dawn of the twentieth century the Battle Creek Sanitarium consisted of the main building with two added wings, a charity hospital, an annex building, more than 20 cottages, a resort at nearby Goguac Lake, and approximately 400 acres of farmland that produced garden, fruit, and dairy products for institutional use. During one peak summer season a staff of nearly 1,000 took care of 700 patients. The expanded facilities had resulted only through a heavy program of deficit financing. The institution borrowed large sums of money for short periods from commercial sources and secured smaller sums for longer periods from hundreds of Adventist laypeople and sanitarium patients. In addition, Dr. Kellogg had contributed his surgical fees; and the low wages sanitarium employees cheerfully accepted made possible the diversion of a considerable portion of income to capital expansion.

During the 1890s Dr. Kellogg spent a great deal of time planning the legal reorganization of the sanitarium. At the time the institution had received a charter from the state, the law limited the lifetime of corporations to 30 years. Hence the sanitarium charter would expire on April 7, 1897. Nearly 10 years beforehand Kellogg succeeded in getting the stockholders to go on record as opposed to any division of the sanitarium's assets at the expiration of its charter. As his next move he applied to the state legislature for a special act of incorporation that would extend the sanitarium's life and would recognize the institution's philanthropic and nonprofit nature.

After the legislature refused to approve the request, the sanitarium management decided to ask the state district court to appoint a receiver to take over the sanitarium property when the charter expired. Meanwhile they would organize a new association that would then attempt to purchase the old institution from the receiver for the cost of its debts alone.

Several possible complications worried John Kellogg. A small minority of the stockholders appeared to favor a distribution of sanitarium assets to the shareholders when the charter expired. He determined to prevent them from capitalizing on the institution's greatly expanded net worth, for which he was to such a large degree responsible. Also the possibility existed that some non-Adventist person or group, sensing the sanitarium's commercial possibilities, would appear at the public auction that the law required the receiver to hold. Such a group might outbid the projected new Adventist association and thus wrest the valuable facility from its denominational affiliation. To guard against such a possibility, John Harvey had all the sanitarium doctors and staff members prepare bills for the difference between the normal wages being paid in Battle Creek and the much smaller compensation they had received. Then he showed them to one or two persons who had ideas about purchasing the sanitarium. They quickly realized that wages would have to go up if they bought the institution because the staff would not work for the old pay without religious motivation.

As a result of such careful preliminary preparations, Kellogg encountered no difficulties in carrying out the plan of transfer he and his associates had worked out. When the old charter expired, the court appointed Dr. Kellogg to serve as receiver, and one year later, after a new Michigan Sanitarium and Benevolent Association had organized and incorporated, the sanitarium went up for sale at public auction. No bidder other than the new organization appeared, and so the purchase price equaled the exact cost of the outstanding debt.

In later years the contents of the articles of association for the Michigan Sanitarium and Benevolent Association, which Kellogg had personally written, caused considerable controversy between the doctor and Adventist leaders. After Kellogg had formed the new association, it allowed the old sanitarium stockholders to nominate one person for membership in the new organization for each share of stock they held in the first corporation. In this way a large number of Seventh-day Adventist ministers became members of the Association.

All members of the new Association had to sign a declaration of principles, which included a specific statement approving the nonprofit purpose of the Association and agreeing that the work of the sanitarium should be "of an undenominational, unsectarian, humanitarian, and philanthropic nature." The document guaranteed each member of the Association the right to an equal vote at all meetings, but they had to exercise it in person. In effect the plan placed control of the Association in the hands of those members in or near Battle Creek who could attend meetings without difficulty. Those present at a regularly called meeting could expel other members of the sanitarium Association by a two-thirds vote. Kellogg maintained that such a voting procedure would prevent any member of the Association from trying to profit financially from his membership in the way that some stockholders had done in the old corporation. He had decided, he wrote General Conference President George A. Irwin, that the sanitarium could avoid future difficulties "by making character rather than money the basis of the organization, and providing that a person's membership in the Association shall lapse when his character ceases to be such as to make him of service to it or a properly qualified member in it."

Some of the prospective members of the sanitarium Association almost immediately expressed concern about what the wording characterizing the work of the sanitarium as "undenominational" and "unsectarian." When asked to explain, Kellogg stated that the words meant simply that the sanitarium was "to be conducted as a medical institution, that it may have the advantages of the statutes of the state; as a hospital, it must be carried on as an undenominational institution. It cannot give benefits to a certain class, but must be for the benefit of any who are sick. The institution may support any work it chooses with the earnings of the Association, but cannot discriminate against anyone because of his beliefs." The Association's members readily accepted his explanation.

Soon, however, Dr. Kellogg began to broaden his definition of "undenominational" in a way that frightened Adventist leaders. As an undenominational institution, the doctor stated, the sanitarium was not to be used "for the purpose of presenting anything that is peculiarly Seventh-day Adventist in doctrine." Several years later he told a newspaper reporter that the sanitarium had "no connection with the Seventh-day

Adventist denomination as such" and that "membership in the Association governing it is as open to a Catholic as to a Seventh-day Adventist." To many Adventists his statements sounded dangerous indeed, for more than 20 years earlier Ellen White had plainly stated, "It was in the purpose of God that a health institution should be organized and controlled exclusively by S.D. Adventists." Some Adventist leaders decided that Kellogg's use of the words "undenominational" and "unsectarian" in the new sanitarium charter was part of a scheme to separate the institution completely from denominational control. Denying the charge, he stated that the sanitarium was "owned and controlled by those who have owned it during all the years since its organization. There has been no change in ownership, no change in principles, no change in management; and no change of any sort has been contemplated."

In the light of later events it appears that the suspicions Adventist leaders harbored toward Kellogg's designs on the sanitarium had some foundation. After his separation from the church (see chapter 16), Kellogg indicated that for years, both prior to and during the sanitarium reorganization, he believed that certain Adventist ministers had tried to place the institution under the direct control of the Adventist General Conference and that "it [had] required constant vigilance" for him to "baffle the various plots and schemes" they used. Kellogg confided to an old associate in 1905 that he had anticipated the probability of an eventual break between himself and the church 15 years earlier, and that he had been preparing for the possibility for the previous 10 years. For that reason, he wrote, he had insisted on maintaining the sanitarium as a "private, distinct, independent corporation."

Within several years after the successful reorganization of the sanitarium, John Harvey once more began to think that it needed larger facilities. Then a disastrous fire, which broke out in the early morning hours of February 18, 1902, brought the whole question of the proper size of the Battle Creek Sanitarium into sharp focus. The fire, whose cause was never determined, began in the sanitarium pharmacy and spread rapidly. By daylight the entire main building, the charity hospital, and several small adjoining buildings lay in ruins. The staff safely evacuated all of the 400 patients in the sanitarium except for one man who reentered the building in an unsuccessful attempt to rescue his wallet, which contained his life savings.

At the time of the fire, Dr. Kellogg was returning to Battle Creek from the West Coast. He first learned of the disaster from a newspaper reporter while changing trains in Chicago. When the reporter asked if the sanitarium would be rebuilt, John Harvey, although shocked by the news, replied that of course it would. As soon as he was seated on the Battle Creek train, he ordered his secretary to secure a desk and spent the remainder of the trip drawing preliminary plans for a new building.

Although he may never have had any doubt about the sanitarium's reconstruction, some uncertainty existed as to whether or not the institution should remain in Battle Creek. Recently Ellen White had spoken out against the tendency to center so many Adventist institutions and families in one location. Although four days after the fire the sanitarium directors voted to inform Battle Creek city officials that they were ready to begin rebuilding if the city would raise $20,000 to support the project, promise better fire protection, and remit all of the institution's personal and real estate taxes, they did not make a final decision to stay in the city until five weeks later. During the period they considered a number of other sites. The city of Niles, Michigan, offered to give 45 acres of land and raise $200,000 in cash if the sanitarium would relocate there. Other offers came from Benton Harbor, Michigan; Atlantic City, New Jersey; and several cities in California.

A number of factors influenced the directors to rebuild in Battle Creek. Thousands of former patients associated the sanitarium with Battle Creek and recommended that it stay there. C. W. Post, already a cereal magnate, threatened to build a new competitive institution in Battle Creek if Kellogg and the Adventists left. Prominent citizens of the city pledged considerable financial support. Also, even after the fire, there remained some $250,000 worth of usable sanitarium property that the institution would probably have had to sacrifice for a much smaller figure had it moved. Sanitarium officials called together a number of leading Adventist ministers to provide counsel, and after a week's deliberation the group voted to rebuild in Battle Creek. On May 12, 1902, an estimated 10,000 persons gathered for elaborate cornerstone-laying ceremonies.

It proved to be easier to decide to rebuild the sanitarium than to finance the project. The destroyed property, valued at an estimated $350,000, had carried insurance worth only $150,000. At the time of the

fire the sanitarium already had an outstanding debt of $250,000. Not sur-
prisingly, the sanitarium directors voted that total expenditures for both
building and equipment should not exceed a $200,000 ceiling. The new
building ultimately cost at least twice, and perhaps three times, this
amount. The reasons for the greatly increased costs are not entirely clear.
Dr. Kellogg blamed them on "various circumstances over which we had
no control."

Raising the money necessary for rebuilding became a major problem.
Although local citizens had pledged liberal donations if the sanitarium
would remain in Battle Creek, they paid only a fraction of such pledges.
Immediately following the fire Dr. Kellogg suggested that the entire denomination mobilize its membership to sell copies of *The Living Temple*—
a new book that he had recently completed—directly to the public.
Kellogg offered to donate his normal royalties to the rebuilding of the sanitarium. Church leaders agreed to Kellogg's proposal on the condition that
he include none of the new theological ideas he was then propounding.
The denominational leadership laid plans to attempt to sell 500,000
copies of the book at a price that would yield a net profit of approximately
one dollar a book. Any funds secured above the needs of the Battle Creek
Sanitarium would aid other denominational sanitariums. The plan of financing never materialized, however, because Adventist leaders became
concerned over the theological implications of some statements in *The
Living Temple* and refused to implement it (see chapter 16).

After the collapse of the book plan, the sanitarium management
turned to the sale of mortgage bonds and life annuity agreements. They
also issued a general call to all Adventists and former sanitarium patients
for contributions or loans. When such methods succeeded in providing
only a fraction of the necessary funds, the institution tapped the earnings
of both the subsidiary Sanitarium Food Company and Dr. Kellogg's private food manufacturing business. Fortunately, the boom in prepared
breakfast cereals that developed after 1906 provided sufficient funds to
complete the financing of the new building. At the same time the
Adventist church terminated John Harvey's membership. His careful planning, however, allowed the doctor and his associates to retain legal control of the sanitarium. Some of its most profitable days still lay ahead.

CHAPTER VII

SANITARIUM UPS AND DOWNS

A S ADVENTIST LEADERS questioned the wisdom of labeling the sanitarium a nonsectarian institution, the majority of Battle Creek citizens were asking whether it was really the nonprofit, charitable institution that Dr. Kellogg claimed. Conscious of the seemingly continuous expansion of the sanitarium plant and impressed by the increasing number of wealthy and famous people who came there as patients, local people generally assumed that those running the sanitarium were becoming wealthy.

Several years before the great fire, Kellogg attempted to persuade the local tax board to grant the sanitarium exemption from property taxes as a nonprofit, benevolent institution. Such a step would not only allow money spent for taxes to go for charity programs, but it would also be a public recognition of the sanitarium's true character. The doctor's effort failed because the board feared that public opinion would not approve such action.

The sympathy evoked by the 1902 fire seemed to offer another opportunity to press for tax exemption. Representatives of the Battle Creek Business Men's Association and the city council received invitations to examine sanitarium records so that they might be convinced of the institution's philanthropic character. The modest salaries received by all sanitarium workers from Dr. Kellogg down to the staff in the treatment rooms came as a surprise to the investigators. They had also been unaware of the large number of charity cases treated at the sanitarium. In a report of their findings, the committee confessed that the community had largely misjudged the sanitarium and its management. For the next several years Battle Creek's citizens raised few objections to a local court ruling that exempted the sanitarium from taxes on the major portion of its properties.

Then, in 1905, the Battle Creek city government reopened the question of the taxability of sanitarium properties, and for the next five years the matter caused considerable local agitation. The climax came in January 1910 when the Michigan Attorney General filed a motion in the circuit court at Jackson asking to have the sanitarium management ousted and the institution placed under a receivership on the grounds that the sanitarium had violated its charter as a charitable institution. One month later Judge James A. Parkinson issued the requested judgment of ouster, but at the same time he suggested that the matter immediately go to the state supreme court.

With this threat hanging over them, the sanitarium directors welcomed the attempts by a group of Battle Creek merchants to effect a compromise. Everyone temporarily suspended further legal action while Mayor John Bailey and Attorney General John Bird negotiated with the sanitarium managers. On May 7 came an announcement that all parties involved had agreed to a compromise in which the sanitarium would pay one fourth of the $100,000 in assessed back taxes. In the future the city would levy no taxes against the main sanitarium building, but would consider subsidiary properties to be taxable. Dr. Kellogg went on record as satisfied with the arrangement, maintaining that the chief objective of the sanitarium had always been not to escape taxes, but rather to secure official recognition of its position as a benevolent and charitable institution.

The intervention of Battle Creek merchants in the tax case may have resulted in part by their concern over current rumors that Kellogg and his associates were considering the development of a branch of the Battle Creek Sanitarium somewhere on the east coast. In 1908 a former patient of Dr. Kellogg's, C. E. Wood, of Washington, D.C., had passed away. His will bequeathed a substantial sum for the purpose of starting a branch of the Battle Creek Sanitarium in Atlantic City, New Jersey. Although a legal contest kept the New Jersey project from materializing, the next year New York businessman Nathan Straus and Arthur Brisbane, an executive of the Hearst publishing empire, proposed underwriting the development of a sanitarium branch at Lakewood, New Jersey. It, too, failed to get beyond the discussion stage. Yet the idea of a competitive institution, which would certainly attract many of the wealthy and famous who now made the pilgrimage to Battle Creek, cannot have but alarmed local merchants who had benefited from the guests' patronage.

A born publicist, John Harvey Kellogg had long recognized the values one could reap from inducing newsworthy personalities to seek restoration of their health and energy at the Battle Creek Sanitarium. He made it a point to show famous guests special attention. When, for example, patrons such as Sir Horace Plunkett, internationally known Irish agronomist, and Gifford Pinchot, former Chief Forester of the United States and the future governor of Pennsylvania, arrived, John Harvey met them at the railroad station and gave a banquet in their honor. Amos Pinchot followed his brother to Battle Creek, took a short course in hygienic cookery, and departed an announced convert to the Battle Creek diet.

Visiting Chautauqua lecturers also rated a news story. Kellogg considered it worth the time and effort to prepare a banquet honoring former Missouri governor Joseph Folk, and to entertain and give free medical advice to William Jennings Bryan. Prominent guests such as Oklahoma Democratic Senator Robert Owen and Denver's pioneering juvenile court judge, Ben Lindsey, frequently agreed to speak before sanitarium audiences. On such occasions they commonly made approving references to their host and his program. The casual mention in the press that U.S. Attorney General George W. Wickersham and Senator Charles Townsend were guests at the sanitarium for a few days seemed to put an official stamp of approval on the Battle Creek "system." When former President William Howard Taft registered as patient number 100,000 and received a complete physical examination, Kellogg realized a real propaganda bonanza.

Many notables came to the sanitarium partly because Dr. Kellogg either entertained them without charge or arranged for them to receive reduced rates. Just which celebrities were so privileged it is impossible to say, but it is likely that the 25-percent discount provided publisher S. S. McClure may also have extended to other journalists. Entertainers such as comedian Eddie Cantor, pianists Percy Grainger and José Iturbi, and champion juggler Edward N. Bradford probably received their room, board, and treatments in exchange for performing for other patrons. Colorful personalities such as Arctic explorers Vilhjálmur Stefánsson and Roald Amundsen, big game hunters Carl Akeley and Martin Johnson, and world travelers such as Richard Halliburton and Lowell Thomas may have received special rates so that they would ornament the big sanitarium veranda. Their presence would attract other guests who might thus be converted to biologic living.

It would be difficult to estimate the number of prominent visitors to Kellogg's establishment who permanently accepted part or all of his health program. Statistician Roger Babson, naturalist John Burroughs, and philosopher-historian Will Durant are a few, however, who adopted the diet system the doctor recommended. The Wall Street financial wizard C. W. Barron, a frequent visitor to Battle Creek during the 1920s, repeatedly attempted to adhere to Kellogg's system but constantly "backslid." He talked freely of the virtues of biologic living, however, and persuaded industrialists such as Alfred DuPont and John D. Rockefeller, Jr., to make the trip to Battle Creek. Rockefeller, at least, practiced a part of the Kellogg regimen for several years.

Many prominent business executives returned to the sanitarium as guests on frequent occasions. In 1938 a news report indicated that grape juice producer Edgar Welch had visited the sanitarium 32 times; textile manufacturer Joseph Cannon and W. A. Julian, the treasurer of the United States, 22 times; and Yale economist Irving Fisher, 19 times. Joseph H. Patterson, the founder of the National Cash Register Company, was not only himself enthusiastic about the Battle Creek system, but also sought to expose his employees to Kellogg's ideas. He had some of his executives sent to Battle Creek to learn the Kellogg "gospel," and hired a sanitarium doctor as plant physician at his Ohio factory. Other prominent businessmen frequently visiting at the Battle Creek Sanitarium were J. C. Penney, Montgomery Ward, S. S. Kresge, and Harry F. Sinclair.

Since Dr. Kellogg recognized educators and the clergy as important formulators of public opinion, he granted them special rates. Not only did local public school teachers take advantage of Kellogg's generosity and emerge to spread bits of the gospel of biologic living, but on various occasions the presidents of such academic institutions as Northwestern, Wellesley, and the University of Chicago visited the Battle Creek Sanitarium. In 1895 Admiral A. P. Niblack accepted many of Kellogg's ideas and proceeded to introduce some of them at Annapolis. He indicated at a later time that the Naval Academy owed its entire program of physical training to John Harvey Kellogg. Prominent clerical guests at the sanitarium included Charles Sheldon, author of the best-selling religious novel, *In His Steps;* Dr. Francis Clark, founder of the Christian Endeavor movement; and New York clergyman Newell Dwight Hillis, who once told his huge congregation that Dr. Kellogg was one of the five most useful men in the world.

A good example of Dr. Kellogg's public relations abilities appears in the three-day extravaganza he arranged in October 1916 to celebrate the golden anniversary of the sanitarium's founding. He sent invitations to the jubilee to all former patients and secured a host of prominent speakers. On the evening of the first day of the celebration a two-mile-long torchlight parade wound through the heart of Battle Creek. It included seven bands, 23 floats, and more than 50 decorated automobiles. An extensive fireworks display ended the evening.

During the three days former Michigan governor Chase Osborn, Methodist bishop J. E. Robinson, and the Michigan State Medical Society president, Dr. A. P. Biddle, publicly extolled the values of Dr. Kellogg, the sanitarium, and biologic living. Among others on hand to help celebrate were Gov. Woodbridge Ferris, who had been a fellow student with Kellogg at the University of Michigan; John Harvey's old professor at Bellevue, Stephen Smith; and Yale economist Irving Fisher, the professor with the "wrinkle in his stomach." On the final day of the jubilee, William Jennings Bryan, three-time Democratic candidate for the United States presidency and more recently United States Secretary of State, delivered the major address. Bryan announced that he spoke as a special friend of Dr. Kellogg.

The sanitarium treated more than 7,000 patients during its golden anniversary year, but the physical facilities constructed after the 1902 fire were not really strained until the economic boom of the 1920's. During the same period, active control of the sanitarium, which Dr. Kellogg had exercised for 40 years, began to slip into the hands of a group of his colleagues headed by Dr. Charles Stewart. Dr. Stewart had been closely associated with Kellogg since the crucial early years of the twentieth century, and many observers considered him as John Harvey's heir apparent. Although a brilliant physician, Stewart had long shown more interest in institutional management than in developing a wide medical or surgical practice.

A combination of events opened the way for his group to play an increasingly dominant role in establishing sanitarium policies. Following

American entry into World War I, Dr. James T. Case, a former Kellogg secretary and probably the doctor's most intimate associate on the sanitarium staff, joined the Army Medical Corps, where he made a considerable reputation as a radiologist. Case's army service, however, took him away from Battle Creek during a crucial period in 1918-1919 when a serious respiratory illness confined Dr. Kellogg in Florida. Leadership at the sanitarium during the period fell rather naturally to Dr. Stewart. Even after Kellogg returned to Battle Creek, expert medical authorities held the opinion that at best he had only a short time to live. In such circumstances it probably seemed wise to many at the sanitarium to follow Dr. Stewart's lead rather than that of a man "with one foot in the grave."

After Dr. Kellogg regained his health, he sought to prevent a reoccurrence of his pulmonary troubles by spending each winter either in Florida or in some other area with a mild climate, allowing Dr. Stewart and his colleagues to chart their own course for a number of months each year. Kellogg's influence at the Battle Creek Sanitarium further diminished when his staunch supporter, Dr. James Case, decided to leave Battle Creek permanently to join the medical faculty of Northwestern University. Since the Stewart group recognized the great value of Dr. Kellogg's name in attracting patients to the sanitarium, they continued to allow him to occupy a position of nominal leadership. They had the votes to initiate their own policies, however, as they clearly demonstrated in the matter of enlarging the sanitarium in 1927.

Increased patronage during the "Coolidge prosperity" caused the sanitarium directors to conclude that it needed larger facilities. Dr. Kellogg, remembering the earlier pressures of debt incurred in building operations, wanted to limit the cost of the proposed addition to $1 million. Stewart and his associates, believing that Kellogg had become timid as a result of old age and that he was losing his vision, insisted on a new $3 million structure. The addition of an elaborate lobby and dining room and expensive furnishings later pushed the cost of the "towers addition" to $4 million. Dr. Kellogg gloomily predicted that it would take 30 years to pay off the last million dollars borrowed.

The sanitarium issued $3 million in first-mortgage bonds to meet the major cost of the 15-story addition begun in 1927. Since the sanitarium had shown an average net profit of more than $135,000 a year from 1920 to 1925, the bonds sold quickly. In the first two years after the new addition opened, the expanded facilities seemed none too large, and the sanitarium retired $1 million of its indebtedness. But its prosperous picture changed rapidly after the great stock market crash of 1929. By the middle of the next year, the height of the season, facilities designed to accommodate 1,300 held only 300 patients. John Kellogg, now nearing 80, did not feel like fighting another desperate financial battle. He willingly allowed those who had pressed the hardest for the gigantic expansion to shoulder the main burdens in Battle Creek while he turned his attention toward a new project in the South.

Prior to his serious illness in 1918, he had generally ridiculed the idea of going south for the winter. Cold weather was more healthful than warm weather for most people, he maintained. His own personal experiences during the 1920s led him to greatly modify his earlier views, however. During the winter of 1929-30, John Harvey rented a house in Miami Springs and began to consider how he might open a health institution in Florida. When the doctor's possible intentions became known, salesmen for all kinds of property in many different parts of the state deluged him. Kellogg made many visits but found nothing that suited the purposes he had in mind.

Several blocks away from the Miami Springs house he occupied, Glenn Curtiss, the pioneer aircraft manufacturer, had several years earlier built a large hotel. Of Spanish American design, it was decorated artistically with Indian motifs and beautiful hand woven Navajo rugs. Handcrafted solid mahogany furniture graced each guest room. One morning John Harvey informed his secretary that he had decided that the Country Club Hotel was just what he needed to begin a Florida venture.

Almost immediately Kellogg telephoned Mr. Curtiss's attorney, who indicated that he was quite certain Mr. Curtiss would be interested in selling, but that since he had made a large investment in the building, the price would certainly be quite high. Kellogg suggested to his associates back in Battle Creek that the sanitarium purchase the Curtiss property and operate it as a branch. Dr. Stewart's group expressed polite interest, but pointed out that the sanitarium's financial difficulties made it impossible. Dr. Kellogg then announced that he would assume personal responsibility for establishing a sanitarium in Florida. The Battle Creek group raised violent objections to such a plan, realizing that it would mean competition at an especially inopportune time. John Harvey, they maintained, should remember his obligations to Battle Creek.

Undaunted by his colleagues' objections, Kellogg began negotiations with Curtiss. The two men were not strangers, as Curtiss had been a patient at Battle Creek. The aircraft manufacturer became enamored with the plans outlined by the 78-year-old Kellogg. After several conferences he agreed to draw up a contract donating the Country Club Hotel to Kellogg, providing the latter would agree to operate it as a nonprofit institution and would keep it open a minimum of six months out of every year. To comply with the legal technicalities, Dr. Kellogg would pay Curtiss one dollar. When they finished signing the contract, John Harvey opened his wallet, and with a twinkle in his eye, said, "Mr. Curtiss, I think $1 is too cheap." Whereupon he handed the industrialist a $10 bill. Kellogg still had a good bargain—the hotel and 14 acres of land had a conservative value of more than $200,000.

On December 1, 1930, Kellogg officially opened his new enterprise, which he called the Miami-Battle Creek Sanitarium. The 100-bed establishment had capacity patronage during most of the winter months for the remaining 13 years of Dr. Kellogg's life. The Florida sanitarium emphasized specialized baths, diets, exercise, sunshine, and an extensive program of health education through lectures. The institution, however, handled almost no surgery cases. Dr. Kellogg established a board of trustees to hold and operate Miami-Battle Creek that did not include any of the group who now controlled the original sanitarium. Misses Angie and Gertrude Estell, who had joined the Kellogg household as literary and business assistants a quarter of a century earlier, carried on much of the day-to-day management. The new venture in Miami Springs provided John Harvey great satisfaction after the past few years in Battle Creek. "I confess," he wrote to an old friend, "it is a pleasure once more to be in a place where I can get everything done as I wish to have it done and when I wish to have it done."

CHAPTER VIII
A TORRENT OF WORDS

FOR NEARLY TWO THIRDS of a century, John Harvey Kellogg made extensive use of the lecture platform in his campaign to promote biologic living. During that time, in more than 5,000 public lectures, he presented his ideas to hundreds of thousands of Americans in all parts of the country at church gatherings, Chautauqua assemblies, and professional meetings. Thousands more read about them in press accounts of Kellogg's lectures. Although no one can accurately measure the exact results of such a speaking campaign, it must have contributed materially to the change of American dietary and hygienic habits.

He did much of his lecturing before sanitarium patients. When in Battle Creek or Miami Springs, the doctor spoke in the sanitarium gymnasium or parlor at least two or three times each week. Prominently advertised, the lectures usually drew an audience of from 75 to 200. The most popular lecture each week was one devoted to answering questions that patients had dropped into a large box kept in the sanitarium parlor. Many of the lectures someone recorded stenographically and later duplicated and made copies available at a nominal fee.

Kellogg was not a great orator, but the enthusiasm with which he presented his subject enabled him to hold the attention of his audience in spite of his tendency to be repetitious. He frequently went on for one and a half to two hours and spoke at a rapid rate. Even so, Kellogg's ideas often seemed to come faster than he could express them. In such instances his sentence structure would become involved and difficult to follow, and his enunciation might become indistinct. His large vocabulary and the frequency with which he cited detailed medical data further confused—and impressed—his listeners.

The typical Kellogg speech began with a brief introduction, during which the doctor attempted to capture the audience's attention through some startling statement or impressive rhetorical question. The main body of the address would generally include a liberal sprinkling of simple axioms and homilies, spiced with an occasional touch of humor. His abilities as a storyteller and actor, along with his effective use of comparison and contrast, helped to relieve his tendency to bore his listeners with abundant references to scientific authorities and experiments. Like many prominent evangelists, he also knew the effectiveness of emotional appeals, particularly that involving fear. He frequently interjected into his discourses graphic descriptions of the unpleasant consequences of wrong living.

Although the offhand way in which Dr. Kellogg sometimes referred to medical data may have confused some in his audiences, he made a conscious effort to explain most technical terms and processes. To help accomplish this, he on many occasions employed a wide variety of visual aids, including blackboard drawings, charts, models, and simple scientific experiments. His obvious concern for his listeners' welfare impressed many, but at the same time his repeated emphasis on his "pet" theories antagonized others. Some of his most telling points he made in the question periods that often followed his lectures. In such sessions his apt repartee generally discomfited the scoffers, to the delight of the rest of the audience.

His position as the head of their first and largest medical institution made him an authority among Seventh-day Adventists on matters of healthful living. Kellogg first addressed denominational leaders assembled in General Conference when he was only a newly graduated doctor, 23 years of age. At many subsequent General Conferences he presented lectures showing the scientific basis for health reform principles. On one occasion he so impressed those in attendance that nearly 100 ministers prolonged their stay in Battle Creek for 10 days to study health principles under his direction. When speaking to Adventist audiences, the doctor's lectures became virtual health sermons, liberally laden with quotations from the Bible and the writings of Ellen G. White.

In the early 1880s Dr. Kellogg became convinced that many Adventist ministers had lost interest in health reform, and that some of them even regarded it with definite antagonism. He decided that he must counteract this state of affairs by presenting reform principles directly to large numbers of Adventist laity. With the encouragement of the sanitarium directors and G. I. Butler, the current General Conference president, the doctor began soliciting invitations to speak at camp meetings across the country.

For the next two decades Dr. Kellogg visited a number of Adventist camp meetings, trips made entirely at his own expense. On such occasions he spent much of his time giving free medical examinations and recommending specific treatments to curious inquirers. At first the doctor believed that his efforts were not accomplishing his main purpose. Frequently, it seemed, he only received permission to speak at the early morning service, which began at 5:00 a.m., and he noted that the provision tents continued to stock tea, coffee, canned salmon, and other foods of which he disapproved. Gradually, however, as Adventist young people began to come to Battle Creek in larger numbers to train for medical service, John Harvey saw the fruits of his efforts. Emboldened by increasingly enthusiastic receptions, the doctor often dramatically purchased all of the meat at a camp-meeting provision stand and ceremoniously buried it. Dr. Kellogg's colorful personality and style frequently drew the largest audiences of any of the camp-meeting speakers.

Some of his first invitations to speak to non-Adventist audiences came from temperance groups that welcomed his views on alcohol. Also his wife's WCTU connections may have brought John Harvey, in 1882, the first of several invitations to address the annual temperance convocation at Lake Bluff, Illinois. Of a three-day visit to a similar gathering at Waseca, Minnesota, Kellogg wrote enthusiastically that "the people were as greedy for truth as a flock of hungry sheep for food. There were quite a number of clergymen there from various denominations, and they laid hold of the truth eagerly." On such occasions John Harvey seldom confined his remarks to the denunciation of John Barleycorn. He almost always presented other aspects of healthful living.

Kellogg's temperance contacts led him rather naturally into accepting engagements in the Chautauqua series that were a feature of the American social scene in the late nineteenth and early twentieth centuries. He began such appearances as early as 1892, and within five years he received more requests to deliver health lectures as part of Chautauqua series than he could possibly accept. The Chautauqua season coincided with the Battle Creek Sanitarium's busiest period, and thus John Harvey found it impossible to agree to appear at other than the largest assemblies. In 1898, for example, he presented a five-lecture series at the original assembly in Chautauqua, New York. After a speech before a convention of Chautauqua managers in Chicago a few years later, the doctor contracted for some of his sanitarium associates to present 28 schools of health at various assemblies during the 1905 season.

The random mention of some of Kellogg's lecture appearances indicates his widespread impact on turn-of-the-century America. In Chicago, for example, the doctor addressed large audiences at the Central Music Hall and at Willard Hall on the campus of Northwestern University. At the request of reform mayor Samuel M. "Golden Rule" Jones, Kellogg presented his health doctrines before an open-air meeting in the Toledo, Ohio, municipal park and followed it with another address in the city's main lecture hall. Responding to an invitation from Mormon president Wilford Woodruff, John Harvey outlined correct health practices before 7,000 persons in the Salt Lake City Mormon Tabernacle. It led to later appearances before the Salt Lake City Women's Club and the students at the University of Utah. He also lectured on a variety of other campuses, including the University of Michigan, Tuskegee Institute, Stanford University, and the Boston College of Physicians and Surgeons.

During one extensive tour of the Western states, Kellogg described the reaction to his lecture at the Denver YMCA: "I told them the straight truth, and they asked me scores of questions," he said. "I stood and answered for an hour after my lecture." A similar experience took place in Los Angeles, where he spoke to a full house in the city's largest public auditorium. Once, in Austin, Texas, he shared the platform with former President Theodore Roosevelt.

In later years the doctor loved to relate stories indicating some of the successes of his speaking tours. One of his favorites concerned the conversion to biologic living of Mrs. Mary F. Henderson, a leading Washington hostess and the wife of Missouri Senator John Brooke Henderson. Following a Kellogg lecture in the nation's capital, Mrs. Henderson poured all the contents of her famous wine cellar, reputed to be the finest in the city, into the gutter. Later she sent her chef to Battle Creek to learn how to cook the proper kind of vegetarian foods. She also authored a book, *The Aristocracy of Health,* which promoted the full program of biologic living.

Somewhat akin to Kellogg's public lectures were his arrangements to advertise Battle Creek health principles at some of the major public attractions in the country. The sanitarium staged an exhibit and conducted a cooking school at the great Columbian Exhibition in Chicago, and had similar representation at the St. Louis World's Fair of 1904. John Harvey even managed to have September 29, 1904, designated as Battle Creek Sanitarium Day at the latter fair. On it he and other sanitarium physicians spoke for more than four hours in the exhibition's Hall of Congresses and touched on almost all aspects of biologic living.

Professional meetings provided a convenient forum for Kellogg to present the fundamentals of his program of healthful living to fellow physicians. Although such audiences were frequently much smaller than those the doctor might reach in a public lecture, any converts he made there had potentially greater value. John Harvey's most ambitious efforts to promote biologic living among the medical fraternity included papers presented before the Pan-American Medical Congress in Toronto in 1895 and the following year in Mexico City. Kellogg frequently received requests to address local medical groups, state medical societies in various parts of the country, and regional meetings of doctors such as the Mississippi Valley Medical Association. One may infer the type of presentation he would usually make before such groups from his account of an address in 1896 before the New York Academy of Medicine. After noting that his paper "was applauded again and again" and that the physicians "greeted with vigorous applause" his remarks during the subsequent discussion period, Kellogg wrote that "this was not because I said anything smart, or because my paper was a brilliant one. . . . It was the principles which the paper presented, the principles which the Lord has given us, and which we have found so sound and so successful. I have always tried to keep these principles to the front, and have sought to hide myself behind them."

Always primarily a teacher at heart, Kellogg accepted numerous invitations to speak before national and state educational meetings. On such occasions he pointed out what he considered to be the twofold duty of all teachers: to maintain the best possible hygienic condition in the classroom, and to give pupils adequate instruction in personal hygiene.

His dietary views brought him a number of invitations to speak before various trade associations. He addressed several meetings of the Northern Nut Growers Association, an organization whose enthusiasm for Kellogg's advocacy of a wider consumption of nuts is quite understandable. John Harvey also made appearances before groups interested in milk production and distribution, including the National Milk Congress, the American Association of Medical Milk Commissions, and the Holstein-Friesian Association of America. At other times he filled speaking engagements before the Potato Association of America, the American Soybean Association, and the National Restaurant Association. At the close of one of the doctor's addresses before the National Association of Life Underwriters, its president declared Kellogg's paper to be worth $50,000 to the Association.

Dr. Kellogg understood the transitory effect of the spoken word, so from the start of his career he made a major effort to get his views before the public in written form. At the time of the Battle Creek Sanitarium's Golden Jubilee in 1916, the doctor estimated that he had sold approximately one million copies of his major books and that more than five million copies of the magazine *Good Health* had been printed. He had also promoted aspects of biologic living in hundreds of thousands of tracts and leaflets that he had either written or edited. One of them, "The Simple Life," had a circulation of approximately one million. For many years John Harvey edited a health almanac that sold as many as 200,000 copies annually. In addition to their wide circulation in the United States, Kellogg's books were marketed in England, Australia, New Zealand, South Africa, Germany, and India. One or more of his treatises on food and nutrition had translations into Danish, Swedish, Norwegian, French, German, Spanish, and Chinese. Toward the end of Kellogg's life, Mohandas Gandhi remarked to American journalist Louis Fischer that Dr. Kellogg was probably among that group of individuals whose work and teachings were better known abroad than in their own country.

In the 75-year span during which he committed his health tenets to print, John Kellogg produced nearly 50 books. The doctor's initial venture into book publishing took the form of a hygienic cookbook that he prepared the year prior to his graduation from medical school. At least 30,000 copies of it sold. Its recipes included early versions of his later food creations. In that same year, 1874, Kellogg published his first major statement advocating a vegetarian diet—a 48-page booklet entitled *Proper Diet for Man.*

The task of directing the Battle Creek Sanitarium at first appeared likely to threaten the literary career he had envisioned as a medical student. He solved the problem by writing late into the night in order to meet what he considered to be a real need. "When I get a book on my mind and on my heart and soul," the doctor once remarked, "it is a real burden and does not give me any rest or peace of mind until I get it off. I often think when I have finished a book that I know something about how a woman feels who has given birth to a child. It seems a wonderful relief." At another time he indicated that each time he completed a book he felt that he never wanted to write another one.

Kellogg wrote a number of his books in an extremely short time. One of his early ones, *The Uses of Water in Health and Disease,* took just eight days to write. The original text of his *Plain Facts About Sexual Life,* which went through a number of editions and enlargements and sales of half a million, called for 14 days of work. The doctor usually wrote entirely from memory, with only a brief outline of chapter headings as a guide. Constantly revising as he worked, he dictated many of his literary compositions.

Kellogg's literary style was simple and direct, almost conversational in nature. Although easy to follow, it lacked polish and was often repetitious and discursive. The doctor confided to his wife after 45 years of writing that he did not believe it necessary to get new material or even a new method of treatment or style when producing a new book. One needed only to give the appearance of a new volume through changing the wording, chapter order, and headings. He often recycled entire sentences and paragraphs from earlier works.

The Review and Herald Publishing Association published John Kellogg's early books. Soon, however, the doctor became convinced that the denominational publishers were not promoting his titles with sufficient vigor. Since the small royalties allowed also dissatisfied him, he borrowed enough money to establish a small press in the back of the sanitarium laundry, and there he proceeded to publish his own books. After a few years he sold his printing equipment to the Good Health Publishing Company, which had been organized as a nonprofit-making subsidiary of the sanitarium. Either the Good Health Publishing Company or a later Kellogg enterprise, the Modern Medicine Publishing Company, produced his subsequent books.

Seventh-day Adventist door-to-door salespeople sold many of Kellogg's books. Later, as the denomination began to offer more of its doctrinal works on a subscription basis, the doctor shifted to using non-Adventist personnel. For a time, a future governor of Michigan, Woodbridge Ferris, handled the promotion of Kellogg's books. Although Kellogg's statement to a reporter in 1903 that he had "made over a million dollars" with his pen appears to have been an exaggeration, his income from his publications was substantial. The doctor recalled late in life that for more than a quarter of a century he had received book royalties of $8,000 or $9,000 annually.

In more than a dozen of his volumes Kellogg attempted to present all aspects of biologic living. His most extensive and probably his most widely circulated book of this type was *The Home Handbook of Domestic Hygiene and Rational Medicine*. First published in 1880, it contained in its more than 1,600 lavishly illustrated pages not only a statement of the Kellogg health principles, but also an extensive discussion of human anatomy and specific directions for treating common diseases in the home. The volume went through several revisions by the end of the century. The first 20 years of the twentieth century saw several more editions, somewhat altered in format and title, published.

Almost as numerous as the books that treated biologic living in a general way were the ones he devoted to the problem of proper diet and nutrition. His most comprehensive book on the subject was *The New Dietetics*, which appeared in 1921. Although the medical profession generally seemed unimpressed with his enlarged statement of the advantages of a vegetarian diet, some in the general public thought highly of the book. Henry T. Finck, an editor of the New York Evening Post, suggested that the volume's evidence of Kellogg's research qualified him for a Nobel Prize as a "life saver," and philosopher Will Durant wrote that *The New Dietetics* was worthy of a place among the 100 best books ever published.

In addition to his pioneer *The Uses of Water in Health and Disease,* John Harvey published a number of other volumes dealing with the use of natural curative agents, including electricity and massage as well as water. The results of 27 years of experimentation went into *Kellogg's Rational*

Hydrotherapy, issued in 1901. Within three years of its publication, he had sold 15,000 copies, principally to physicians. For many years the medical profession recognized it as the most important single treatise on hydrotherapy, and as late as 1960 the Mayo Clinic still reportedly used it.

John Kellogg's old desire to teach bore fruit in seven textbooks on anatomy, physiology, and hygiene that he prepared for schools. The first one appeared in 1881, designed primarily for use in Adventist secondary schools and colleges. Five years later Harper and Brothers persuaded Kellogg to begin work on a similar text for the primary grades. In 1888 his *First Book in Physiology and Hygiene* appeared. The American Book Company, which had acquired the rights to the earlier volume from Harpers, prepared and published a *Second Book* several years afterward. Twenty years later, in collaboration with Professor M. V. O'Shea, of the University of Wisconsin's Education Department, Kellogg produced a four-volume Health Series of Physiology and Hygiene for the Macmillan Company. Although the general school textbooks did not specifically advocate the vegetarian diet he preferred, the use of meat received scant treatment and, at least by inference, John Harvey suggested the superiority of fruits, grains, nuts, and vegetables as foods. In the textbooks he placed his main emphasis on the values of fresh air, exercise, and sunshine, and the dangers involved in the use of alcohol and tobacco. In such areas his views closely paralleled those of the majority of informed physicians.

Only one of Kellogg's many books concerned itself with other than health topics. Early in his career the doctor had received an invitation to address a General Conference of Seventh-day Adventists session on the "Harmonies of Science and Religion." The enthusiastic response given his presentation encouraged him to expand his lecture into a book in which he discussed, from a scientific viewpoint, the nature of the human soul and the doctrine of the resurrection of the body. Although it was Kellogg's only avowedly religious book, the theological implications in one of his later general discussions of health principles, *The Living Temple,* played an important role in the controversy that resulted in his separation from the Adventist church (see chapter 16).

As a lad John Kellogg had set type for some of the first articles published in the *Health Reformer.* At the time he probably never dreamed that he would use the journal and its successor, *Good Health,* to promote his health teachings over a 70-year span. The summer after Kellogg returned from Trall's Institute, James White, who was then the *Reformer's* editor, pressed the 21-year-old youth into service as his chief editorial assistant. Since church responsibilities overburdened White, one year later John officially became editor of the *Reformer,* a position he held until his death 61 years later.

Shortly after he began work on the *Health Reformer,* he found himself involved in an acrimonious exchange with his old teacher, Dr. Russell T. Trall, a regular columnist for the journal during the previous five years. The argument began over some statements Kellogg had made about sugar, a substance Trall had violently attacked for years. Soon the two men vigorously traded insults. At the same time John Harvey became concerned over Trall's tirades against members of the regular medical profession. He decided that the venerable reformer must go and convinced White to end Trall's association with the *Health Reformer.*

Several years after he assumed the editorship of the *Health Reformer,* Dr. Kellogg decided that it needed a new name if the magazine and its teachings were to gain wider acceptance. He reasoned that public reaction to the word reform had changed. No longer did it call up visions of progress, advancement, and the substitution of truth for error. Rather, he felt, the average person associated reform with revolution, controversy, discord, and radicalism. A more positive name was essential. He decided to rechristen the periodical *Good Health* and make it into a journal that would tell its readers how to find and maintain their health. A year after the name change, the Battle Creek Sanitarium officially acquired *Good Health* from the Seventh-day Adventist Publishing Association. Thus what had begun as a Seventh-day Adventist publication remained under Kellogg's control even after his separation from the church.

Within a few months after he began his program of rejuvenating *Good Health,* he had succeeded in increasing its circulation to 20,000 copies a month. The doctor hoped that it would be possible with a little effort to double the number of subscribers, but apparently the subscription list never grew much beyond 25,000, and it probably stayed considerably below that number during most of the time. The popular *Literary Digest* frequently reprinted material from the health periodical during the early years of the twentieth century.

The basic ideas promoted in *Good Health* remained the same throughout the years until it ceased publication in 1955. During the period of his
editorship Dr. Kellogg generally prepared the lead article for each monthly
issue as well as several editorials and often one or two other pieces. He
also conducted a department in which he answered questions sent in by
readers. Not only did some aspect of biologic living receive endorsement
on almost every page of *Good Health,* but the periodical repeatedly called
attention to the Battle Creek Sanitarium, encouraging readers to come to
the institution, where they might experience the practical values of
Kellogg's health gospel. In turn, the sanitarium urged its patients to subscribe to *Good Health.* Thus his enterprises reinforced one another and
deepened the impact of biologic living on those exposed to its concepts.

Throughout the years John Kellogg managed to get his ideas in print
in a variety of other journals that he either edited or controlled. From
1908 until the onset of the Great Depression, the Battle Creek Sanitarium
published a small weekly entitled *The Battle Creek Idea,* which it mailed to
all former sanitarium patients for a time after they had returned home.
Most issues of the *Idea* carried a Kellogg article, often a transcript of one
of the doctor's lectures at the sanitarium. He also conducted a question-
box feature in the *Idea* similar to the one he operated in *Good Health.*

As early as 1889 Dr. Kellogg expressed interest in starting a publication, directed specifically at doctors, that would contain scientific articles
based on the research and experience of members of the sanitarium staff.
Two years later *Bacteriological World and Modern Medicine* appeared under
Kellogg's editorship. The journal continued under a variety of titles until
1909, and then, after a temporary lapse, he reinstituted it from 1922 to
1931 as the *Bulletin of the Battle Creek Sanitarium and Hospital Clinic.*
Through it John Harvey managed to get a number of his ideas before the
medical profession in conventional scientific form.

In 1891 the International Health and Temperance Association, an
Adventist organization that Kellogg headed as president, launched a new
magazine entitled *Medical Missionary,* a monthly published until the end
of 1914. Dr. Kellogg also edited this magazine. Unlike *Good Health,* the
Medical Missionary originally was planned solely for Adventists. In addition to promoting the cause of health and temperance, it sought to develop a genuine missionary spirit among church members. When John

Harvey's controversy with other Adventist leaders reached its height, he temporarily expanded the *Medical Missionary* into a weekly journal in an effort to present his ideas more fully to the Adventist rank and file. He attempted to continue the *Medical Missionary* as a nondenominational enterprise, but the expense of publishing for a decreasing subscription list proved too great, and the journal ceased its existence.

Dr. Kellogg started two other periodicals to promote specific aspects of biologic living. In 1893 he began publishing the *American Medical Temperance Quarterly* to convince physicians that alcohol was not a proper stimulant, but rather contributed to numerous health and social problems. The doctor continued to edit it for a decade before arranging its merger with the *Journal of Inebriety*. Early in the twentieth century he decided to publish a small journal to promote the cereal and vegetarian foods that he had developed, but *The Battle Creek Food Idea* apparently failed to survive for more than one issue.

Over the years he wrote many articles advertising some facet of his health dogma for a variety of trade and medical journals. He told potato growers and dairymen, for example, how their particular products fit into the ideal diet. Articles written by Kellogg also appeared in more than 40 different medical journals, including some published in Austria, France, Germany, Great Britain, and Canada. In addition, he had papers published in the transactions of at least five different learned societies. Although many of them concerned his career as a surgeon, a large number stressed one or more of his particular health tenets. The man who had been fascinated with words as a boy proved unusually apt at enlisting them in his service throughout his long life.

CHAPTER IX

VARIATIONS ON A BOYHOOD DREAM

TWELVE-YEAR-OLD JOHN'S dream of himself as the friendly and inspiring teacher of a roomful of boys and girls never materialized beyond the one year's experience in rural Hastings. Yet in a real sense John Kellogg was a teacher all of his life. Even before he accepted leadership of the future sanitarium, which he frequently referred to as a University of Health, he had, in the summer of 1875, accepted an appointment as professor of physiology and chemistry at the Seventh-day Adventist Battle Creek College. Concurrently the Seventh-day Adventist Educational Society, the legal body responsible for operating the first Adventist institution of higher education, also elected him a trustee. He continued to serve as a trustee for most of the next quarter of a century.

Dr. Kellogg taught at Battle Creek College for five years before the burden of managing the growing sanitarium forced him to give up regular classroom instruction. His college students considered the energetic young doctor to be one of the most stimulating and demanding of their instructors. In his final spring of college teaching, however, he became so irregular in meeting class appointments that his chemistry students finally drew up a formal petition requesting him to begin and end his lectures on time. The next day Kellogg frankly admitted his past irregularity, announced that he could see no way for correcting the situation, and summarily terminated the class two weeks before the close of the term. Although the experience ended his official membership on the college faculty, he came back to give occasional health lectures during chapel periods and served as a guest lecturer during special institutes that the college conducted periodically for Adventist ministers and educators.

In his capacity as a college board member, Kellogg took a strong stand in favor of demanding a high standard of student conduct. Although he

Battle Creek College buildings

approved of coeducation, he also believed in close supervision of all social contacts between the young men and young women. On the curricular side, he pushed for a program of instruction that would emphasize intensive study of the Bible.

The early 1880s were critical years in the history of Battle Creek College. A number of Adventist leaders believed that the college should place more emphasis upon vocational training and should establish industries in which students could learn manual and domestic arts. No one more enthusiastically promoted such reforms than John Harvey Kellogg. Among the college faculty, Professor Goodloe Harper Bell, who had taught grammar to Kellogg in his youth, became the chief advocate of the educational reform program. The proposed changes proved too foreign to the experience of college president Brownsberger, however, and he resigned his post in the spring of 1881. Brownsberger's successor, Alexander McLearn, proved no more receptive to the new ideas, and he soon found himself in open conflict with Professor Bell and a majority of the college board. The board discharged McLearn after a year in office, and the college remained closed during the school year 1882-1883.

In the controversy that had developed between McLearn and Bell, Dr. Kellogg staunchly supported Bell, in spite of the fact that a majority of the Adventists residing in Battle Creek had backed McLearn. By the time the college reopened in the fall of 1883, the reform group had gained complete control. They introduced courses in typesetting, broommaking, shoemaking, and tinsmithing. Also they rented enough land to offer students experience in cultivating small fruits and garden vegetables. In addition, the school launched a major building program to provide additional space for recitation rooms, a library, gymnasium, museum, and student dormitories. Kellogg played a major role in each activity.

The basic educational philosophy that Dr. Kellogg expressed was similar to that of Margaret Fuller and Friedrich Froebel, whose works he had studied in his youth. John Harvey believed that the true purpose of education was "to make useful, noble men and women, not simply scholars." To accomplish it the school should not concentrate simply on teaching facts, but should impart the "ability to discover new facts and apply old ones. The aim of education should be to prepare an individual to make the most of himself in life." He advocated giving more attention than customary to developing the moral and physical side of the student's nature. In a commencement address at Battle Creek College on June 18, 1895, Kellogg outlined his basic ideas on education. He maintained that "knowledge obtained in books is chiefly of value only as it calls attention to, and opens the way for, the objective study of things not in books." Children, the doctor suggested in what sounded like a preview of John Dewey's progressive theories, should be allowed to learn those things that they wanted to as they instinctively sought to know what was most essential.

Although many of Kellogg's ideas prevailed at Battle Creek College, it took some years before he won complete acceptance of his dietary views at the institution. In the early 1890s he had not yet persuaded the college administration to ban meat and spices from the school dining hall. The situation improved in 1897, when Edward Alexander Sutherland, a believer in vegetarianism and a staunch friend of Kellogg's, assumed the college presidency. Before long, however, Sutherland became a leader in the movement that in 1901 relocated the college in rural surroundings near Berrien Springs, Michigan. Although Dr. Kellogg did not openly oppose the transfer, he regretted losing the students who had long provided a cheap source of labor for the sanitarium. (For more information about Kellogg's relationship with Battle Creek College and its successor, Emmanuel Missionary College, see E. K. Vande Vere's *The Wisdom Seekers* [Nashville: Southern Publishing Association, 1972]).

Shortly after completing his own medical course, John Kellogg began giving private lessons in chemistry, anatomy, and other basic medical subjects to E. J. Waggoner and several other young Adventists desiring to become physicians. At that time medical schools commonly accepted such instruction as fulfilling a portion of the requirements for a medical degree.

In the autumn of 1877 Dr. Kellogg decided to broaden his teaching and to open a School of Hygiene in connection with the Battle Creek Sanitarium. Some church leaders urged that the school should grant an M.D. degree to those who finished its course of instruction. In view of the standards of medical education then current, such an arrangement might have been possible, but he firmly opposed the proposal. He believed that one could obtain a first-class medical education only in a large city that had an abundance of clinical material. Kellogg's main objection to the established medical schools was their lack of attention to practical matters of hygiene and diet. He opened the School of Hygiene to provide a background in both areas for those who wanted to begin the study of medicine, and to inform interested individuals in basic health care.

Approximately 80 students attended its first lecture on January 14, 1878. By the tenth evening, the number had increased to 150. The session lasted 20 weeks. In addition to daily lectures and recitations in hygiene, Kellogg and other sanitarium physicians offered elementary instruction in anatomy, physiology, chemistry, physics, and mental philosophy. For several years the school repeated its course every spring and fall. Then Kellogg discontinued the School of Hygiene, but during its existence it had better equipped many to spread the gospel of healthful living through demonstrations, lectures, and personal example.

Several years after launching the School of Hygiene, Dr. Kellogg attempted to interest the Adventist leadership in organizing a denominational school for training nurses, possibly in connection with Battle Creek College. Failing to awaken any response, the sanitarium doctors decided to act on their own. In the spring of 1883 they issued a public invitation to young women to come to the sanitarium and enroll in a three-month course in the fundamentals of nursing and massage. Even though only two young women responded to the initial announcement, the lack of response did not discourage the program's promoters, for the following autumn they announced the organization of a Training School for Nurses in connection with the sanitarium. The first six-month course, which began on November 1, 1883, cost $150, including board, room, and tuition. A girl could meet expenses by working at the sanitarium. In fact, in later years, Kellogg announced that such a procedure was the preferred way since it provided the student with additional practical experience.

The course at the Sanitarium Nursing School soon lengthened to two years. By the end of the century attendance had increased to such a degree that a single graduating class numbered more than 150. In the early days two women physicians on the sanitarium staff—Drs. Kate Lindsay and Anna Stewart—carried on most of the instructional program of the Nursing School, though Dr. Kellogg also gave some of the lectures.

As the popularity of the Sanitarium Nursing School increased, Kellogg decided not to admit those interested in the profession simply for monetary rewards. For a time the school accepted no students unless they agreed to work for five years in the Battle Creek Sanitarium or a similar philanthropic institution after their graduation. In later years prospective students had to sign a declaration that they would use their training to serve as missionaries. Even after completing their course of study, sanitarium nurses did not receive their diplomas until they had worked for a period of time in some missionary enterprise.

After a lapse of some years, Dr. Kellogg decided in 1889 to reactivate the School of Hygiene under a new name: the Sanitarium Training School for Medical Missionaries, sometimes referred to as the Health and Temperance Missionary School. For the next decade it offered a variety of courses designed to prepare health lecturers, hygienic cooks, practical nurses, and other paramedical personnel. The special 10-week summer session that the Missionary School offered in 1897 provides an example of what Kellogg and his associates attempted to do. They had designed the course especially for ministers and their wives, missionaries under appointment to overseas posts, teachers in Adventist schools, and a group of evangelical and educational personnel whom the denomination was preparing to send to work among African-Americans in the Southern United States. The students received instruction in hygiene, healthful cookery and dress, physical culture, the administration of simple hydrotherapy treatments, and methods of personal Christian evangelism. Other programs offered by the Missionary School varied in length from one month to two years. After the beginning of the twentieth century and Kellogg's relationship with the Adventist Church deteriorated, the school closed.

In the spring of 1888 Dr. Kellogg, assisted by his wife, began a School of Domestic Economy at the sanitarium. The 25-week course included lectures, recitations, demonstrations, and drills in "all branches of

Scientific Cookery, Laundrying, Dress-Making, General Housework, and Household and Personal Hygiene." Thirty young girls and women enrolled in the first class. Although the School of Domestic Economy was scheduled to be repeated each spring and fall on a regular basis, it appears that the Missionary Training School absorbed it during the decade that followed its birth. After Kellogg discontinued the latter school, however, the School of Domestic Economy reappeared sometime between 1904 and 1906 as the Battle Creek Sanitarium School of Health and Home Economics. The one-year course had as its major goal preparing dietitians for hospitals, private clubs, and school and factory cafeterias. In 1919 it initiated a two-year course designed to educate young women to teach home economics in elementary and secondary schools.

A decade earlier, at Kellogg's suggestion, the Battle Creek Sanitarium had organized a Normal School of Physical Education to train young women for positions as directors of physical education in schools, YWCAs, and community social centers. Shortly after the initiation of the new program, it turned coeducational. The School of Physical Education offered a two-year course that stressed the therapeutic values of recreational programs and gave special attention to aquatic sports and summer camps.

The Sanitarium Schools of Nursing, Home Economics, and Physical Education were among the earliest of their types in the United States. For many years their two-year curricula remained adequate for the purposes envisioned. A general tightening of educational requirements about the time of World War I, however, made it difficult for graduates of the sanitarium schools to achieve certification for teaching purposes. Dr. Kellogg initiated discussions with officials of the North Central Association of Colleges and Secondary Schools on the advisability of combining the sanitarium schools with courses in the arts and sciences to form a liberal college.

Late in 1920 John Harvey received a gift of $75,000 in securities to use in founding a health college. At about the same time conversations with dowager socialite Mrs. Mary B. Henderson, of Washington, D.C., led him to believe that he could expect an eventual contribution of three quarters of a million dollars from her to help support such a college. As a result, during the summer of 1921 the sanitarium directors voted to initiate a four-year degree program in physical education and home economics. It took two years, however, before they could work all details out, but on September 10, 1923, a new Battle Creek College officially opened with an all-feminine student body of nearly 600.

As chairman of the board, Dr. Kellogg assumed major responsibility for the college development. He determined from the start that it should operate in harmony with the principles of biologic living. Its articles of association specifically stated that it would offer instruction "in coordination with, and subordinate to, the principles of race betterment and biologic and physiologic living." The school expected students to learn to correct faulty habits of eating, sleeping, exercise, and posture. The sanitarium board agreed to allow the new college to use sanitarium facilities and also to hire college students whenever possible so that they might earn a portion of their expenses. The Race Betterment Foundation, another Kellogg philanthropic organization, undertook to supply a central administration and classroom building.

For the first two years of its existence Dr. Kellogg served, in effect, as president of Battle Creek College as well as chairman of its board. The doctor took an active part in selecting an enlarged teaching staff. Then, in the summer of 1925, the board persuaded Dr. Paul F. Voelker to exchange the presidency of Olivet College for that of Battle Creek College. At once substantial progress began in adding curricula to those of the old sanitarium schools. President Voelker received authorization to establish departments of chemistry, history and sociology, psychology and philosophy, physics and mathematics, physiology, biology, English, education, and foreign languages. At the same time the board transformed the college into a coeducational institution.

As might be expected because of Kellogg's views, the initial social regulations governing Battle Creek students were extremely conservative. As late as 1929 the directors ordered a set of rules drawn up making it mandatory for college students to wear correct, healthful clothing and shoes. Even though the school strictly supervised student conduct, the college enrollment increased to nearly 800 by 1929, and John Harvey expressed the belief that twice that number would have enrolled if facilities had been available.

Dr. Kellogg had originally hoped that the Battle Creek College football team would be so successful as a result of the special biologic diet and regimen that it required its members to follow that attention would focus on the superiority of his system. After one season, however, the college administration discontinued intercollegiate football because they decided that metabolism studies of the players showed that football was too violent a game to be healthful, and because they feared that the sport might attract "undesirable" students. Local residents maliciously whispered that the team's poor record of wins was the real reason that it came to an end.

Part of the success of Battle Creek College undoubtedly resulted from the excellent programs of the continued sanitarium schools. Dr. Kellogg also attempted to recruit a superior faculty. In 1929 he boasted that the quality of his college faculty stood second only to that of the University of Michigan among the state's institutions of higher learning. In addition to individuals of the caliber of President Voelker and his successor, Dr. Emil Leffler, later graduate dean at Andrews University, the faculty included a number of distinguished instructors. Among them were biologist Luther West, subsequently graduate dean at Northern Michigan University; English instructor David I. Henry, who would serve both Wayne State and the University of Illinois as president; and Dr. Helen S. Mitchell. Dr. Mitchell, professor of nutrition at Battle Creek, headed the United States Army's dietetics service during World War II and later taught at the University of Massachusetts.

The financing of Kellogg's Battle Creek College proved to be a difficult problem from the start. The substantial gifts he had hoped to receive for the college failed to materialize. Instead, the institutional operating budget had to subsist on tuition and on grants that he made through his Race Betterment Foundation and the Battle Creek Food Company. Although President Voelker wanted to solicit a minimum endowment of $700,000 to make the financial future of the college relatively secure, Kellogg was reluctant to approve any nationwide drive for endowment funds. He always feared that outside contributions would lead to outside control, placing the principles of biologic living at the college in jeopardy. When Kellogg in 1930 finally approved a national drive to raise a $5 million endowment, the times were hardly auspicious for the success of such a campaign.

After the opening of the Miami-Battle Creek Sanitarium in 1930, Dr. Kellogg shifted a major part of his interest to its development. Battle Creek College fell almost completely under the control of President Leffler, although the doctor continued to underwrite a large share of its budget through gifts and loans from his Race Betterment Foundation and the Battle Creek Food Company. By 1938 Kellogg's financial resources would no longer permit him to contribute the additional $60,000 a year necessary to keep the college solvent, and that fall Battle Creek College closed its doors. At first he hoped that it would be only temporary and that the college could, in the meantime, operate a correspondence school offering courses in health and nutrition. His hopes never materialized. Three years after the doctor's death Battle Creek College officially went out of existence. Its remaining assets reverted to the Race Betterment Foundation, to which it had become heavily indebted.

Dr. Kellogg's earlier attempt to operate a medical college had also ended in disappointment and failure. By the 1890s recognized medical schools would no longer accept the private instruction that Kellogg had given for years to aspiring medical students, as satisfying part of their required classwork. In counsel with Seventh-day Adventist leaders, he therefore decided that the Battle Creek Sanitarium should bear the financial burden of sponsoring a number of Adventist youth at the University of Michigan's Medical School. Since the doctor insisted that all such students maintain the health principles taught at the sanitarium, he had a private rooming and boarding house secured for them in Ann Arbor. Here they lived in a homelike atmosphere, complete with a vegetarian diet. During the school year 1891-1892 more than a dozen young men and women studied at Ann Arbor under sanitarium direction. In order further to indoctrinate the future doctors in health reform ideas, Kellogg arranged for them to spend a major part of their summer vacations in Battle Creek, where they attended special lectures and observed sanitarium methods.

Several years after his plan for the training of Adventist physicians started, Ellen White began to express doubts as to its wisdom. Kellogg and his associates also found that, in spite of their best efforts, some of the medical students they sponsored began to discard parts of the sanitarium health program. The Battle Creek group decided that it would be easier to establish a medical school of its own than to eradicate what it considered to be the wrong concepts being absorbed by Adventist students at conventional medical schools. In the spring of 1895 the directors of the sanitarium, in collaboration with the Seventh-day Adventist Medical

Missionary and Benevolent Association, agreed to organize a medical school large enough to accommodate 100 students.

On July 3, 1895, the Illinois legislature granted a charter to the new school, named the American Medical Missionary College. Although it did not limit attendance to Adventists, it did expect all applicants to be practicing Christians and required them to pledge to devote their training to missionary endeavors. The college divided its instruction between Battle Creek and Chicago, where two years earlier Kellogg had opened a branch of the Battle Creek Sanitarium and where the Medical Missionary and Benevolent Association also operated a medical mission in the slum district bordering Chicago's Loop. The American Medical Missionary College made no tuition charge, but expected each student to engage in two hours of practical work at the sanitarium daily. They could also meet the cost of room and board by several additional hours of daily labor.

The promoters of the new medical college hoped to enroll at least 25 students in the first class. The actual number turned out to be 40. At the inaugural ceremonies, Dr. Kellogg, who served both as the school's president and as professor of surgery, principles of rational medicine, and medical physics, announced that the faculty consisted of 17 qualified physicians, and he indicated that the school had excellent laboratory facilities available, thanks to the cooperation of the sanitarium and Battle Creek College. Charity patients at the sanitarium hospital in Battle Creek and the Chicago Medical Mission provided a good variety of clinical material. Contrary to the practice in many medical schools, the AMMC began clinical instruction during the student's first year. Its president announced that the new educational institution's goals included providing thorough instruction in "rational medicine" rather than in "drugging," surrounding its students with a Christian influence, and offering each student practical missionary experience in addition to theoretical instruction.

The American Medical Missionary College took great care in selecting its students. When S.P.S. Edwards, a member of the first class, arrived in Battle Creek, Dr. Kellogg personally quizzed him for two hours. During that time the doctor surveyed the prospective student's knowledge of mathematics, history, literature, and ancient and modern languages. After the interrogation, John Harvey assigned young Edwards to the sanitarium matron, who gave him some of the most undesirable tasks that needed attention around the sanitarium, such as cleaning a long-neglected urinalysis laboratory. When Edwards had completed his jobs in a satisfactory way, Dr. Kellogg decided that he would make an acceptable medical student.

By the end of its fifth year of operation, the American Medical Missionary College had gained admission to the Association of American Medical Colleges, and the Medical Examining Boards in such important states as New York and Michigan recognized its graduates. Rush Medical College was the only other medical school in Chicago whose instruction had as wide acceptance. Several years later the London Medical Council, which Kellogg called the "highest examining body in the world," granted recognition to the AMMC.

In the course of its 15 years of existence, the AMMC enrolled 408 students and graduated 187 doctors of medicine. Although other affairs occupied Dr. Kellogg too much for him to be a very satisfactory teacher at the school, he once reported that instructing medical students was his favorite work. Probably one of his most valuable contributions to the students at the AMMC was the regular weekly surgical clinic that he conducted. A report of the judicial Council of the Association of American Medical Colleges indicated that his surgical instruction was "not surpassed by any similar clinic in the country."

As was later true of Battle Creek College, the financing of the work of the American Medical Missionary College presented a major problem. Battle Creek Sanitarium met the school's principal expenses in its early years. By the time the sanitarium suffered the disastrous fire of 1902, it had expended nearly $100,000 in support of the AMMC. The financial drain occasioned by its rebuilding operations, however, made it impossible to continue such heavy support of the medical school. Kellogg and his associates turned to the Adventist Medical Missionary and Benevolent Association for aid. It solicited funds for the AMMC from Adventists and former sanitarium patients. For a brief time some hoped that they might persuade the Rockefeller or Vanderbilt families to provide the medical college with a $1 million endowment, but such support never came. After Kellogg's Adventist connections ceased, the doctor committed a large share of the income from his cereal creations to the AMMC's support. In its final years the school also met a substantial part of its expenses by having its staff perform laboratory work for the city of Battle Creek.

The controversy between Dr. Kellogg and the Adventist leadership, which grew more pronounced as the twentieth century advanced, not only jeopardized the financial position of the American Medical Missionary College, but also seriously affected its enrollment. During the first decade of its existence, the overwhelming majority of the students had been Adventists, but one year following Kellogg's dismissal from the church, a freshman class of 38 included only two Adventists. The doctor continued to insist, however, that AMMC should admit only students promising to devote their lives to missionary work. In 1908 he indicated that he did not wish his medical school to become large, but he would like it to be noted for its quality. He professed to believe that its future was brighter than it had ever been.

To those behind the scenes, however, his words must have had a hollow sound, since the Illinois State Board of Health had recently decided to drop the American Medical Missionary College from its list of approved schools, an action taken after an investigating committee of the board had submitted a report highly critical of the AMMC's Chicago facilities and of the quality of its instruction. For some years several of Kellogg's chief associates had been convinced that the days of small medical schools not connected with a university were numbered. When the substantial financial and moral support that John Harvey hoped to receive from some of the country's evangelical mission boards did not materialize, their pessimism deepened. In the spring of 1910 the AMMC graduated only nine doctors, and two months later the college administration announced that it had arranged to merge the school with the Medical School of the University of Illinois.

John Kellogg did not confine his educational activities to the two Battle Creek colleges, the American Medical Missionary College, and the variety of schools associated with the Battle Creek Sanitarium. He had entered the modern field of audiovisual education as early as the 1880s, when he prepared a series of 10 colored charts depicting the harmful effects of alcohol and tobacco. Temperance lecturers used them widely. Several years later he developed two series of charts for school use. Going beyond the conventional fundamentals of anatomy and physiology, the charts showed the effects of bad habits in dress and posture and the results of neglecting to secure sufficient exercise.

The doctor also participated in a wide variety of adult education ventures. Along with James and Ellen White and G. I. Butler, he had organized the American Health and Temperance Association in 1878 in an effort to expose the dangers of alcohol, tobacco, tea, and coffee. Kellogg served as the Association president during its 15-year life-span and actively organized public meetings and campaigns to distribute temperance tracts and pledges. In later years he served as president of the Michigan Anti-Cigarette Society, and following World War I he became a member of the Committee of Fifty to Study the Tobacco Problem. Kellogg assisted the latter group—which included Henry Ford, George Peabody, and John Burroughs—in producing one of the first educational motion pictures devoted to the dangers of tobacco smoking.

In cooperation with Horace Fletcher, Dr. Kellogg, in 1909, organized the Health and Efficiency League of America. During the next several years the League actively propagandized for healthful living through promoting health lectures on various Chautauqua circuits. Five years later he joined the board of directors of the Life Extension Institute, an organization founded by Irving Fisher to publicize the value of regular physical examinations for all Americans. Drs. William Gorgas and Will Mayo and famed athletic coach Alonzo Stagg associated with Kellogg in the institute.

The transitory existence of the schools and educational societies with which John Harvey Kellogg had connections for more than half a century might, at first glance, seem to indicate that the doctor was a failure as an educator. But one must remember that his schools sent out hundreds of doctors, nurses, dietitians, cooks, physical education instructors, and health lecturers. They carried with them the doctor's concern to make Americans health conscious—to teach them the rules for good health. Kellogg's disciples passed on his message that good nutrition required a variety of fruits, nuts, grains, and vegetables in the diet; that it was essential to drink only pure water, and to use it liberally to keep clothes and premises clean. And they carried with them his concern for proper ventilation, posture, and healthful clothing. In a definite way his students served as an extension of Kellogg himself. They brought the doctor's message to hundreds of thousands whom he could not reach personally. Thus, as spreading ripples from a stone dropped into a pond, John Harvey's influence diffused. What teacher could ask for more?

CHAPTER X

THE UNWILLING SURGEON

THE TENDER-HEARTED LAD who wept over the accidental killing of a robin and was horrified by the kitchen-table surgery performed on a boyhood chum could hardly have dreamed that as an adult he would have the reputation of being one of America's foremost surgeons. Although required at Ann Arbor to observe the surgical techniques of Professors Donald Maclean and Edward S. Dunster, the experience failed to inspire young Kellogg to follow the life of the surgeon. The effect of his final year at Bellevue was the same.

In retrospect it would not have seemed strange if the Bellevue staff had been able to claim Kellogg as a convert to surgery, for certainly the surgeons he saw in action there were among the most able in the nation. Dr. James Wood, one of the founders of the Bellevue Medical School and a man with an international reputation as a surgeon, headed the surgical staff. His associates had scarcely less skill. The United States Army had offered Dr. William Van Buren the post of Surgeon General during the Civil War, and Dr. Frank Hamilton had commanded the Union field hospital at the first battle of Bull Run. Several of the surgical staff had no peer in the country in the areas of their specialty. Dr. Edward Peaslee was the nation's foremost authority on gynecological surgery; Lewis Sayre occupied the first chair of orthopedic surgery established in an American medical school; and E. L. Keynes, Sr., had pioneered the development of genitourinary surgery on this side of the Atlantic.

Yet Bellevue's brilliant galaxy failed to shake Kellogg's abhorrence of deliberately slicing into human flesh. The sight of blood nauseated him so that he could only glance sporadically at the operations the school required him to observe. Always sensitive to unpleasant odors, Kellogg likewise found himself repelled by the heavy smell of disinfectants and the stench of infected wounds.

In view of his reaction to operations, it is not surprising that during his early years as medical superintendent of the Battle Creek Sanitarium John Harvey performed none himself. Instead, whenever he or another staff member judged that a sanitarium patient needed surgery, Kellogg employed specialists from Chicago or Detroit. Gradually, as he assisted some of the visiting surgeons and thus watched their technique more closely, his attitude began to change. He began to feel that not only could he master the necessary skills, but also that he could improve on some of the procedures he had observed. It also seemed to him that the patient's chances for recovery would be better if the sanitarium had a surgeon in residence instead of more than 100 miles away. On the practical side, the sanitarium could retain the money that now went in large amounts to the experts and use it to help finance the medical center's growth.

It particularly appalled Kellogg to find that mortality rates in abdominal surgery were extremely high. Physicians expected from 15 to 20 percent of the patients to die. John Harvey decided to obtain the best instruction available in the hope that he could reduce the rate at the sanitarium. Since many during the nineteenth century considered European methods to be more advanced than those in use in America, Kellogg began his specialized surgical study with a five-month tour of Europe. For nearly a month he attended clinics at the famous Hospital of St. Thomas and St. Bartholomew in London. Then he proceeded to Vienna to observe Theodor Billroth, the founder of modern gastric surgery and regarded by some authorities as the greatest surgeon the nineteenth century had produced. In the Austrian capital Kellogg not only watched the great master, but also took private instruction from Billroth's first assistant, Anton Wölfler.

Upon his return to Battle Creek, Dr. Kellogg fitted up several special wards at the sanitarium and began to perform a considerable amount of surgery. Soon an increasing number of complicated cases began to appear, and John Harvey recognized that he still had many things to learn. Consequently he arranged to work for several weeks in the private clinic of Dr. Horace T. Hanks, a leading New York City gynecological surgeon. While in New York, Kellogg also had the opportunity of observing Dr. Thomas Emmet, long-time surgeon at Women's Hospital, in action. Emmet had perfected the major surgical techniques used in repairing injuries resulting from childbirth.

Not yet satisfied with his surgical preparation, in 1889 Kellogg journeyed to Birmingham, England, where he spent nearly five months as surgical assistant to Dr. Lawson Tait. At the time, Tait, who specialized in abdominal and gynecological surgery, had a record of 116 successive operations without a death. His record remained unsurpassed in America for several years until Dr. Kellogg, using Tait's techniques coupled with his own distinctive biologic regimens, established a new record of 165 successive operations without a fatality, a record set in the days before it became the regular procedure for surgeons to use sterile rubber gloves in their work. During his visit to England in 1889, John Harvey also spent a month in London, observing the methods of leading surgeons at the Good Samaritan Hospital and the special techniques employed by Joseph Lister.

After a lapse of nearly 20 years, Kellogg returned to Europe on two different occasions to catch up on new surgical developments. He again visited Wölfler, who now dominated the field in Vienna, and made other stops in Bern, Paris, London, and Berlin. By then John Harvey had become interested in the problems of autointoxication, so he spent considerable time with Sir Arbuthnot Lane, one of England's most famous gastrointestinal surgeons, who was also experimenting in an effort to develop a surgical remedy for the supposed colonic malady. Although Kellogg did not adopt Lane's radical surgical techniques, he learned much from the Englishman, as he did in Berlin, the center for experimental renal surgery.

Although Dr. Kellogg last visited Europe in 1911 in the interest of improving his surgical skills, he did make several subsequent visits to the Mayo Clinic in Rochester, Minnesota. Here, at what had become the chief center for experimental surgery in the United States, he cultivated the friendship of both Drs. Will and Charles Mayo. The Mayo brothers quickly recognized his abilities. On one occasion, Dr. Charlie astounded a patient whom he was examining by saying, "I see that Dr. Kellogg performed an earlier operation for you."

"You are right," came the startled reply, "but how could you know who had done the operation?"

"That's easy," Mayo replied. "The scar is small and neat, just like a signature."

On at least one occasion the Mayos spent several days at the Battle Creek Sanitarium in order to observe the methods in use there. By that time John Harvey's surgical proficiency had received official recognition through his election as a member of the American College of Surgeons.

Part of his talent as a surgeon undoubtedly resulted from his manual dexterity. In boyhood he had demonstrated unusual natural ability as he deftly sorted broomcorn or type faces. Throughout his adult career he continued to cultivate his skill with his fingers. While traveling by train he frequently practiced making minute stitches on a small piece of cloth in order to improve the speed and precision needed in closing a wound. During his first visit to Vienna he took several lessons in freehand drawing from an artist whose shop he passed on the way to the Vienna Polyclinic. In later years he frequently sketched, not really for relaxation, but because he believed that the practice of training the hand to follow the eye was of great value to any surgeon.

As might be expected, Dr. Kellogg incorporated a number of the features of biologic living into his treatment of surgical patients. He firmly believed that the quick recovery most of his patients experienced came from the fact that he did not allow them to eat any meat for a number of days before and after their operations. Also he insisted that patients use liquids freely as an integral part of their postsurgical care. In certain types of operation the doctor, convinced that it contributed to an easier convalescence, gave patients a large tepid enema immediately following the surgery while they were still under the anesthetic.

In contrast to the modern practice of putting patients on their feet and having them walk soon after their surgery, surgical patients in Kellogg's day had to stay quietly in bed for a number of days, perhaps even for several weeks. As a believer in regular exercise, John Harvey deplored the custom. Although he did not break with it, he did develop a carefully graded set of bed exercises that he required all of his surgical patients to perform regularly. He also devised a way to cause muscular contractions in bed patients through the application of a mild and painless electric current. Believing that it helped to eliminate blood clots, pneumonia, and other postoperative complications, he frequently started the passive exercise the day following the operation.

Attendants packed all of Dr. Kellogg's surgical cases in warm sandbags before they left the operating room. He developed the method to help prevent surgical shock and found it effective. The doctor also prescribed hot footbaths rather than drugs for the relief of postoperative pains, again with good results. On one of his European trips Kellogg became acquainted with some experimental work being done with lactose, a milk sugar that seemed to have antiseptic properties. Beginning in 1916, he regularly sprinkled lactose over the dressings he applied to surgical wounds, considering it beneficial in preventing infection.

He did not attempt a wide variety of operations, but became adept at those to which he confined himself. At first he specialized in hemorrhoidectomies and ovariotomies, but later he expanded the scope of his gynecological surgery, devising several new operations to correct specific defects. After the start of the twentieth century he concentrated almost entirely upon gastrointestinal surgery. By limiting the kinds of operations that he performed, Kellogg learned to go through the complicated procedures involved much more rapidly than the average surgeon of the day. He remained careful, however, not to let speed interfere with the meticulous performance of his work. After a day in which he watched Dr. Kellogg perform nine operations in rapid succession, Dr. Howard A. Kelly expressed the opinion that John Harvey had just completed some of the most skillful surgery that he had ever seen. Since Kelly was himself one of America's foremost abdominal surgeons, a member of the renowned surgical team developed at Johns Hopkins University Medical School early in the twentieth century, his tribute had special significance.

Throughout much of his career Kellogg regularly devoted two or three days a week to surgery. He frequently operated for eight or 10 hours without a break and might perform as many as 25 operations in a single day. In the course of his lifetime he performed more than 22,000, the last when he was 88 years of age.

In spite of his renowned surgical skill, he frequently expressed dislike at being known as a surgeon, stating that he had less interest in surgery than in any other facet of his work. John Harvey never completely banished a distaste for the sight of blood and what he called "the terrible thought of cutting into people."

From the start of his career as a surgeon, he followed the practice of assembling his surgical team for prayer before they began the operation. Numerous patients commented on the strong reassurance they received from his procedure, and Kellogg himself frequently testified that his communion with God calmed the fears he inevitably experienced on each surgical case. He felt certain God imparted to him the particular skill necessary to cope with each situation.

Ellen White, who reported being shown by God that it was John Harvey's dependence upon divine aid that accounted for his surgical skill, shared his assurance. She also indicated that in vision she had observed a heavenly being standing at his side and guiding his hand as he operated. In later years the doctor tended to resent Mrs. White's statements about his angelic helper as he claimed they led people to expect too much of him.

The surgical fees that John Kellogg would normally have received could have made him a wealthy man. At the time of the great sanitarium fire in 1902 a local businessman estimated that the doctor's earning power was more than that of any two other residents of Battle Creek combined. But Dr. Kellogg refused to use his surgical talents for private gain. He made it a practice to assign all surgical fees to the Battle Creek Sanitarium or to other sanitariums where he operated, for, as Seventh-day Adventists established sanitariums from Massachusetts to California, he followed a regular pattern of visits to the infant institutions. At each he operated on difficult cases that the local staff had reserved for his attention. The fees from such operations were his contribution to the growth of the family of sanitariums.

At the peak of his career Dr. Kellogg estimated that his surgical fees had already amounted to more than $400,000. Significantly, while he was earning such large amounts for the various sanitariums, he was also performing from one third to one half of his operations upon charity patients, to whom he made no charge. Kellogg believed in the policy of assessing wealthy patients large fees so that they might, in effect, contribute to the cost of the surgery needed by those who were deserving but poor. On one occasion he reported charging $1,000 for one case so that he could afford to operate on some of the poor for nothing. At another time he received $400 for an operation that took him not quite four minutes to perform. Although John Harvey embarked upon his surgical career rather unwillingly, he employed his skill in it to support the great educational program of the Battle Creek Sanitarium and its sister institutions, and to finance the charitable work in which he so fully believed.

CRAPTER XI
PRODUCTS OF AN ACTIVE MIND

IN MUCH THE SAME WAY that his skilled fingers played a large role in John Harvey's success as a surgeon, so his active imagination and inventive mind led naturally to his devising a number of products designed to improve the user's health. As a result of preparing his own food during his student days at Bellevue, he had become convinced that a real need for healthful ready-to-eat foods existed. He devoted a major part of his spare time in New York to dietary experiments. They served as the basis for the health-reform cookbook that he later compiled.

Shortly after becoming medical superintendent at the Battle Creek Sanitarium, he became aware of the patients' general dissatisfaction with the food served them. They commonly complained that the menu was both meager and monotonous. At once Kellogg decided that he must find some means of making it more attractive and, at the same time, more healthful.

In his study of food chemistry, Dr. Kellogg had learned that one of the first steps in digestion is the conversion of starch into dextrin. The process begins in the mouth through the action of the saliva. Eating too rapidly and without proper mastication inhibits dextrinization, and hence the digestive process. He reasoned that it would be advantageous, particularly for patients with digestive disorders, if starchy foods were already partially digested.

Cereal grains, which John Harvey regarded as the basic element in a natural diet, have a high starch content. He conducted a variety of experiments that resulted in the discovery that prolonged baking almost completely dextrinized the starch contents of the multigrain biscuits he had prepared. Kellogg had the biscuits ground up and served to sanitarium patients in a form similar to the modern cereal Grape-Nuts. The preparation resembled the Granula made at Dansville, New York, by Dr. James Caleb Jackson, except that longer baking made it more thoroughly dextrinized, and it also consisted of several grains rather than wheat alone as did Jackson's product. Since many persons interested in a reform diet already knew of Granula, John Harvey called his creation Granola. At first he apparently had no thought of selling it. He intended it solely for sanitarium patients.

Laboratory building at Battle Creek Sanitarium

Gradually, however, as former patients and others interested in dietetic improvement sent to the sanitarium for Granola, a small commercial business developed, and Battle Creek thus took its first step toward becoming the "Breakfast Food Capital of the World."

To stimulate the flow of saliva as an aid to proper digestion, Dr. Kellogg commonly required his patients to begin their meals by eating a saucer of dry Granola or several pieces of hard zwieback. One day he discovered the dangers in such a program when an irate woman stormed into his office to complain that she had cracked her false teeth while following his prescription. When she suggested that he should pay her $10 to purchase new dentures, he immediately decided that he must do something to keep the foods that he believed to be essential to good health from becoming a health hazard. He ordered the experimental food laboratory—established at the sanitarium in the early 1880s—to begin searching for a method that would make cereal products both thoroughly dextrinized and more easily soluble.

Sometime during 1893 or 1894, while Dr. Kellogg was busily outlining a series of experiments that he hoped would result in the kind of cereal product he desired, a patient called his attention to Shredded Wheat, recently developed in Denver by Henry D. Perky. Obtaining a supply of the little whole-wheat biscuits, Kellogg served them to sanitarium patients, who complained that eating Shredded Wheat was like munching straw or whisk brooms. In spite of the comparison, the possibilities of the new product sufficiently impressed him to cause him to visit Perky and to secure from him a promise to sell the sanitarium a machine so that it might produce Shredded Wheat for its patients. Kellogg may even have offered to buy Perky's entire interest in Shredded Wheat, but may have been unwilling to pay the price the manufacturer demanded. For his part, Perky apparently learned from Kellogg about the long, high-temperature baking process necessary for the complete dextrinization of a wheat cereal. When he shifted his manufacturing operations from Denver to Massachusetts and later to Niagara Falls, Perky began to use the thorough baking process John Harvey had discovered. He found that the change not only increased the digestibility of his biscuits but also the length of time that they would last without spoiling.

Although Kellogg's contact with Perky did not result in getting the desired Shredded Wheat machine, it did make him more confident than ever that someone could develop an improved cereal food. His goal became the discovery of a process for turning each grain of wheat into a small flake of toast. At first the doctor tried to produce such flakes by feeding raw wheat, which he had soaked in water, between a pair of rollers. Instead of flakes, he obtained a combination of watery starch and coarse bran. Kellogg next tried cooking the wheat for periods of up to an hour before putting it through the rollers, but he found that it simply formed a pasty mass that stuck to the machinery. Then a fortunate accident occurred. John Harvey had cooked up a batch of wheat in his kitchen at home. Before he could put it through the rollers, something interrupted and called him away for several hours. When he returned to his experiment, he decided that rather than waste the wheat that he had previously cooked, he would just run it through the rollers. He fed the wheat into a small pair of rollers while one of his foster children turned the crank and another used a large bread knife to scrape off the distinct flakes that emerged. Success had come. Unknowingly, the doctor had stumbled upon the principle of "tempering," a process basic to the future of the flaked cereal industry.

While elated with his discovery, he still did not know just how it had happened. He discussed the problem with his brother Will, and the two men agreed to carry on further basic experimentation together. Working at the sanitarium one day, the brothers cooked up a batch of wheat, expecting to attempt to flake it later the same day. But other work intervened, and they could not process the wheat until a day or so later. Although they found that the delay had allowed the grain to accumulate a little mold, to their delight the flakes that they secured were larger and thinner than any they had previously made. Baking some of the wheat flakes in the oven of the big sanitarium kitchen range, the Kelloggs found that, although they possessed a slightly moldy flavor, they were otherwise crisp and quite edible.

Many problems still demanded solutions. Will Kellogg suggested that they fasten a paper-cutting knife, similar to those used in printshops, against the rollers. A local mechanic fixed up the blade for them. Although the new adaptation was an improvement over the old bread knife, it took quite a bit of adjusting to keep the flakes from being compressed into masses as the knife scraped them from the rollers. It also required time to discover the proper rate to feed the cooked wheat into the rollers in order to secure flakes of uniform size. The brothers noticed that changing atmospheric conditions interfered with the tempering process, a factor they had to control in order to keep the wheat from molding. At first they air-dried the flakes, but later they discovered that the flavor of the flakes improved if they baked them quickly at temperatures of from 400 to 480 degrees. Once the Kellogg brothers had made the initial flakes, employees of Dr. Kellogg, working under his general direction, carried out much of the experimentation necessary to perfect the product for mass manufacturing and marketing.

Kellogg named the new cereal discovery Granose Flakes, deriving "Gran" from "grain," and borrowing the suffix "ose" from the field of physiological chemistry, which frequently employed it to indicate a digestion product. After having spent nearly $2,000 in the experiments that finally resulted in Granose Flakes, John Harvey on May 31, 1894, filed for a patent on "flaked cereal and process of preparing same." The patent covered flakes prepared from barley, oats, and other grains as well as those made from wheat. While he did not plan to use his discovery for personal profit, he did hope that the sale of flaked cereals would provide funds for spreading the gospel of biologic living. He showed his initial attitude toward any financial profit that might result from the cereal foods in a lecture in which he described to a large Adventist audience the process for making Granola at home. "You may say that I am destroying the health food business here by giving these recipes," John Harvey stated at the end of his talk, "but I am not after the business; I am after the reform; that is what I want to see."

In spite of all the trouble he had taken to develop wheat flakes, Kellogg was not completely certain that the public would accept them in such a form, so different from the old standard Granola. Consequently he had a portion of the flakes rubbed through a sieve to make small particles that mushed up instantly in milk. He called them Granose Grits. Will Kellogg, however, was confident that the flaked form of the cereal would eventually prove more popular, and he insisted upon developing it further.

Although Kellogg had originated Granose Flakes primarily for his sanitarium patients, the new cereal's popularity soon spread far beyond Battle Creek. The first year that the product was available saw more than 50 tons manufactured and sold in spite of rather primitive production facilities. Success invited competition, and soon cereal manufacturing companies sprang up all over the country. The competitors soon discovered that they could easily infringe upon Kellogg's Granose patent, and in a short time the bulk of the flaked cereal business went to men less financially conservative and less idealistic than John Harvey Kellogg. The doctor was understandably bitter, particularly when a firm in Quincy, Illinois, took the name "The Battle Creek Breakfast Food Company." However, he saved his deepest antagonism for his brother Will, who eventually made Corn Flakes into the biggest success in the entire prepared cereal trade.

Another important item in the modern American diet that Kellogg first introduced was peanut butter. Shortly after 1890, he had a quantity of roasted peanuts ground up into a paste for use by patients who had difficulty in masticating nuts or peanuts (which are a legume) well enough to digest them properly. Later he decided that roasting caused the fat content to begin to decompose, irritating the digestive organs. From that time forward the sanitarium made its peanut butter from steam-cooked rather than roasted peanuts. Kellogg also devised a variety of nut butters that he claimed were "sweeter, more palatable, and more digestible" than regular butter. Making no attempt to secure patents that would let him control the production of either peanut butter or any of his nut butters, he announced that he believed that they were products that "the world ought to have; let everybody that wants it have it, and make the best use of it."

During the decade following the appearance of peanut butter, Dr. Kellogg developed several other food products with a nut base. In 1896 he patented a product labeled "Bromose," which he claimed to be a vegetable equivalent of malted milk. Composed of a combination of nuts and dextrinized starch, Bromose was manufactured in the form of small cakes. It, he said, contained in a predigested form all the food elements difficult to digest in regular malted milk. At about the same time, John Harvey originated a similar product that he named Malted Nuts. Derived principally from peanuts and almonds, one could mix Malted Nuts with water to form a vegetable milk that he maintained looked "exactly like milk, and tastes so nearly like it that it is a very satisfactory substitute." Although he designed the latter product primarily for infants who could not tolerate cow's milk, the doctor also recommended its use by persons suffering from biliousness, hyperpepsia, nervous headache, and Bright's disease. In 1897 Kellogg patented a nut meal that he claimed was particularly valuable for the blood- and tissue-building elements it contained. One could eat it either as a gruel or in combination with a variety of fruits.

Although peanut butter was the only one of Dr. Kellogg's nut products to gain wide public acceptance, health-conscious persons expressed approval of and used several of the others. Clara Barton, founder of the American Red Cross, wrote him that although she did not as a rule lend her name to the promotion of any particular products, she would be happy to make an exception in the case of Bromose and Nut Butter. She had found both foods to be not only wholesome, but nutritious and "very pleasant to the palate."

During the years in which he directed the experiments that led to the production of flaked cereals, Bromose, and Malted Nuts, Dr. Kellogg also attempted to develop a substitute for meat from plant sources. He traced his interest in such a product to conversations with Dr. Charles W. Dabney, noted agricultural chemist and former president of the University of Tennessee. When Dabney was serving as President Cleveland's assistant secretary of agriculture, he had discussed with Kellogg the problem of supplying adequate protein for the world's rapidly expanding population. The men agreed that it was better economics to use grain for human food than to feed it to animals and then use them for food. The problem, as

Dabney saw it, was to produce a grain product that would have all the nutritional value and taste appeal of meat.

In 1896 Kellogg announced that he had perfected the ideal substitute for meat in Nuttose, a nut product that he could prepare to taste much like beef or chicken. By then he was much too busy to carry out food experiments personally, but kept a full-time assistant performing the numerous tests that he outlined. The doctor's interest in new vegetarian meatlike protein foods continued until shortly before his death. Among some of the more popular creations later developed in his laboratories were Protose, Battle Creek Steaks, and Battle Creek Skallops. Varying combinations of nuts and wheat gluten composed the principal ingredients of the imitation meats.

During the series of legal battles that developed with his brother Will, John Harvey claimed to have invented more than 75 different foods. In addition to those already mentioned, the most successful was Caramel Cereal Coffee. The sanitarium had been manufacturing a coffee substitute made from a mixture of burned bread crusts, bran, molasses, and corn at the time that Kellogg joined the institution. The doctor's attempts to make the product both more healthful and more tasty resulted in Caramel Cereal Coffee. Although he never showed much enthusiasm about his coffee substitute, publicly calling it "a very poor substitute for a very poor thing," the product enjoyed a considerable sale. It sold about one ton a day when C. W. Post began to market a similar creation that he called Postum.

Through extensive and clever advertising Post captured the coffee-substitute market. Ironically, he built his fortune on products that he had learned to know at the Battle Creek Sanitarium. At the time Kellogg was experimenting with Caramel Cereal Coffee, Mr. Post was a patient at the sanitarium. Since the Post finances were in bad shape, the sanitarium took him in as a semi-charity case. Door-to-door sales of suspenders made by his wife provided his main source of income. Both Mr. and Mrs. Post showed unusual interest in the sanitarium's experimental food laboratory, visiting it often and asking many questions. One of the laboratory workers reported their curiosity to Dr. Kellogg and further voiced the suspicion that the couple was planning to put out a cereal coffee themselves. When someone suggested that the management bar the Posts from the laboratory, Kellogg replied, "No! The more people there are who make such products, the more there are who are likely to use them. That is the important thing."

Kellogg had all of his food creations developed in an effort to encourage biologic living. To satisfy the American taste for sweets, he invented a health candy made from malt sugar and chocolate minus the theobromine. In his later years, after he became concerned over the problem of bowel regularity, he developed a number of natural laxative foods, the most successful of which was a sterilized bran breakfast cereal. He also devised Paramels, a mineral oil preparation in the form of chocolate-flavored caramels; Laxa, a combination of sterilized bran and Japanese seaweed; and L. D. Lax, a derivative of psyllium seed, lactose, and dextrins.

Kellogg's last major food discovery was an artificial milk made principally from soybeans. He was particularly enthusiastic over soymilk because it proved an excellent host for the acidophilus bacteria that the doctor believed the intestinal tract needed in order for it to function perfectly. Shortly after Kellogg had developed soy acidophilus milk, he chanced to read that Marie, smallest of the Dionne quintuplets, was suffering from bowel trouble. Immediately wiring the quints' physician, Dr. A. R. Dafoe, he announced he was sending him a supply of soy acidophilus milk, which he was certain would cure Marie's problem. About 10 days later he received a letter from Dafoe that indicated that it had indeed corrected the situation and requested a continuous supply be sent to Callander, Ontario, for the five little girls.

Demonstrating his inventive talents in an entirely different area, Dr. Kellogg devised a variety of instruments for use in the types of operation in which he specialized. They included a special set of hooks and retractors, an operating table heated by hot water as an aid in preventing surgical shock during long operations, and an aseptic drainage tube for use in abdominal surgery.

Early in his career Kellogg exhibited interest in mechanical exercisers. Two years after becoming sanitarium superintendent, he purchased several hundred dollars' worth of exercise equipment for the use of sanitarium patients. His visit to Sweden in 1883 allowed him to become better acquainted with the variety of mechanical exercisers that Gustav Zander had been building for a number of years. Shortly after his return to Battle Creek, John Harvey devised a vibrating chair to stimulate the bodily organs located in the lower trunk. The device was quite simple. It consisted of a regular wooden armchair placed upon a small platform made to oscillate mechanically at the rate of 20 times a second. He maintained that the resulting vibrating movements increased blood circulation with beneficial results.

Toward the end of the century, Dr. Kellogg organized the Sanitarium Equipment Company. It manufactured a variety of apparatus designed by the doctor to provide stimulation to many different parts of the body. His devices included a vibratory bar for use on the hands, arms, upper spine, and head; a mechanical kneading machine for stimulating the abdomen in order to relieve chronic constipation; a moving belt that became a standard piece of equipment in weight-reduction programs; a tilting table that alternately raised and lowered a patient's head and feet eight times each minute; and a revolving ribbed cylinder designed to apply friction to the bottom of the feet. Zander had first built many of them, but Kellogg made adaptations that he claimed improved their effectiveness.

In 1884, while experimenting with a high-frequency oscillating electrical current later named the sinusoidal current by French physicist Jacques-Arsine d'Arsonval, Dr. Kellogg discovered that it offered great possibilities as a means of passive exercise. He noted that when applied to the body, the sinusoidal current produced vigorous muscular contractions but

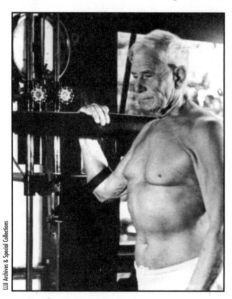

no pain. To his delight, he had discovered a way by which he could make the benefits of exercise available to paralyzed persons and others who, because of obesity, arthritis, or diabetes, could not engage in vigorous physical activity. Utilizing the sinusoidal current, John Harvey devised a passive exerciser that, when used for 20 minutes, provided the patient with the stimulation of a brisk four-mile walk.

Dr. Kellogg believed that symmetrical muscular development was essential for good health, but he recognized that

A machine to test muscle strength

observation alone was a deceptive method for estimating the extent to which the body's various muscle groups had grown. He felt certain that it should be possible to devise some kind of apparatus to test muscle strength. In 1894, after 10 years of experimentation, he perfected the universal dynamometer. Based on the same mercury principle used in blood-pressure machines, it soon became a part of the physical education programs at West Point, the University of Wisconsin, Yale, and a number of other leading colleges.

By using the dynamometer over a period of years to make a series of strength tests, Kellogg developed a table of average norms for the various muscle groups. It then became possible to test a patient, to ascertain the extent that he varied from the norms, and to prescribe a special set of exercises designed to strengthen improperly developed muscles. In 1907, when Admiral A. P. Niblack became commander of the naval squadron attached to the U.S. Naval Academy at Annapolis, he decided that the equipment in the school's new gymnasium was useless without Kellogg's dynamometer. Niblack personally went to Battle Creek, purchased two of the divices, and secured instruction in their proper use. For a quarter of a century thereafter every cadet who entered the Naval Academy took dynamometer tests.

One evening in the early 1890s as Dr. Kellogg turned on an ordinary incandescent reading lamp, he noted that his fingers took on a red glow as he held his hand in front of the light bulb. Convinced that he had found a valuable new source of heat penetration that he could use to treat bodily disorders, he immediately set to work sketching designs for a cabinet bath that would utilize electric light bulbs as the source of heat. A few days later the sanitarium machine shop built the first electric light cabinet bath. Kellogg introduced his new invention at the Chicago World's Fair of 1893, but it aroused little interest there. Even though the Battle Creek Sanitarium installed a number of them and patients used them regularly, little widespread public demand developed for the cabinet baths in the United States until after they became popular in Europe. Introduced in Vienna by Kellogg's friend Dr. Wilhelm Winternitz, the Kellogischen Licht Bade soon became fashionable, and the royal palaces of Great Britain, Germany, and Sweden installed them. For years the electric light cabinet bath was popular in athletic clubs, where it frequently replaced the old Turkish steam baths.

Kellogg's interest in proper breathing led him in 1888 to construct a device that he named the pneumograph. It provided a graphic representation of an individual's respiratory habits. Equipment attached to the subject's chest activated a stylus, which in turn drew a tracing of the regularity and depth of the breathing. On another occasion, an invention the doctor had devised to correct faulty night breathing had humorous results.

One morning a male patient approached John Harvey and confided that he planned to leave the sanitarium the next day. The doctor expressed surprise as the man had only recently arrived.

"Aren't you pleased with your treatments?" Kellogg queried.

"Very much so," came the reply. "I am receiving a great deal of benefit, but a difficult situation has arisen. I have become quite well acquainted with a maiden lady who sits at my table in the dining room and who occupies the room next to mine. This good woman snores so loudly all night long that I can't get a wink of sleep. If I ask to be transferred to another room, she will want to know why. I don't want to risk hurting her feelings, so I will check out and come back some other time."

Dr. Kellogg smilingly indicated that he thought that he could correct the situation without embarrassment. "Snoring results from breathing through the nose and mouth at the same time," the doctor stated. "Without mentioning snoring, I will see the lady you mention and prescribe a device that will improve both her health and her appearance by preventing her jaw from dropping when asleep."

To the great satisfaction of the disturbed guest, the doctor's plan worked perfectly. On the second day, however, Dr. Kellogg happened to walk into the lobby just as the man was checking out. "What is the matter now?" the doctor inquired.

"Shortly before midnight last night," answered the departing guest, "I thought of the inconvenience I had caused my neighbor, and I just had to call her on the telephone and apologize." At that moment the woman in question, obviously much disturbed, entered the lobby. Both Dr. Kellogg and his companion decided that it would be wise to move along, and the doctor never made any attempts to market his snoring cure.

During the early years of the twentieth century John Harvey became interested in the idea of an electrically heated blanket as the result of

JOHN H. KELLOGGS'
WORLD

Above: John Harvey Kellogg in later years

Right: John Harvey's parents, Ann J. and John Preston Kellogg

Early view of Battle Creek Sanitarium taken from a stereopticon slide

Health Reform Institute

Dr. Kellogg with staff of Battle Creek Sanitarium

Left: Fire destroying the
Battle Creek Sanitarium

Below: The main Sanitarium
building as it looked before
the 1902 fire.

Women's in-door swimming pool

A Christmas greeting card from the Sanitarium

Merry Christmas 1910 FROM THE
SANITARIUM BATTLE CREEK MICH

Laying the cornerstone of the new Sanitarium building. May 11, 1902

Battle Creek Sanitarium band

Left: Dr. Kellogg with Ivan Pavlov, far left

MAIN DINING ROOM SANITARIUM BATTLE CREEK MICH. 22

Kellogg's Battle Creek home

Women's bathing room
at the Sanitarium

Views of John Harvey Kellogg through the years

Aerial view of the Battle Creek Sanitarium before the towers addition

Battle Creek College and girl's dorm

The doctor always projected a dynamic personality.

An older Dr. Kellogg

President William Howard Taft speaking at Battle Creek Sanitarium

something he had read about some experimental work in France. He arranged for the preparation of a carpet that had a silver wire woven along the side of every sixth thread. The doctor then connected the wires electrically and found the resulting warmth particularly comforting when used on the bed on his outdoor sleeping porch in midwinter. Although Kellogg apparently had several of the primitive electric blankets made for use in his home, he never attempted to develop the product for public sale.

Throughout the years his fertile mind devised many other contrivances useful to his system of biologic living. The doctor's interest in fresh air led him to design a type of canvas tube to bring fresh air into a bedroom at night without cooling off the entire room. With one end attached to an open window, the other ended in a tent-type contrivance fastened over the sleeper's head. Several other inventions reflect his interest in fresh air and proper respiration. They included a simple device for testing the carbon-dioxide content of the air in a room and some improvements on a pioneer mechanical artificial respirator originally designed by Zander to train individuals to correct poor respiratory habits. Kellogg also developed and patented a menthol inhaler to aid in clearing nasal passages congested because of a cold or some other minor ailment.

His insistence on pure water led him in the early 1880s to construct a water filter that he claimed was superior to any similar equipment then available. Several years later he developed an apparatus for the home sterilization of milk, and extravagantly claimed that it was so satisfactory that milk sterilized according to its directions would keep "indefinitely." John Harvey's concern about proper posture resulted in his development of several different types of chairs.

In no instance did Dr. Kellogg make a sustained effort to reap personal financial profit from any of his inventions or adaptations. A statement that he made in 1916 relative to his food manufacturing business applies equally well to the promotional activities connected with his other inventions. "I desire to make clear," the doctor testified, ". . . that the food business I have been carrying on is a part of my general scheme to propagate the ideas of health and biological living. Otherwise, I should not have engaged in it as a commercial enterprise, but I have carried it on as a part of the general philanthropic work in which I was engaged."

CHAPTER XII

ALL WORK, BUT LITTLE PLAY

PHYSICIAN, SURGEON, AUTHOR, lecturer, administrator, educator, inventor, propagandist—how could John Harvey Kellogg accomplish so much in so many different areas? For one thing, he loved to work hard, and he thoroughly enjoyed what he did. At the age of 80, he maintained that he could not remember a dull day in his entire life, or one that seemed too long. Several years earlier he had expressed the wish that life could go on for a thousand years so that he might really be able to accomplish something.

Another secret of his success centered in his willingness to extend his workday much beyond today's normal eight-hour limit. During the early part of his career he often began work at 4:00 in the morning and seldom quit before midnight. On many days his wife would bring him four or five hot lunches, only to have them remain untouched because the doctor was too occupied with his tasks to take the few minutes required to eat. John Harvey's mother, who was still living at the time, became worried, because she realized her son could never maintain his strength under such circumstances. She finally conceived the plan of sending him regularly a glass of whole cream, which he would sip while working.

Kellogg seemed able to tap almost superhuman sources of energy to keep going full tilt for extended periods. Before he had built up a corps of efficient assistants at the sanitarium, he reported that for 10 of the days in the preceding two weeks he had been unable to take his clothes off except to take baths. Frequently he would work 30 to 40 hours at a stretch, taking a break only to eat a little fruit.

To maintain such an arduous work program, he developed special techniques that enabled him to summon forth reserve energy. Often immediately after someone awakened him at 4:00 or 5:00 in the morning, he would begin the day with a warm, stimulating bath. When the habit proved too exhausting over an extended period, he switched to a long lukewarm bath before retiring. Sometimes he would relax for up to two hours in the tub, dozing off for short periods, awakening to add more hot water as the bath cooled. It prepared him for five or six hours of sound sleep. He would begin the next day with a cold bath and then be able to work continuously for periods extending up to 40 hours.

Even at 60 the doctor could work for weeks at a time on an average of only about four hours of sleep a night. At the end of one of his study trips abroad, he reported, "I had hard work to finish . . . before I left London, and during the last 48 hours I did not close my eyes to sleep. The last four days I had only ten hours sleep, and worked every minute of the rest of the time. I only stopped to eat one small meal a day, and I was glad to find I had endurance enough to do it. I was very glad to see that I felt no worse for it."

Even in his later years he still worked at top speed for long periods of time. His efficient staff, both at his home and at the sanitarium, adjusted their schedules to his every whim in order to enable him to make the best use of his time. He might arrive at his office, where two or three stenographers always waited to take dictation, at any time between 7:00 in the morning and 3:00 in the afternoon. Kellogg's average day might include four or five hours of dictation, an equal amount of time in surgery, several hours of consultation with sanitarium patients, an hour or two devoted to a consideration of sanitarium business with staff doctors and officials, plus a lecture of perhaps an hour and a half. Two private stenographers kept their bags packed and in the office so that they could accompany the doctor on a moment's notice on one of his frequent cross-country

Dr. Kellogg dictating to his secretary, August Bloese, about 1935

trips. On such occasions they would barely be seated on the train before Kellogg would begin to dictate, usually for some book or article that he was writing. The dictating might continue for as long as 18 hours, with time out only to munch some fruit and nuts. Then, at a convenient station, the stenographer would return to Battle Creek to transcribe his notes while the doctor continued to his appointment.

Eventually Kellogg preferred to do his literary work late at night, when no one would interrupt him. Often he would begin dictating shortly before midnight and would continue until 4:00 in the morning. Contrary to what one might expect, his efficiency seemed to increase during the early morning hours, and he was at his best between 3:00 and 4:00 a.m. During his night and early morning sessions Kellogg preferred to lie down while dictating. He maintained that a prone position relieved tension and allowed his brain to get added blood so that he could think more clearly. If the night was at all warm, a nurse or the chauffeur rubbed the doctor's forehead with a towel dipped in ice water for as long as he dictated. A favorite Kellogg working spot was the glider on the open porch of his Battle Creek residence. In cold weather he would lie there for hours, comfortably wrapped in blankets, while dictating to a benumbed secretary.

The wide variety of Kellogg's interests and activities necessitated an extensive correspondence. On a normal day he would dictate between 25 and 50 letters. Since he never acquired the habit of brevity, many of them were lengthy epistles, ranging up to 15 or 18 typewritten pages. Kellogg dictated rapidly, and his failure to enunciate clearly, coupled with his use of an exceedingly large vocabulary, increased his stenographers' difficulties. To save time, he occasionally dictated while taking his morning bath, and he almost never bothered to reread or sign his letters, a chore he delegated to his private secretary. Kellogg had the ability to do several things at the same time. Regularly he examined reports and medical literature while dictating.

An agile mind and a tremendous memory contributed to his ability to accomplish more than the average man. It was not unusual for him to dash off a paper for a scientific meeting in three hours' time. John Harvey was 78 when he took the Florida state medical licensing examination, and although he made no effort to review for the test before boarding the train at Battle Creek for the trip south, study during the journey enabled him to complete the two-day test with a score higher than that received by most of the younger examinees.

The doctor also possessed the enviable ability to drop off to sleep almost instantly under any circumstances and to awake after a five- or 10-minute nap sufficiently refreshed to continue his labors. On such occasions he would immediately return to the conversation or dictation at the exact point at which he had fallen asleep. His secretary would not need to read back his previous words even if he had stopped in the middle of a sentence. Kellogg's subordinates found it expedient to carry a notebook to jot down all of the doctor's instructions, as he would invariably inquire to see if they had carried them out, even if he did not see the person again for a number of days.

Finally, when he reached the age of 80, Kellogg began to cut his workday to 12 or 15 hours. In emergencies, however, he still could carry on a program most younger men would have found exhausting. Shortly before making his final trip to Battle Creek from Florida at the age of 91, for example, he dictated for 16 hours at a stretch and appeared no worse for the experience.

The punishing work schedule he adopted is even more remarkable in view of the fact that as a child and youth John Kellogg's health had not been particularly robust. In later years he blamed chronic gastrointestinal problems on his unwholesome childhood diet, specifically his excessive consumption of meat and candy. Probably more significant for Kellogg's later life was the touch of pulmonary tuberculosis that he contracted in his early teens. Although he made a relatively good recovery from it, it permanently weakened one of his lungs.

Like all mortals, Dr. Kellogg occasionally became ill and had not only to abandon his punishing work schedule but, much to his embarrassment, had to take to bed. Early in his tenure as superintendent of the sanitarium, he found himself confined to his private quarters for a number of days. Rumors soon spread that the doctor was a victim of typhoid fever, but in reality he was simply suffering from a severe cold and the effects of overwork.

A few years later Kellogg revealed in vivid manner the physical discomforts his heavy schedule sometimes induced. "My head and spine have been giving me great inconvenience and often acute suffering," he

wrote to his longtime friend and mentor, Ellen White. "I reel and trem-
ble, and get blind and have so many nervous symptoms I am ashamed to
tell them all. Worst of all, my mind seems to stop sometimes, and I cannot force it to go. I am not frightened, for I have been through the same
thing before, and more than once. I know that a little rest will restore me
to myself again."

To be ill for any reason was a matter of real embarrassment for a man
who had bound up his whole life with preaching the gospel of health.
Consequently, when he felt himself approaching the breaking point,
Kellogg almost invariably left Battle Creek in a hurry. He probably also
recognized the impossibility of his securing the rest he needed there. Early
in his career Florida became a favorite retreat. Since his wife's health was
rather delicate, the need to take her to a warmer climate offered a convenient excuse for the doctor's periodic absences.

After a brief rest Kellogg then plunged back into the same punishing
schedule. It was almost as if he were under a compulsion to work, even
under "fearful physical odds." "The condition of my brain and nerves,"
he wrote once, "was so worn out with anxiety, that every day was a hor-
ror and a terror, and I plunged into my work every morning with sheer
desperation, . . . although so perplexed that everything seemed in a
whirl." He commented on another occasion that the work of the previous few years had been so arduous that "sometimes I feared that I should
lose my mind, and I do not know but that I have been off my mental balance a little sometimes."

In the winter of 1891-1892, after he had followed a work program of
18 to 20 hours a day steadily for nine months, Kellogg suffered a real physical collapse. For weeks a high fever confined him to his room, and not
until the following summer was he able to resume a normal program again.
It was Kellogg's most serious illness since his youth. Yet within a year he
was back working from 5:00 a.m. until midnight, sandwiching in his meals
while dictating and maintaining that he never felt better in his life. Had he
not worked so hard, John Harvey always maintained, the sanitarium would
not have made any progress. Several years later he boasted that his muscles were "hard as wood" and that he could pick up a 200-pound man from
the floor, throw him over his shoulder, and carry him off.

At other times, however, physical exhaustion set in, and Kellogg declared that his eyes seemed "like balls of fire." He spoke of not having known even once during the previous 10 years what it was really like to feel rested. His tendency to drive himself continually led some of the doctor's closest associates to fear lest he suffer a nervous breakdown. They urged him to get away periodically for a real vacation. At some times Kellogg himself recognized that the regimen he was following made such a breakdown a real possibility.

Ellen White, who advised him with more frankness than most of his associates could muster, repeatedly cautioned the doctor to work more moderately, to eat regularly, and to get sufficient rest. "I feel deeply for you," she wrote on one occasion, "and you must change your course of action. You are living two years in one, and I utter my protest against this."

Periodically, Kellogg would resolve to change his ways. He would admit that improper eating and insufficient rest impaired his effectiveness and caused him concern lest he disgrace the principles he professed and taught. But always less concerned about what happened to his own health, he believed that it was a person's duty to sacrifice themselves completely to the cause of humanity and trust God to care for them as long as He had a work for them to do. At the age of 60, John Harvey frankly admitted he did not always follow his own advice. "I am under no obligation to practice what I preach," he argued. "My business is to preach, and really I haven't time to practice. I am putting out fires; that is my business. I belong to the fire department, and I haven't time to look after my own health. I am looking after other people's health, and my own health has to take the best chance it can."

His tendency to neglect his own health nearly cost Kellogg his life in 1918. When several members of the sanitarium staff joined the American Expeditionary Force in France, Dr. Kellogg, then 66, added much of their work to his own full program. For months he slept a maximum of five or six hours a night. At the same time he often ate only one meal a day, and that on the run. As a result, his resistance to infection so lowered that he suffered a reoccurrence of the tuberculosis of his boyhood. In the fall, it forced him to go to Florida, where he spent more than seven months in bed.

The period of convalescence was a trying one for Kellogg. He complained of considerable pain in his left side and a shortness of breath. A severe neuritis that especially affected his shoulders, legs, and feet, further complicated his condition. Some days he felt better, some worse. On the latter occasions, he thought himself "pretty near to the end of my rope." He would have preferred to be at home, but he thought that it would be too embarrassing to be there and not to be active. He was, indeed, anxious that the seriousness of his condition not be generally known.

Shortly after he returned to Battle Creek, a number of the leading lung and chest specialists of the United States gathered at the sanitarium for a national meeting of the Trudeau Society. John Harvey had several of the doctors examine him, and he asked them if an entire year of rest would enable him to live for five more years. They answered in the negative and told him that his condition would get progressively worse. Most of the doctors thought that he could anticipate living for a maximum of three years. Kellogg fooled them all—he survived almost a quarter of a century more. From then onward, however, he avoided cold weather and spent most of his winters in Florida.

Although, contrary to his own teaching, he was extremely irregular in his eating habits most of his life, he did eat only the type of food he advocated to others. When traveling, he always made it a point to carry fruit and nuts with him. He was particularly fond of fresh green figs, mangoes, and alligator pears. Also he regularly ate the cereal and meat substitutes that he had developed. While working, he often kept nuts or dried fruits in his pockets and would munch on them until he had a chance to get a regular meal.

In later years, when his schedule became more regular, Kellogg generally ate only two meals a day, but they were substantial ones. A typical breakfast might consist of two large fully ripe bananas, one or two good-sized apples, several tomatoes in season, half an avocado, half a pound of ripe papayas or other fresh fruit, and perhaps a baked potato, some boiled rice, and toast. The second meal of the day was similar but with smaller quantities of fruit and with green garden vegetables and parsley sauce added.

During the last 15 years of his life Dr. Kellogg's hearing became progressively worse and, as he approached 90, his eyesight also deteriorated. He disliked wearing glasses, however; and he tolerated a hearing aid only on occasion. Although his mind remained clear until the last, he became increasingly forgetful and showed more than his normal tendency to repeat himself. During the last several years of his life, John Harvey suffered from Bell's palsy, which led him to restrict his public appearances. He also became somewhat anemic, due probably both to the low protein diet upon which he insisted, and to advancing age.

If he had only followed the advice he gave others and had learned to rest and to spend more time in recreation, Dr. Kellogg might well have experienced even better health throughout his nearly 92 years. But he enjoyed only a few common recreations—

Dr. Kellogg playing the piano at the age of 91

among them music. The doctor found relaxation in playing the piano or violin during an evening with his family, and he often listened to some favorite violin or accordion recordings before retiring.

Kellogg also enjoyed motoring. After a hard day's work he liked to have someone drive him over backcountry roads at a high rate of speed. Since he never became a skillful driver himself, it was fortunate that he was content to entrust the driving to a chauffeur. In his later years he liked to ride in a motorboat. Again he always wanted the boat to go as rapidly as possible. During the last 15 years of his life John Harvey frequently traveled by airplane. Once he even rode in an early type of helicopter piloted by Amelia Earhart. But he never really enjoyed flying, probably because it did not provide him with the sensation of speed that he experienced in a fast-moving boat or automobile.

From the time of his youth he was a bicycle enthusiast. For years he regularly bicycled the five blocks from his home to the sanitarium. At work he sometimes took a few minutes to pedal around the circular drive in front of his office. Often, in order not to waste any time, his brother Will or a secretary jogged along by his side, taking down orders and memos for the day.

Although Dr. Kellogg frequently recommended gardening as an excellent recreation, he was always too busy to engage in it himself. He enjoyed observing plant and animal life, however, and especially appreciated a hike through the neighboring woods and fields, where he could study

Kellogg golfing

the local flora and fauna. His love of animals led him to keep a number of pet deer on his estate and to visit many of the world's major zoos, where the monkeys and big apes always fascinated him. The doctor's interest in animals probably helps to account for his enjoyment of the circus, which he attended whenever possible.

While considering most games to be a waste of time, he still in his 60s took up golf as part of a bargain whereby a patient agreed to give up cigars if Kellogg would play the game with him once a week. The doctor soon learned to enjoy his visits to the links and came to realize that golf provided valuable exercise. Although he never became proficient at the game, he always played it with great vigor. Immediately after teeing off, John Harvey would start after the ball at a trot, not even waiting until it had stopped rolling.

Although most of Dr. Kellogg's frequent trips were for business or professional reasons, they also brought him relief from his full schedule at Battle Creek and gave him time for meditation and relaxation. A business trip to Colorado, for instance, permitted him to go horseback riding along mountain trails, and a medical convention in Minneapolis provided him with the opportunity to visit historic and scenic spots in the area. During his 1883 trip to Europe the doctor spent a week in the Alps and visited many of the customary tourist attractions. In the 1890s he began a series of periodic visits to Mexico, where he visited the Aztec and Maya ruins. An avid photographer, he took numerous pictures that he later had converted into stereoptican slides. One of his Mexican trips, a week of camping in the central Mexican mountains, provides an excellent example of the doctor's habit of mixing work and recreation. On the horseback rides, a daily feature of the vacation, he occupied his rest stops by dictating a translation of a book on dietetics by the French nutritionist Gautier. The mixture of work and recreation was in a sense symbolic of John Harvey Kellogg's complex character. He was, one good friend recalled, both "the kindest and the harshest man I ever knew."

CHAPTER XIII
WHAT MANNER OF MAN

EVERY INDIVIDUAL POSSESSES both attractive and unattractive traits of personality. In this respect, John Harvey Kellogg was no different from the rest of humanity. With him, however, both types of trait appear to have been more highly developed than in the average American. Perhaps a number of his personal characteristics had a direct relationship to his physical size.

As an adult, Kellogg measured five feet four inches. Always conscious of his short stature, he may well have felt a psychological need to demonstrate his abilities through directing and dominating others. Frequently John Harvey commented on the advantage of being short, but those that knew him believed his statements simply masked a fond wish to be six feet tall. On numerous occasions he pointed out that it was only his legs that were short. When a tall visitor would come into his office, Kellogg often invited his guest to sit in his chair. The doctor would place a mark on the wall corresponding to the top of the visitor's head. Then seating himself in the chair he would demonstrate that his head reached or even surpassed the line he had marked on the wall. With a chuckle he would proclaim, "You see, it's all in the legs—all in the legs!"

His tendency in childhood and youth to be headstrong and self-willed caused his father concern. Shortly before his death, John Preston Kellogg requested Ellen White to take a special interest in helping his doctor son to overcome that trait and to develop a character pleasing to God and humanity. Through the years, Mrs. White kindly, but persistently, counseled John Harvey to beware of the dangers of too much ambition and the tendency to take too much personal credit for his successes. Repeatedly she referred him to the example of Nebuchadnezzar's humiliation when he exhibited excessive pride over his kingdom. The doctor candidly admitted that he sometimes had quite a struggle to remember the virtues of humility.

Some of Kellogg's most admiring disciples noted that he harbored a very real desire for personal recognition. It was not unusual for him to attend a medical meeting expecting to stay four or five days, but then to leave on the second day because he had not secured the initial attention and deference to which he felt himself entitled.

A tendency to assume complete control over any activity he was associated with was one of Kellogg's lifelong traits. Less than six months after he had accepted responsibility for directing the Health Reform Institute, some Adventist leaders suggested that his half-brother Merritt should return from California to help supervise it. The younger Kellogg bridled at the idea. He professed willingness to turn the entire enterprise over to Merritt. "But," he continued, "I find it difficult to carry a fraction of a burden and leave the rest. If I have any responsibility in a matter, I somehow cannot avoid feeling a burden of the whole." Years later a close medical associate charged that John Harvey ignored any actions of the sanitarium's governing board with which he did not agree.

His inclination to attempt complete personal control of his various enterprises persisted to the end of his life. Only four years before the doctor's death one of his literary assistants quit because he felt that John Harvey found it impossible to delegate authority. As a result of his urge to dominate, the doctor had difficulty in accepting constructive criticism—he tended to become suspicious of those who disagreed with him, and to accuse them of undercutting his program. Although Dr. Kellogg attempted to be scientific in his approach to a problem, a person had little chance of persuading the physician to change his mind once he had reached a decision on a particular point, because he found it extremely difficult to admit a mistake or to apologize for something he had done or said.

At times, in a straightforward manner, Ellen White reproved John Harvey for his failure to share responsibility with his colleagues. "There is with you a love of supremacy whether you see it or not," she wrote, "and had it not been cherished, you could have had by your side men who would have been developing as useful physicians, men who would be constantly growing, and upon whom you could have depended. But you have not given them all the advantages which you yourself would have claimed had you been in their place." To some, Kellogg's failure to share responsibility stemmed from his jealousy of any potential competitors. They observed that he refused to give a completely free hand to associate doctors at the sanitarium even when they were experts in fields other than his own specialties. And when a surgical assistant began to build an independent reputation, he soon received an invitation to go elsewhere.

As is frequently the case, Dr. Kellogg had difficulty in recognizing in himself his need to dominate. When others sought to point it out to him, he would usually reply that he received no satisfaction from sitting in an office and running things. He insisted that the only reason that he was involved in so many activities was because there seemed to be no one else to do them. John Harvey even tried to belittle his role, characterizing his career as quite ordinary and undistinguished. He maintained that he was naturally shy and retiring without any desire for greatness.

Occasionally a feeling of being unappreciated, almost a persecution complex, surfaced in his mind. Three years after he had taken charge of the Health Reform Institute, he confided to James White that so many difficulties faced him and he had so much to do that he felt he would probably work himself to death and "no one will thank me for it." Looking back on his years as a Seventh-day Adventist, he believed that a majority of the denominational leaders had opposed him and his activities.

A certain amount of antagonism toward Kellogg undoubtedly did exist. In part, the doctor's sharp tongue, which often lashed out at those who opposed any of his plans, brought it on. John Harvey often interpreted opposition as a personal affront. In quieter moments he recognized that he sometimes spoke "too strongly," but he professed to be "quite unconscious of it until afterwards." Always having a fondness for words, he developed great skill in putting them together in a clever and witty way, which often included a heavy dose of sarcasm. His talents as a mimic contributed greatly to his ability to satirize an opponent's viewpoint

Dr. Kellogg could be extremely persuasive in conversation or debate. His agile mind frequently enabled him to anticipate an opponent's possible objections, and he would proceed to smother them with a constant flow of words. Sometimes such a stream of words made him appear to poor advantage. Especially during his later years, some of his friends believed that he tended to "talk a great deal without really saying much." His propensity to talk made it difficult for him to keep confidences. The doctor at times recognized his problem. In his last conversation with his brother Will, he said, "I talk too much. I have to overcome it. I talk too much."

In moments given to introspection, Kellogg was willing to admit that it was not his only undesirable trait. To few persons during his lifetime did he write about such matters with the complete frankness that he did to Ellen White. Through the years he confessed to her that he realized that "selfish pride" plagued him and that he was inclined to be "high-headed and hasty, suspicious, stubborn and irritable, hypersensitive, morbid and fretful." He admitted further to being "awfully selfish and narrow-minded" and "naturally strong-willed, pugnacious, controversial, and skeptical." The doctor believed that he could generally keep his shortcomings under control, but that they became most evident when he was overworked and weak from lack of sleep and proper food.

Patience was a virtue Dr. Kellogg never claimed to possess. He clearly demonstrated its lack one day in 1911 during a trip to present a Chautauqua lecture at Winona Lake, Indiana. When he learned that he could not catch a train to Battle Creek until the following day, John Harvey telephoned his chauffeur to fetch him home in his new Oldsmobile. Considering the state of the highways in 1911, such an undertaking was fairly risky. After an all-night trip during which they averaged 23 miles per hour, the doctor reached home in time for his next day's surgical schedule.

Although he was himself short tempered, others had to exercise considerable patience in dealing with him. He was invariably late for appointments, and the stationmaster at the Michigan Central depot in Battle Creek often had to hold a train for several minutes until the doctor arrived in a "mad dash" from the sanitarium. Perhaps his habitual late arrivals in such instances partially resulted from the fact that he always feared he would run out of work on his trips and so insisted on packing and taking along five or six suitcases filled with medical books and journals. Others suspected that he deliberately timed his late arrivals to draw the passengers' attention to the importance of the little man in white for whom the train had been held.

During the first decade of the twentieth century Dr. Kellogg adopted a distinctive style of attire that he adhered to for the rest of his life—he began, whatever the season, to dress completely in white from his hat to his shoes. Some have suggested that Horace Fletcher influenced him to adopt the style, but as early as January, 1886, at least a dozen years before he met Fletcher, the doctor had written that "from the standpoint of health, white is superior to all other colors at all seasons." White clothing, he argued, allowed more of the beneficial rays of sunlight to penetrate to the body than did clothing of other colors. He carried on many experiments that he maintained proved his theories, demonstrating, for example, that flowers grown under white coverings developed more satisfactorily than those raised under pale yellow, green, red, and black cloth. This, he assumed, was because the ultra-violet rays penetrated the white.

In spite of the doctor's rationale for a completely white wardrobe, some who knew him well believed that his distinctive mode of dress was only a good example of his showmanship. Such unusual clothing would almost certainly elicit questions, and they provided an excellent opportunity for him to express his views on the values of sunlight and personal cleanliness. It was also true that a vigorous little man whose white overcoat and spats matched his white goatee left a visual image hard to erase.

In spite of certain unattractive aspects of his personality, even Dr. Kellogg's opponents recognized his great powers of leadership, his tremendous mental versatility and ability, and his great vision and the kindness he demonstrated in many concrete ways to the poor or disadvantaged. Learning at one time that one of his research assistants was concerned for an ill friend, the doctor immediately insisted that his subordinate put aside his work and travel 400 miles to his friend's home in order to arrange his transfer to the sanitarium for treatment. Kellogg personally supplied the funds necessary to move the patient, and he also paid the entire cost of the man's stay in the sanitarium.

Taking a deep interest in his patients, Kellogg felt keenly his inability to restore them all to perfect health. No matter how busy he was, he had the knack of making a patient feel that his case was the only matter of importance to the doctor at the time. Dr. Kellogg exhibited a similar concern for his subordinates at the sanitarium. If illness or tragedy struck their homes, he frequently employed someone to help with the necessary household tasks, and he made it a point to check the situation regularly until conditions had returned to normal.

He insisted that his colleagues and subordinates be men and women of high Christian ideals and standards. In most cases John Harvey was an excellent judge of human nature, but occasionally colorful personalities or a man who possessed cultured and refined speech and bearing deceived him. He was less likely to be fooled by the feminine sex.

Although Dr. Kellogg worked with hundreds of individuals during the course of his many years, few of them became his intimate friends. He was unable to consider a person a close friend unless he respected that individual's mental abilities, education, and general cultural tastes. Among the small group of men really intimate with him over the years were Drs. Percy T. Magan, David Paulson, W. S. Sadler, George Thomason, and James T. Case. Loathing self-seeking, John Harvey was always concerned lest some colleague or relative try to use their association with him for personal advancement. The suspicion often led Kellogg to appear sharp and critical and undoubtedly kept many of his associates from becoming really friendly with him.

Most of the time he realized that the success of his work in Battle Creek largely resulted from the faithful service of devoted colleagues. After his first 30 years at the Battle Creek Sanitarium, he boasted that he had never had a serious conflict with his governing board. In fact, his personal influence over his associates was so great that Ellen White several times warned him that he was in danger of surrounding himself entirely with yes-men. Some of those who worked with him, she stated, did not always approve of all his suggestions, but they followed them nevertheless. Dr. Carolyn Geisel, for some years a member of the sanitarium staff, once referred to the doctor's influence over his associates as practically hypnotic.

Although John Preston Kellogg had joined the Republican Party at its beginning and his son inherited his political inclinations, the doctor could never get very much interested in politics. Shortly before the election of 1900, John Harvey did declare himself to the extent of stating that he did not understand how an honest man could vote any but the Republican ticket. Even in the Grand Old Party's darkest hour, Kellogg maintained his formal loyalty, introducing Gov. Alfred M. Landon at a 1936 Battle Creek appearance as "the next president of the United States." According to one of Kellogg's close friends, the statement was about typical of the doctor's political judgment. Although he was always an avid temperance supporter, he failed to take an active role in the drive to establish national prohibition. He did lend his name to endorse the presidential candidacy of an old acquaintance, former Gov. J. Frank Hanly, of Indiana, when Hanley ran on the Prohibition ticket in 1916.

As a young medical student John Kellogg had found it necessary to practice the most rigid economy in order to stretch his limited finances as far as possible. The habit thus formed remained a lifelong trait. Several years after he became superintendent of the Battle Creek Sanitarium, Ellen White warned Kellogg not to let his economy "degenerate into avarice and sharp practice." The extent to which the doctor heeded her warning is a disputed point, but it is certain that he sought for years to keep salaries at the sanitarium at a very modest level. He criticized the neighboring Review and Herald Publishing Association for paying wages that he regarded as too generous. After years during which the sanitarium's employees had worked for as little as seven cents an hour, an outside adviser suggested in 1907 that it establish a 10- or 12-cents-per-hour minimum wage. Dr. Kellogg objected strenuously to the proposal. A former secretary remembered years later that the only arguments he had ever had with the doctor concerned the subject of wages. On such occasions John Harvey was likely to become quite upset and to lose his temper.

It would be possible to cite numerous examples of his inclination to be rather miserly. Mrs. White once reproved him for serving the sanitarium workers inferior quality food in an effort to save money. Although Kellogg was always interested in the latest therapeutic equipment, he sought to acquire it at the lowest possible price. On one occasion he informed the German manufacturers of some electrical machinery he wanted that he would not consider ordering it unless they agreed to a 20 percent discount. Sometimes his miserly attitude had far reaching consequences. The tendency to haggle over prices cost John Harvey thousands of dollars and the use of the profitable name "Pep" for one of his cereal creations. He attempted to buy the trademark for $5,000 from the original owner. At the time he was making a net profit of approximately $2,000 a day on the sale of the cereal he wished to call "Pep." While the doctor bargained, his brother Will's firm bought the trademark for $7,500.

"I think I never would have made any success in business," John Harvey declared, "for I have no liking for business and business details."

It is not difficult to agree with his judgment, for although his food products and books netted him a considerable fortune, the major credit for turning them into profitable enterprises must go to his younger brother, Will. The doctor was too preoccupied with his many activities to give the necessary attention to his personal finances, which Will Kellogg managed for more than 30 years.

At various times throughout his career John Harvey Kellogg maintained that he had worked all of his adult life for the Battle Creek Sanitarium without a salary, and that he never received any fees for the operations that he performed. Like the doctor's casual remarks that he had never had a vacation, the salary statement requires qualification. Even good friends recognized that he sometimes had a tendency to stretch his interpretation of the facts in order to meet his needs. In 1903 Kellogg told reporter Karl Harriman that many times the sanitarium had voted him a large salary, "but I never took a cent." Under oath in court a dozen years later, he modified the statement to indicate that he had never accepted more than a nominal salary from the sanitarium. The sum he received, Kellogg maintained, failed to equal what he had spent to further the work of the sanitarium. In actual practice, the sanitarium regularly set aside a salary account for the doctor, which he used for professional expenses and to support charity cases at the institution.

It is impossible to state with any degree of certainty just how large Dr. Kellogg's income was. He appears to have begun work as a young sanitarium doctor on a salary of $15 a week, part of which came from the denominational publishing house for editing *Good Health*. During the closing years of the nineteenth century the idea that he was becoming wealthy as a result of his position at the sanitarium circulated widely in Battle Creek, but available evidence indicates that the opposite was true. In 1894, for example, the doctor told a friend that during that year he had spent at least $75 more in promoting the sanitarium's interests than the $600 salary he had received from the institution. An investigating committee of local citizens found a few years later that although the sanitarium treasurer credited Kellogg with a regular salary each month, the bulk of the funds went—under the doctor's supervision—to pay the expenses of patients financially unable to settle their accounts.

The first half of his lifetime Kellogg met his personal expenses largely from the royalties he received on the books that he wrote. In later life profits from his food products supported him. For a number of years the doctor actually lived on credit, and in 1899 he was $25,000 in debt. Probably a substantial portion of his debt resulted from his building a $35,000 residence for his growing family. Kellogg's personal indebtedness continued to be large until the success of his cereal creations after 1907 brightened the financial picture for him. Since during the same years the sanitarium was also heavily in debt, it is understandable that the doctor declared when he endowed the forerunner of the Race Betterment Foundation, "I desire to belong before I die to one organization which has no debts, and I wish it understood that this board will not contract debts."

The funds that Kellogg received beyond those needed to support his family he soon expended on charitable causes. In 1895, for example, while supporting a family of 29, he also paid the salaries of a Methodist and a Baptist missionary in India, met half of the expenses of 10 boys in a mission school, and endowed two charity beds in the Seventh Day Baptist hospital in Shanghai, a bed in the Adventist medical mission in Mexico, and one in the Battle Creek Sanitarium.

"I could have accumulated a fortune," Kellogg once told a reporter, "but what is money for except to make the whole world better, to help people have a better life?" C. W. Barron, the Wall Street genius and a Kellogg friend during the 1920s, once commented that the doctor should have been one of the richest men in the country but that he had let money slip through his fingers too easily. In reply John Kellogg pointed out that he had always been interested in human service rather than money. He maintained that it took too much time to make and keep money, and that the attempt to accumulate a fortune kept people from doing many other things that they wanted to do.

CRAPTER XIV
FATHER TO 42 CHILDREN

KELLOGG'S MULTITUDINOUS activities made it virtually impossible for him to enjoy a normal family life. It is frequently said that some men are married to their work. In Kellogg's case the saying comes close to the truth. Yet John Harvey Kellogg was too filled with affection and respect for his parents, too committed to a youthful idealistic mission to help children, too much a child of the Victorian Age, not to desire a conventional family.

Shortly after he finished his medical course, he assumed the major financial responsibility for the care of his parents. During the last years of his life, John Preston Kellogg, plagued by poor health, lived in comparative retirement. The discipline and direction of John Harvey's younger brothers and sisters fell to the new doctor, who also kept a sharp eye on his parents' financial assets, since he feared that some of his older brothers might manage to dissipate them. When J. P. Kellogg died in the spring of 1881 at the age of 73, John Harvey accepted the responsibility of caring for his mother. He also financed the education of those children who remained at home.

Ann Stanley Kellogg survived her husband by almost 12 years. Her death from heart failure at 69 came as a shock to her children and friends since she had always appeared to be in good health. Dr. Kellogg particularly felt the loss of his mother. He often recalled that she always had seemed to have a smile for him, and he determined that he could best honor her memory by helping to train young adolescents in useful work. Even at the age of 80 Kellogg cherished the fondest memories of his mother, remembering that she had invariably been ready to help those in need. He also recalled her efficiency—the way in which she could bind up a wound, administer a wet-sheet pack, or prepare a tempting meal. "I have never met anyone who was able with greater readiness to meet new emergencies, and to render more varied and efficient service in promoting human welfare," the doctor wrote his brother Will. It would be hard to escape the conclusion that much of John Harvey Kellogg's inspiration for a life of service to humanity came from the example his mother supplied.

Just as he had few really intimate friends, so John Harvey was not especially close to his brothers and sisters. The one real exception was his sister Clara, who accompanied the doctor and his wife on their first European trip. Clara married Hiland Butler, son of G. I. Butler, but about the time of Dr. Kellogg's break with the Seventh-day Adventist Church, her marriage ended in divorce. Shortly thereafter she joined the doctor's household, and she lived with him most of the remainder of her life. She idolized her older brother and served him as a confidential secretary in a way no one else could.

With the exception of Clara, none of John Preston and Ann Kellogg's other children were as close to him as was Will. John Harvey had persuaded his parents to give Will the little advanced schooling the latter received. In 1879 the two brothers started a close business relationship that lasted for more than a quarter of a century. During it Will practically submerged his own personality in that of his older brother. Although John Harvey appreciated his faithful service, it was not his nature to give much visible evidence of the fact. Early in the twentieth century the brothers parted company, and their subsequent contacts were largely bitter. Still, although they battled each other in courts of law, occasionally some evidence of brotherly affection appeared above the cacophony of discord.

Of all his half-brothers and sisters, Dr. Kellogg maintained the closest contact with Merritt, who had played a large part in his decision to become a physician. During most of their adult lives, however, Merritt and John Harvey lived and worked thousands of miles apart so that their major tie was through correspondence. Merritt lacked the driving personality

Young Will Keith Kellogg

Review and Herald Collection

shared by John and Will. In his last years, beset by adversity, he had to depend upon John Kellogg for financial support. Dr. Kellogg was always generous to relatives in need and cordial to his many nieces and nephews, but he constantly cautioned the latter not to brag about being a Kellogg or try to turn their family connection to personal profit. The doctor appeared to envy his brothers and sisters their children and grandchildren and to deeply regret that he had no natural children of his own.

On the evening of Washington's birthday, 1879, a number of sanitarium guests had assembled in the big parlor for a social evening. Suddenly the big double doors on one side flung open, the strains of the "Wedding March" began, and, to the general surprise of most of those assembled, Dr. Kellogg entered in his best attire. The bride, Miss Ella Eaton, of Alfred Center, New York, soon followed, and shortly thereafter Pastor Lycurgus McCoy united the couple in marriage.

Dr. Kellogg had known Miss Eaton for a little more than two years prior to their marriage. Many old Battle Creek residents believed that she was not John Harvey's first choice as a bride, for as a young man he had been interested in pretty, energetic Mary Kelsey. Five years Kellogg's junior, Mary had, like him, worked as a proofreader for the Review and Herald. Then while John was away in medical school, she moved to California to work at the newly established Pacific Press. In 1876 she married Kellogg's boyhood friend, William Clarence White, and from that time on relationships between the doctor and Willie White were never quite as cordial as before. Later that same year Kellogg met Ella Eaton.

Ella Eaton Kellogg

An intellectual young woman, she graduated from Alfred University at the age of 19. She spent the next four years teaching school, and then during the summer of 1876, accompanied by a sister, she came to Battle Creek to visit an aunt. Shortly after the girls arrived, Ella's sister became ill with typhoid fever. One of the sanitarium staff, Dr. Kate Lindsay, came to care for her. Ella took over the job of nurse, and although at first opposed to the water treatments Dr. Lindsay prescribed, she carried them out faithfully. Soon the patient's condition began to improve, and she made a complete recovery. About the same time a minor epidemic of typhoid hit Battle Creek. Since good nursing service was vital to recovery, Dr. Lindsay appealed to Ella to remain in the city during the emergency to help care for some of the other patients. At first she demurred, but later she yielded to Dr. Lindsay's repeated requests. During the epidemic Dr. Kellogg first met Ella. From the start she impressed him as a cultured young woman with many talents.

Shortly before Ella returned to her home in New York, Dr. Kellogg made it a point to discuss with her the School of Hygiene that he planned to open at the sanitarium the following fall. She accepted the doctor's invitation to return and take the course, and during her period of study in it, he first became aware of her literary talents. As part of the practical training involved, she did cadet nursing at the sanitarium. John Harvey had occasion to observe the tender care Ella accorded a terminal cancer patient and once more recognized her diverse interests and abilities.

Apparently she liked Battle Creek, because she applied for a position on the faculty of newly established Battle Creek College. She failed to receive the post, possibly because she chose not to leave the Seventh Day Baptist faith she had been reared in. Shortly thereafter, however, Dr. Kellogg asked her to serve as his editorial assistant for *Good Health,* and she accepted his offer. Although their contacts were now more frequent, no evidence exists that an extensive courtship developed. In fact, only about a month before the wedding ceremony, the doctor wrote Ellen White that although Miss Eaton would probably help him for at least another year, she would not become a permanent fixture as she expected to marry a young Seventh Day Baptist whom Kellogg did not know. Thirty-four days later Ella married John Harvey Kellogg. The young couple spent about six weeks on a honeymoon trip to New England, most of it in the vicinity of Boston. It turned out to be a working honeymoon, for part of the time they used to revise his *Plain Facts About Sexual Life* and *The Proper Diet of Man.*

The true inward feelings of John Kellogg for his wife remain something of a mystery. Old friends remembered that although the doctor always treated her with respect and deference, relations between the two never really appeared intimate. A common opinion held that Kellogg probably married his wife largely because of his appreciation of her brilliant mind and literary talents. The doctor's letters to his wife that have survived deal mostly with everyday affairs. Only occasionally do they reveal a touch of sentiment and devotion. For her part, she always made every effort to help the doctor in his work and attempted to make his home a place of relaxation and pleasure.

Although both were fond of children, it soon became apparent that they would be unable to have any of their own. As a result they decided to open their home to needy youngsters. The first child they took in was a little girl of 3 whose mother had recently passed away at the sanitarium and whose father could not give her proper care. Within five years the Kelloggs had acquired an even dozen children, and people were constantly imploring them to accept others.

During the first 15 years of their married life, John and Ella Kellogg occupied an apartment in one of the sanitarium buildings, but their growing family made a continuation of the arrangement impractical. In June 1894 they moved into a large home that he had just built approximately five blocks west of the sanitarium. Shortly before, he had announced that he and his wife planned to make a home for 40 or 50 children. Eventually they assumed responsibility for 42, no more than four or five of whom they ever legally adopted. "The Residence," as the Kellogg home became known in sanitarium circles, contained more than 20 rooms, including individual quarters for John Harvey and Ella, several bathrooms, an office, library, stenographer's room, a small laboratory, and an indoor gymnasium for the children. The house stood well back from the street in the midst of a pleasant grove of trees. A deer park, fruit and vegetable gardens, and eventually an extensive children's playground comprised part of the estate that equaled several city blocks in size.

When the Kelloggs first decided to add needy youngsters to their home, they planned to take in only children with good family backgrounds. However, since both John and Ella firmly believed in the power of environment to overcome, at least to a substantial degree, poor hereditary tendencies, they soon decided to put their beliefs to the test by accepting children no one else wanted. The Kelloggs were certain that with an ideal home setting they could prove that no child was born with a vicious disposition, and that a wholesome and loving environment would produce youth with

outstanding characters re-
gardless of their origins.

Not all of the residents
of Battle Creek's West End
were convinced that the
Kelloggs were carrying out
their environmental experiment in good faith. Some
alleged that the doctor was
quite selective in the chil-

Some of Dr. Kellogg's adopted children

dren he chose to help. John Harvey vigorously denied the charge, maintaining that he and Ella had taken in children "just as they seem to come
providentially." Several they had secured after one or both of their parents
had died at the sanitarium; the rest came in a variety of ways. During his
trip to Europe in 1889 the doctor met a large, but extremely poor, family
of English Adventists. When he returned home, two of their children came
with him. On another occasion the Kelloggs read a newspaper account of
a small 5-year-old boy found gnawing a tallow candle by the side of his
dead mother in a cheap tenement house. They quickly arranged to have
the waif as their own.

As the Kelloggs added children, they drew no lines on the basis of
race, color, or creed. John Harvey's visits to Mexico resulted in at least
four Mexican children becoming a part of his household. Following the
Spanish-American War the Kelloggs accepted a little mulatto boy that an
Ohio regiment brought back from Cuba. Their family also included at
least one Black and one Puerto Rican. Several of the Kellogg children came
from urban slum areas. One of the latter, known originally only as
"Hildah's kid," provides an outstanding example of the "undesirables"
John and Ella were willing to accept and love. In talking to several of his
associates one day, the doctor asked them to find the most miserable child
in Chicago. They brought him "Hildah's kid," the son of a prostitute. The
authorities had found the boy foraging for food in a garbage can, his only
shelter being under the steps of a filthy tenement house. The Kelloggs
willingly accepted the unwanted lad, named him George, and set out to
try to make him into a model young man.

Dr. Kellogg and his wife sought to rear their foster children in harmony with the latest theories of child development and psychology. They were particularly eager to demonstrate their love and provide the security that many of the children had not previously known, an attempt well illustrated in the case of one little boy whom the doctor discovered during one of his periodic trips. Before returning to Battle Creek, John Harvey inquired what the child wanted more than anything else in the world. The boy confided that he had always dreamed of owning a pony, but never expected to do so. Immediately the doctor telegraphed Ella when she might expect him and their new "son," and he further requested that she have a pony waiting on the driveway when they arrived. The thrill the lad received upon his arrival at the Residence is easy to imagine.

That evening as Dr. Kellogg sat reading, he heard a peculiar noise in the front hallway. At first he paid no attention, but glancing up a little later, he noticed that the new member of the Kellogg family was coaxing the pony through the living room toward the stairway leading to the bedrooms. At the stairs the animal balked, and no amount of the boy's pleadings could convince him to mount them. After a time Dr. Kellogg sauntered over and inquired if the boy was having some trouble, never intimating that bringing a pony into the house was not a normal procedure. Tactfully he suggested that the pony probably preferred his comfortable stall in the barn, and together they led the animal out to its quarters.

The Kelloggs shared a firm belief that early education should be "natural and practical." In order to secure such instruction for his family, John Harvey hired private teachers to conduct a school in his home. Among them was Mary Lamson, later widely known among several generations of Seventh-day Adventists because of her many years of service as a college dean of women. The Kellogg home school encouraged pupils to investigate and observe as their interests dictated in the hope that it would lead them to become original thinkers. The teachers kept the youngsters on a planned program, which included regular periods of gymnastics and work. Once the Kellogg boys reached 15, John Harvey expected them to earn money for their books and clothing. To enable them to do so, the doctor, during the summer months, paid them a dollar a day to labor in the garden and yard. As they grew older, he urged both boys and girls to work summers in one of the sanitarium enterprises and to save a major part of their earnings for their future education.

Although Dr. Kellogg's busy program necessarily forced Mrs. Kellogg to assume major responsibility for the children's supervision, the doctor found playing with the youngsters very relaxing, and he attempted to do so whenever possible. He also regularly conducted a brief, simple family worship service for them each morning. The children in most cases generously returned the love he felt for them. Not believing in arbitrary punishment, Dr. Kellogg claimed never to have struck or spoken harshly to one of the children. He believed instead in a program of natural correction best illustrated by several examples.

Faced with constant misbehavior from one of the boys, the doctor informed the lad that since he insisted on acting like a little animal, he would have to sleep with the animals in the barn. That night he had a cot placed in the hayloft and the boy put to bed there. After the boy was asleep, John Harvey, not wanting him to be alone so far from the rest of the family, set up another cot and spent the night in the loft with him, arising before the youth awoke. Kellogg had to continue the procedure for a number of nights, but the doctor's patience finally got its reward when the boy came to him one evening and said, "I don't want to be an animal anymore. I want to be a little boy." The child's future behavior, the doctor remembered later, was all that could be desired. On another occasion the Kelloggs required a boy who could not seem to remember to hang up his clothes to spend an entire half day simply going into the house, hanging up his coat and hat, then putting them on again and repeating the entire procedure. Dr. Kellogg claimed that when the correction was directly related to whatever the child had done improperly, it provided a natural cure for the bad habit.

He hoped that his foster children would develop strong social consciences and would dedicate their lives to humanitarian service, and, in part, they did fulfill his desires. One of the Mexican boys the Kelloggs reared, Alberto Garcia, later took the medical course at the University of Illinois and served for some years as a company doctor with the Guggenheim mining interests in Mexico. Another, Richard Kellogg, became a successful Battle Creek dentist. A number of the foster daughters became nurses or teachers. Several married young sanitarium doctors.

Not all of Kellogg's children turned out as the doctor had hoped, however. "Hildah's kid" proved a particular disappointment. He turned into a dissolute drifter who frequently demanded financial assistance in order that his activities might not become an embarrassment to his foster father. Generally loath to admit failure in his efforts to show the corrective influences of environment, Kellogg, when he did acknowledge a disappointment, would generally blame it on his wife's declining health, which prevented her from giving the children the careful supervision accorded them during earlier years. Several Kellogg associates noticed that the children the doctor had secured from fairly normal homes were later a credit to Ella and him, but those who had come from shiftless or dissolute families failed to shake off the influences of their early childhood.

Kellogg's generosity in providing a home for more than twoscore unfortunate children became widely known. The impact of his example can never be measured accurately, but it is interesting to note one case that indicates just how one man's influence can multiply. Floyd Starr frequently credited Kellogg's experiment with being a major factor in his decision to launch the Starr Commonwealth for Boys near Albion, Michigan. Through the years "Uncle Floyd" Starr helped thousands of socially handicapped boys to become useful young men.

Ella Kellogg's interests and activities complemented her husband's career in many ways. For approximately 43 years she served on the editorial staff of *Good Health*. During that period most of the monthly issues of the journal contained at least one article from her pen. Toward the end of his wife's long association with the magazine, Dr. Kellogg commented that the quality of her writing was better than ever. Her journal articles reflected two of her major interests: the care and training of children and food preparation. Mrs. Kellogg also authored three books. *Her Talks With Girls* contained advice concerning the emotional and physical problems of the teen-age girl. Her principal book, *Science in the Kitchen,* consisted of a record of her experimental work in dietetics and cookery and included a number of recipes for vegetarian foods. In *Studies in Character Building,* Ella Kellogg summarized her philosophy of child training and recorded personal experiences in applying the principles that she advocated.

As part of his effort to provide more palatable menus for sanitarium patients, Dr. Kellogg persuaded his wife to engage in research in dietetics. She first visited the leading schools of cookery in the eastern United States, and then returned to Battle Creek to establish an experimental kitchen at the sanitarium. For nearly 20 years she experimented extensively with new recipes, food combinations, and methods of preparation, always being careful to emphasize the palatability, wholesomeness, and digestibility of the finished product. She carefully kept all of her work within the bounds of the doctor's dietary teachings. At the same time Ella also doubled as sanitarium dietitian, planning all the menus for both patients and staff. The Battle Creek School of Home Economics was an outgrowth of her experimental kitchen and her talks to sanitarium patients about food preparation.

During much of her married life, Ella Kellogg was active in a number of women's organizations. She worked closely with Frances Willard in the Women's Christian Temperance Union, serving successively as its National Superintendent of Hygiene and head of the Social Purity Department. Later she directed the WCTU's Mothers' Meetings and Child Culture Circles. A life member of the Young Women's Christian Association, Mrs. Kellogg also belonged to the Federation of Women's Clubs, the National Congress of Mothers, the Women's League, and the American Home Economics Association. For a time she served as honorary president of the Michigan Women's Press Association.

Mrs. Kellogg never enjoyed robust health, but she never complained. An attack of scarlet fever at an early age had injured her hearing and, in spite of the best treatments available, the affliction gradually worsened until she became totally deaf. She tried hearing aids, but without success. In the late 1890s Ella Kellogg suffered a complete physical collapse, probably occasioned by the heavy burdens associated with rearing her many foster children. Complete rest for a year or more brought some improvement, but chronic invalidism plagued her during the last 20 years of her life. Her final illness began about a year before her death in 1920. Dr. Will Mayo performed an operation that brought temporary relief, but the malignancy discovered was too far advanced for surgery to effect a complete cure.

Whatever John Harvey Kellogg's emotional feelings toward Ella Eaton may have been at the time of their marriage, their common love of nature, children, books, travel, and above all, service in the cause of health and temperance drew the doctor and his wife together. She remained loyal to her Seventh Day Baptist faith until her death. To honor her memory, Dr. Kellogg had a small, but attractive, chapel for her faith constructed just a few blocks down the street from the sanitarium.

CHAPTER XV
HIS BROTHER'S KEEPER

THE CONCERN JOHN KELLOGG evidenced in opening his home to orphans and other underprivileged children provides only a small example of his dedication to social improvement activities. The doctor frequently said that on judgment day God would not ask individuals what they had preached or professed, but rather what they had done to help those in need. It was infinitely more important, he stated, "to be a good Samaritan than to be a good theologian."

He was particularly concerned to see his fellow Adventists commit themselves to a broad humanitarian program. Too many church members, he maintained, had a negative concept of religion. To such persons, Christianity consisted of a list of things one should refrain from doing. He believed that a positive program of practical efforts to aid the distressed motivated by love and concern rather than by a sense of duty was the true way to practice Christianity. In his own way, John Harvey Kellogg attempted to get Seventh-day Adventists to devote their major efforts to social service activities just as Walter Rauschenbusch and others were promoting a similar program among the larger Protestant churches.

Kellogg reasoned that the Christian dedicated to helping his distressed neighbors would also willingly commit his financial resources to such endeavors. He insisted that no one had a right to accumulate money. Rather, a person was duty-bound to distribute what he earned to those in need of assistance. The doctor certainly practiced the financial liberality he preached, but his major problem was that his monetary resources were never sufficient for all the charitable projects his mind conceived.

John Harvey particularly enjoyed helping young people secure an advanced education. Immediately following his own graduation from Bellevue, he began to support needy students in much the same way that

James and Ellen White had aided him. During some years Kellogg helped to finance the education of as many as 30 persons at one time. When his own resources proved insufficient, he even borrowed money.

By 1890 Dr. Kellogg realized that he and his wife could not personally care for all of the orphan children people called to his attention. He decided that a good alternative would be to establish an orphans' home in Battle Creek under Adventist auspices. After discussing the idea with Ellen White and securing her approval, the doctor published several general appeals inviting church members to found both an orphanage and a home for elderly persons. In the spring of 1891 Kellogg placed the needs of the church's orphans and old people squarely before the Adventist leadership assembled for the biennial General Conference. In an emotion-packed address the doctor graphically portrayed a number of poignant cases that needed immediate attention. Among other arguments, he suggested that an Adventist orphanage would offer a splendid place to begin preparing young people for denominational service. Also he expressed the belief that Adventists could easily support both an orphanage and a home for the aged from the money they saved by not using tea and coffee. Several days later, the General Conference officially voted to establish "a home for orphans and destitute aged persons." In harmony with Kellogg's suggestions, they named it the James White Memorial Home.

Selected as the first president of the new project's board of trustees, Dr. Kellogg, with his customary energy, immediately began work. Within a few weeks he had helped make plans to raise $50,000 to build and equip a suitable home on a small farm near Battle Creek. But John Harvey soon found that it was much easier to find future occupants for the James White Memorial Home than it was to raise the funds necessary to build it. After a year of work he had succeeded in accumulating only $20,000 (including a personal donation of $1,000). Meanwhile friends and interested persons had submitted the names of nearly 400 parentless children to him, and 40 homeless youngsters were already temporarily crowding the Kelloggs' personal quarters while awaiting the construction of the church's orphanage.

The generosity of a wealthy non-Adventist guest at the sanitarium, Mrs. Caroline Haskell, eventually solved the fund-raising problem. Mrs. Haskell admired Dr. Kellogg's concern for unfortunate children and offered to give him $30,000 for the orphans' home, only asking in return that he name it in memory of her late husband and that it be operated as a nonsectarian institution. Her unexpected gift made possible its immediate construction. The trustees of the project decided to postpone a home for elderly persons, which in harmony with the original plan they would name in honor of James White.

Dr. Kellogg persuaded the 1893 General Conference to establish the Seventh-day Adventist Medical Missionary and Benevolent Association. The new organization would assume supervision of the Haskell and James White Homes, all denominationally sponsored medical activities, and any future philanthropic programs that the church might initiate. Some Adventist leaders had suggested that the denomination appoint John Harvey as its medical secretary and give him complete responsibility for all Adventist charitable activities. The doctor opposed the idea of a single secretary as centralizing "too much power in one person." He favored control by a separate association that would not be an integral part of the denomination on the basis that such an organization would find it easier to appeal for financial support from the general public. Thus the Seventh-day Adventists established the Medical Missionary and Benevolent Association in harmony with his wishes. The doctor served as the Association's president during its entire 13 years of existence.

The Haskell Home for Orphans was officially dedicated on January 25, 1894. Following Kellogg's ideas, the trustees had organized it in such a way as to minimize the traditional institutional character of such enterprises. The children, combined into "families" of 12 or 13, had a "mother" supervising each group. The orphanage gave special attention to the children's diet, dress, posture, and moral training, and conducted a planned program of physical exercise suitable to their various age levels.

For nearly a decade and a half the Haskell Home received its operational support from semiannual offerings taken up in all Adventist churches. During that period it sheltered 150 to 200 children at a time and helped place more than 500 orphans in foster homes. Dr. Kellogg maintained close personal contact with the Home and encouraged its occupants to use the spacious lawns surrounding his family residence for play and recreation. Frequently the doctor would take a quartet composed of sanitarium employees to sing for the children. On such occasions he would tell the youngsters Bible stories between musical numbers and would encourage them to share with him their favorite stories in return.

As relations between Dr. Kellogg and the Adventist denomination moved toward the breaking point, church leaders decided to cease providing financial support for the institutions under Kellogg's control. They discontinued special collections for the Haskell Home in 1906, but at the same time they offered to secure homes for any orphans in the Home who desired placement. Deprived of the denomination's financial support, Kellogg found himself forced to restrict the number of children the Haskell Home could care for. Then, in 1909, a fire destroyed the orphanage, causing the death of three children. Subsequently the trustees ordered a much more modest structure erected, designed to accommodate about 50 children. By 1921 it sheltered fewer than 15 children, and it closed the following year.

Mrs. Haskell's substantial gift temporarily diverted Dr. Kellogg's interest in the James White Memorial Home for the aged. Several months after the dedication of the Haskell Home, John Harvey wrote Ellen White that, although there was enough money available to put up a good-sized home for elderly people, he doubted the wisdom of such action during the financial depression currently engulfing the nation. The doctor believed that if the trustees built a large structure, they "would be overwhelmed with applicants" whom they would find difficult to reject. A large institution would also be expensive to maintain. Although opposed to the construction of a large old people's home, Kellogg offered the Medical Missionary and Benevolent Association the right to use two houses that he owned. For several years the MMBA operated the buildings as the James White Memorial Home. One accommodated about 20 elderly people, and six widows with small children lived in the other one.

Eventually the Association built a substantial three-story house capable of sheltering 40 aged citizens. For 14 years after the Adventist General Conference discontinued its financial support of the James White Memorial Home, Dr. Kellogg underwrote the expenses of its operation, aided by income from bequests. In 1920 he transferred the Home to the Lake Union Conference of Seventh-day Adventists.

During the decade following its organization in 1893, the SDA Medical Missionary and Benevolent Association helped to establish more than 30 new sanitariums, a similar number of hydrotherapy treatment rooms, more than a dozen vegetarian restaurants, and a variety of urban medical missions designed to aid the poor and unemployed. Local Adventist conferences controlled the enterprises, but the MMBA, and particularly Dr. Kellogg as its president, served as adviser, coordinator, recruiter of personnel, and fundraiser. Throughout this 10-year period Kellogg spent about half of his time traveling all over the nation to attend meetings of local sanitarium boards, perform surgery at the institutions, and give advice on the treatment of patients and the construction of buildings.

As president of the MMBA, Dr. Kellogg also helped to organize Adventist sanitariums abroad. From 1892 onward the doctor was deeply involved in the sanitarium established at Guadalajara, Mexico, visiting it frequently. He also helped personally in establishing medical institutions in Denmark, England, Germany, and Switzerland; and he gave written advice on developing similar facilities in South America, Australia, New Zealand, and South Africa.

The financing of the expanding network of medical centers became a major problem and source of concern for him. He hated nothing more than raising money, even for a worthy cause. Since John Harvey realized that the financial resources of the Adventist church were limited, he determined to help MMBA-sponsored projects develop money-making departments in order that they might be largely self-supporting.

Observing how rapidly the sales of Granose Flakes increased, Kellogg became convinced that the manufacture and sale of his new food products would be an ideal way to finance the charitable work of the MMBA. With this in mind, he spent thousands of dollars from his personal funds to obtain patents on his food creations in both the United States and abroad. Then he helped many of the new sanitariums to develop small food-manufacturing businesses. Others became distribution agents for the cereals, nut products, and meat substitutes produced in Battle Creek. Within only a few years, however, the vicious competition developing in the flaked-cereal industry blighted Kellogg's hopes. He came to realize that profits from the food-manufacturing business would provide no more than a fraction of the funds necessary to support the various Medical Missionary and Benevolent Association projects.

Dr. Kellogg made heavy personal contributions to the MMBA. All expenses incurred while traveling on Benevolent Association business he paid from the profits of his food company. Fees collected for surgery that he performed at the various sanitariums he turned over to the individual institutions. John Harvey personally guaranteed the payment of some of the loans contracted to carry on certain MMBA projects, and he dipped into his private bank account to support projects that appealed to him in a special way. After the Medical Missionary and Benevolent Association dissolved, he claimed that his personal accounts would show that he had made contributions in support of the Association that amounted to as much as or more than that donated by the entire Adventist membership.

Believing that if individual Adventists made substantial contributions to social aid activities, they would identify more closely with such programs, Dr. Kellogg cast about for some plan that he might use to encourage such giving. In 1893 he learned that an Adventist farmer in Oregon had promised to donate for missions the profits received from 10 acres of land planted to onions. The doctor immediately saw possibilities in such a project and launched an aggressive publicity campaign to convince all rural and small-town Adventists to sow a parcel of land with a specific crop and contribute the proceeds to the Medical Missionary and Benevolent Association. "A crop planted for the benefit of the poor," Kellogg wrote, "is a crop planted for God."

The General Conference of 1897 officially approved the scheme of missionary farming and gardening that Kellogg had begun to promote. It agreed that funds turned into the church from such projects should go exclusively to the Benevolent Association. That spring John Harvey announced that Adventists had designated more than 850 acres as "missionary" acres during the previous year, and he expressed the hope that funds from the program would yield $20,000 during 1897 for charitable activities. Kellogg's high hopes for the Missionary Acre Fund did not see realization, however. Hard-pressed financially, many Seventh-day Adventist local conferences found it necessary to divert money received from the Missionary Acre Fund to projects not approved or initiated by the Benevolent Association. The doctor's growing conflict with church leaders prevented him from securing their aid in rectifying the situation, and he gradually allowed his promotion of the program to lapse. On several occasions he lobbied unsuccessfully to have a portion of the tithe paid by all Adventists committed to charitable endeavors. But the doctor did manage to persuade some of the sanitarium employees to contribute their tithe to MMBA projects.

Possibly none of Kellogg's pet projects absorbed more Medical Missionary and Benevolent Association funds than the medical mission the Association opened in Chicago in 1893. Just what sparked Kellogg's interest in aid for the derelicts found in large numbers in every big city is not clear. On a later occasion he declared that initially he had felt a great "physical repugnance" toward the drunken, dirty people encountered in slum areas and that the idea of working with such people had been "terribly disagreeable" to him.

The Minneapolis General Conference of 1888, which Kellogg attended, spent some time in considering the declining fortunes of the evangelical missions that Adventists had attempted to establish in the major urban areas of the United States. The discussion may have aroused his interest. At least the following year, when on his way to Europe for surgical study, John Harvey stopped in New York City to visit the famous Bowery Mission begun by Jerry McAuley on Water Street in 1872. McAuley's goal was to clean people up on the outside while "the Lord cleansed them inside." Tremendously impressed by what he saw at the McAuley Mission, Kellogg reported that prior to his visit he "didn't know what the gospel . . . could do for people," but that at the Water Street Mission he saw that it was possible for religious faith to take away the addict's desire for liquor and tobacco and to cure other undesirable habits as well.

Apparently shortly after his experience at the McAuley Mission, Kellogg began to discuss the idea of starting a similar program in Chicago. About the same time he also came across a little missionary paper published by Dr. George Dowkontt describing the medical mission that Dowkontt was operating in New York City. At his next opportunity Kellogg visited Dowkontt's mission, observed its religious services, medical clinic, and day nursery, and became thoroughly convinced that it was "a most blessed kind of work, and a most fruitful field of labor." The doctor told the next General Conference session that Adventists should not be content to let others operate medical missions when the Lord had given them "special light" and "advantages in this kind of work."

The 1892 visit to the sanitarium of Col. George R. Clarke, founder of Chicago's famous Pacific Garden Mission, may have also influenced

Kellogg's immediate decision to start a medical mission in the city. During his stay in Battle Creek Clarke related many experiences from his 15 years of city mission work. Dr. Kellogg also vigorously promoted the establishment of Adventist missions in non-Christian lands. Both he and Ole A. Olsen, Adventist General Conference president, looked upon the varied ethnic population of Chicago as a natural laboratory to provide prospective foreign missionaries with training in evangelistic and medical missionary techniques. Kellogg also advanced the idea that an urban medical mission program would help eliminate the general prejudice against Adventists.

Concern for the way it might be financed led him to negotiate with social worker Jane Addams about the possibility of adding a medical mission to the settlement project she had recently begun. Miss Addams, however, proved unwilling to add any venture with sectarian connections, forcing him to abandon that approach. Opportunely, early in 1893, two Adventist brothers, Francis and Henry Wessels, whose family lands in South Africa had recently been the site of a rich diamond strike, informed Dr. Kellogg that they were impressed with the humanitarian activities he was directing. When the brothers asked John Harvey what he would do with a gift of $40,000, he immediately replied that he would use it to begin social and evangelistic activities among "Chicago's heathen." The Wessels brothers approved of his idea, and soon the doctor received a check for the indicated amount.

Since a number of wealthy Chicago residents had urged Kellogg for some time to open a branch of the Battle Creek Sanitarium in their city, the doctor decided to use the Wessels' gift to establish such an institution and then to use the profits from the branch sanitarium to finance a medical mission for the city's destitute. The Wessels' donation would become a type of endowment, and while Chicago's wealthy received the benefits of biologic living, they would also provide needed facilities for the city's poor. After quickly converting a suitable building into the necessary quarters, Kellogg opened the Chicago Branch Sanitarium on May 1, 1893, in time to be available to visitors to the great World's Fair of that year.

Less then two months later the Chicago Medical Mission started operation. Before deciding where to establish his mission, Kellogg had visited the Chicago Police Department and asked them to direct him to the "dirtiest and wickedest" section of the city. Sent to the slum district bordering the south edge of Chicago's "Loop," Kellogg searched unsuccessfully for a suitable location until, at last, he persuaded Henry Monroe, then superintendent of the Pacific Garden Mission, to allow him to use a portion of the mission's building on West Van Buren Street.

For the next decade and a half John Harvey attempted to spend at least every other Sunday in Chicago. When in the city, he usually spent his mornings visiting patients at the branch sanitarium, afternoons consulting with his subordinates involved in managing the various mission projects, and evenings interviewing mission employees and converts or perhaps participating in the religious services.

The Chicago Medical Mission originally provided three major types of service: a medical dispensary, free baths, and a free laundry. At the dispensary, several nurses were on duty all day, and a doctor from the branch sanitarium was available for consultation two hours of each day. The medical facility offered free obstetrical care to the neighborhood's poor and unemployed and also provided free medications and special foods from the Battle Creek Sanitarium Food Company whenever the doctor in charge prescribed them. Some idea of the character of the mission's neighborhood may be inferred from Kellogg's report that the dispensary regularly treated from 25 to 30 knife wounds each day.

The basement of the mission building housed the free laundry and baths. Some mission workers had told Kellogg that such facilities were unnecessary, since the gospel of Christ would lead people to clean up on their own accord. The doctor maintained, however, that individuals who had been cleaned up first would be easier to reach with Christian teachings. Since hundreds of Chicago's poor lacked proper bathing and laundry facilities, they soon came in large numbers to the mission to wash both themselves and their clothing. The bathrooms offered special sanitarium water and electrical treatments, particularly effective in sobering up drunks.

Two weeks after the Medical Mission opened, Kellogg reported that an average of 100 persons a day were already using its facilities. The demand continued to grow, and after nine months of operation, the mission during a single month provided 2,116 free baths and 869 other treatments, made its free laundry facilities available to 1,725 persons, prescribed for 199 persons, dressed 427 wounds of various types, and gave away 53 free drug prescriptions, 31 packages of food, and 2,942 used, but serviceable, articles of clothing.

A visiting nurse service also operated in connection with the Chicago Medical Mission. The program had actually begun a year before the mission started as the result of an arrangement made with Dr. Kellogg by a Chicago banker, upon the request of his daughter who had been a patient at the Battle Creek Sanitarium. The banker agreed to pay the salaries of two sanitarium nurses assigned to work in Chicago under the direction of the city's Visiting Nurses Association. The young women's reports inspired a larger group of Battle Creek nurses to go to Chicago, where a portion of them worked for wealthy families as private-duty nurses and contributed their wages to support the rest of the group, who ministered to the city's poor. After the founding of the Chicago Medical Mission, they used it as their base of operations. During the first three years of the mission's existence, the visiting nurses made nearly 9,000 free home calls.

As a part of its original program the Chicago Medical Mission provided a free lunch each Sunday noon, consisting of hot bean soup and zwieback or graham bread. After several months Dr. Kellogg decided that if he required the men who patronized the mission to pay something for the meal, it would help to build their self-respect. The mission instituted a charge of one penny per lunch and, at the same time, offered lunches twice each day instead of just on Sundays. The doctor also ordered one-cent tickets printed and bound into books of 100 each to be sold to businessmen who could then give a ticket to panhandlers in lieu of cash, assuring the beggars of some good food instead of the liquor for which they all too frequently spent the donations. Within a few months' time the mission was serving an average of 500 to 600 penny meals daily. Some days the number reached 1,500. Eventually the lack of funds made it necessary to discontinue them.

In 1896 the Chicago Medical Mission greatly expanded when it purchased an old church near the Pacific Garden Mission. Since its owners had converted the building into a cheap rooming house during the Chicago World's Fair, Kellogg's group could now provide sleeping quarters there for between 300 and 400 men. A modest charge of 10 cents a night for lodging in the newly acquired "Workingmen's Home" also included an evening meal of soup and bread. The men could purchase breakfasts for one cent an

Workingmen's home in Chicago

item. The Workingmen's Home served no meat or condiments of any kind, except salt, and it barred tobacco, alcoholic beverages, and narcotics from the premises. The free baths, laundry, and dispensary moved from the old mission to the Workingmen's Home. Five years later the secretary of the Medical Missionary and Benevolent Association reported that the Workingmen's Home, in one year, had provided more than 70,000 individual night's lodgings, had served nearly 600,000 meals, and had given free bath and laundry privileges on 35,000 occasions.

Since one purpose of the Workingmen's Home was to help the unemployed, its directors set aside a portion of the building to provide temporary work for men seeking jobs. In this section, by weaving rugs or making brooms, an unemployed person could earn his expenses at the Workingmen's Home. Kellogg believed that the system discouraged shiftlessness and vagrancy and was much superior to outright charity.

When the Battle Creek Sanitarium and the MMBA made the decision to found the American Medical Missionary College in 1895, Kellogg decided to integrate its clinical activities with the program of the Medical Mission. A building acquired in a working-class neighborhood some distance south of the main mission served as a combination dormitory, classroom, and social settlement house. It became the headquarters of the mission's visiting nurse service and the center of a number of new social programs, including a free kindergarten and day nursery for working mothers, a cooking school, classes in sewing and manual training, and separate health lecture courses for adults and children. The nurses and workers at the AMMC Settlement Building also sponsored a women's club to provide instruction in child training, housekeeping, and correct principles of dress, diet, and cookery. Working among the city's newsboys, boot-blacks, and street urchins, the AMMC medical students organized more than 70 boys' clubs, that eventually attracted a weekly attendance of as many as 3,000. The Settlement House established a special reading room for the boys' use. Later, at the suggestion of the Chicago Women's Club, the medical students began to make daily visits to the jail in order to carry on a regular program of gymnastics and moral instruction among the younger inmates confined there.

The AMMC Settlement House also maintained a placement service that found homes for orphans and reclaimed prostitutes, and jobs for former alcoholics. Those in charge of the service became convinced that the mission needed a farm far from urban temptations, where reformed alcoholics could work for a time until they had won a permanent victory over their former habits. Dr. Kellogg had expressed a similar idea shortly after the Medical Mission's establishment. As a firm believer in "the pure atmosphere of the country," John Harvey asked the Chicago staff to make the subject of a mission farm a matter for special prayer. A short time later a wealthy sanitarium patient, Edward S. Peddicord, asked Kellogg if he might contribute to some program related to the Chicago mission. John Harvey immediately suggested a mission farm, and before the interview ended, Peddicord had offered Kellogg 160 acres in LaSalle County, Illinois. Mr. Peddicord died shortly thereafter, and his heirs sought to reclaim the farm, but the Illinois Supreme Court eventually awarded the property to Kellogg. For a number of years the farm employed reclaimed derelicts to grow fruits and vegetables, which the Chicago enterprises used.

Each evening pairs of mature nurses left the Settlement House to work among Chicago's streetwalkers, whom they encouraged to turn from lives of prostitution. The Life Boat Rescue Service, as Kellogg called it, put the prostitutes who responded in private Christian homes for a period. Kellogg contended that only such an environment could accomplish any lasting reformation in their lives. The Settlement House also sponsored a maternity home for young unmarried mothers who had run away from home. If a girl desired to keep her child, it helped her to find a new home or to find acceptance and understanding in her old community, and it placed with foster parents the children the young mothers did not wish to keep.

The social service aspects of the Chicago Medical Mission always had stronger emphasis than the strictly religious activities, although the latter were not ignored. At first the Medical Mission conducted joint evening religious services in cooperation with the Pacific Garden Mission. Later the Battle Creek group began a Sabbath school for the children of the area, and in 1894 W. S. Sadler opened the strictly evangelistic Life Boat Mission on South State Street. Sadler, who eventually married Dr. Kellogg's niece, had worked as a youth in the sanitarium kitchens. He later became a salesman for sanitarium health foods and was in the process of introducing them in the Chicago wholesale district at the time the Chicago Medical Mission began. Deciding that he wished to have the young man take over the religious side of the mission program, Kellogg sent him to the Moody Bible Institute for training in evangelistic techniques. Eventually Sadler received responsibility for the supervision of all the mission's activities. The Life Boat Mission was the only part that carried a public Seventh-day Adventist label. The other activities operated on a Christian, but undenominational, basis.

Another evangelistic mission, run by Tom Mackey, was for several years loosely affiliated with the Chicago Medical Mission. Mackey, a former drifter, traced his permanent religious conversion to a chat with Dr. Kellogg, during which the doctor gave him the penny needed to secure a bowl of soup at the mission lunch counter. After some months of street evangelism, Mackey opened the Star of Hope Mission on West Madison Street. For several years Dr. Kellogg personally contributed $100 or more each month to help Mackey with his operating expenses, but when John Harvey had to assume a greater share of the cost of the Medical Mission, he curtailed his gifts to the Star of Hope. Later Mackey closed his Chicago mission and moved to Los Angeles, where he carried on a similar enterprise for a number of years.

Dr. Kellogg firmly believed that the goal of city mission activities should be to "rescue lost souls, not to teach theology," and so he maintained that such missions should not be sectarian endeavors. In harmony with his ideas he arranged for an interdenominational committee, under the chairmanship of S. S. Sherin, a Methodist clergyman, to serve in an advisory capacity to the Chicago Medical Mission. The undenominational aspect of the mission upon which Kellogg always insisted, led to misunderstanding between him and other Adventists and eventually resulted in the termination of the Chicago Medical Mission. Most Seventh-day Adventists were convinced that their only excuse for existence was to proclaim distinctive religious principles. They naturally questioned the value of a program that appeared to be absorbing an increasing amount of both the denomination's financial resources and its potential leaders without at the same time spreading Adventist beliefs. Although Ellen White had indicated approval of Kellogg's initial ventures in Chicago, she later counseled him not to place his major emphasis on work for social outcasts and, in particular, not to solicit funds for such programs among Adventists at a time when the denomination's other financial needs were so great.

John Harvey reluctantly agreed to restrict his attempts to raise funds for mission work from Adventist sources. The branch sanitarium's earnings proved insufficient for the expanding services of the Medical Mission, and so in an effort to increase local support, Kellogg authorized Sadler to begin publishing the *Life Boat Magazine*. A small journal patterned after the Salvation Army's *War Cry,* it described the Medical Mission's varied programs. Sold on the city streets, at its peak it had a print run of more than 200,000 copies per issue. Its sales helped to balance the mission budget, but it was also necessary for Sadler to initiate an extensive solicitation campaign among Chicago businesspeople.

By 1901 less than one tenth of the financial expenses of the Chicago Mission came from Adventist donations. In 1902, however, when Sadler discontinued his connection with the mission in order to study medicine, the local financial support that he had developed began to decline, forcing Dr. Kellogg to contribute an increasing share of the costs of the mission from his personal income. Kellogg might have weathered the financial problem growing out of the withdrawal of denominational support, but when his rupture with the church ended the stream of young people coming to the sanitarium and to the American Medical Missionary College for medical training, his difficulties compounded. The students had formed the bulk of the unpaid, or nominally paid, staff members who operated the Chicago Medical Mission. Unwilling to affiliate with another religious organization, he failed to secure the interdenominational support for which he hoped. As a result the American Medical Missionary College rapidly declined, and the activities of the Chicago Mission discontinued one by one. The last to go was the free dispensary, which closed its doors in the autumn of 1913 after an existence of just over 20 years.

At about the same time that he was laying plans for the organization of the Chicago Medical Mission, Dr. Kellogg was busily promoting another activity that he believed could involve almost every Adventist in humanitarian work. In the late fall of 1892 he organized a number of Christian Help Bands among the employees of the Battle Creek Sanitarium. The Christian Help Bands sought to find those in the community in need of neighborly assistance—families plagued by either illness or unemployment or that had become disorganized because the mother had to work outside the home. Kellogg envisioned Adventist Christian Help Bands busily cleaning up the homes of the poor and sick, demonstrating hygienic housekeeping and cooking, and organizing kindergartens and manual training, sewing, gardening, and physical training classes for children.

At first he believed that most Adventist ministers were unsympathetic toward his idea of Christian Help Bands, but soon, backed by O. A. Olsen, the doctor obtained increased cooperation. In the spring of 1894 John Harvey introduced the idea of Christian Help Bands on the Pacific Coast and in the mountain states. During the next several years he actively promoted such activities, proclaiming the belief that such humanitarian projects would win more converts to Adventist doctrines than would all of the denomination's preachers and publications combined. The plan for Christian Help Bands, like other Kellogg projects, suffered from the doctor's theological and organizational dispute with Adventist leaders. During the conflict all Kellogg-sponsored projects became suspect, and the bands gradually disappeared from Adventist congregations.

An enlightened attitude on racial questions accompanied Kellogg's humanitarian projects. He would allow no color line at the Battle Creek Sanitarium or in any of the schools associated with it. When some of the sanitarium workers once petitioned the institution's directors to establish segregated seating in the employee dining room, Kellogg emphatically declared that if it were done, he would resign as medical director. He vigorously supported the pioneer educational, evangelistic, and medical program that Ellen White's son, J. Edson White, launched among the African-Americans of the deep South. The doctor believed that Adventists should develop a whole system of primary schools for Blacks across the region.

For a number of years he enthusiastically supported and liberally contributed to the African-American orphanage maintained by Mrs. A. S. Steele in Chattanooga. After the Haskell Home opened, he arranged for the transfer of more than 30 Black children from Mrs. Steele's establishment. Earlier, the doctor had taken seven of Mrs. Steele's older girls into his own home in order to help them secure sufficient medical knowledge to teach healthful living among their people.

John Kellogg demonstrated his concern for those about him in many other ways. He constantly agitated for more public recreational facilities. When the city of Battle Creek moved more slowly than the doctor wished in establishing playground facilities, John Harvey converted a section of his substantial estate into a modern play area for the neighborhood children. The playground included a large pool where, during the summer months, instructors provided free swimming lessons.

Early in 1915 Dr. Kellogg pressured the physicians and dentists of Battle Creek into agreeing to provide free medical and dental examinations as part of the public school program. Strange as it now seems, considerable opposition to the plan arose from parents. When the city referred the issue to the voters, they rejected the doctor's offer by the decisive margin of three to one. Perplexed at the rebuff, Kellogg confined himself in the future to urging regular voluntary physical examinations.

With the exception of pure food and drug legislation and national prohibition, John Harvey never showed much interest in government attempts to remedy social ills. He preferred the personal approach that demanded individual involvement. "I do not know of anything I love as well as to do charitable work," the doctor had written Ellen White during the height of his MMBA activities. Although he never renounced his interest in the welfare of others, the severing of Kellogg's Adventist ties deprived him of most of the channels through which he had demonstrated his concern. In fact, the event changed his life in many ways—things were just not the same for John Harvey Kellogg after 1907.

CHAPTER XVI

THE TIES OF 50 YEARS ARE BROKEN

JOHN HARVEY KELLOGG'S parents had inculcated Seventh-day Adventist doctrines in him from infancy. As a young doctor he had testified, "I sincerely believe the whole truth. I love it and love to work in the cause. I could not be happy anywhere else." For three decades the doctor occupied numerous positions of trust and leadership within the Adventist organizational structure. Yet the year 1907 saw his official church ties severed at the culmination of a long and often bitter controversy.

The causes of the controversy were many and varied. Perhaps the most basic, yet at the same time the most difficult to assess, was the quality of Kellogg's personal religious faith. Early in his career, he admitted to Ellen White that he frequently found it difficult to know just what his religious beliefs were. "I have recognized the fact that it was only my early education that held me from becoming a skeptic," the doctor wrote. "I have not had a hold upon God that gave me a living experience of my own."

Several years later John Harvey participated in the 1888 General Conference of Seventh-day Adventists meeting in Minneapolis. During it he evidently experienced a deep religious awakening. Ellen White testified that "after the meeting at Minneapolis, Dr. Kellogg was a converted man, and we all knew it." His busy schedule, however, often crowded out spiritual meditation from his life. Visiting his sickest patients kept him occupied even on the Sabbath. Seldom could he attend a church service without getting called away to deal with some seeming emergency.

From the start, too, a persistent tendency to be critical of the actions of others marred his religious experience. He constantly assailed the failure of many Adventists to practice the entire system of health reform laid down by Ellen White and himself. It is true that, for many years after the introduction of the health tenets, many understood their proper application only imperfectly. John Norton Loughborough used to tell of a conversation with a new Adventist believer in England. Not having seen the man for some time, Loughborough inquired how he was getting along with the reform diet. "Pretty well, I guess," came the reply. "But tell me, Elder, would it be all right to cook the oatmeal before we eat it? I like it raw quite well, but my wife thinks she would relish it better if it were cooked." Such was the state of knowledge concerning a vegetarian diet. Small wonder that many complained that the reform diet made people feel worse rather than better.

To Kellogg, the chief villains responsible for denominational backsliding in regard to health principles were the Adventist ministry. They, the doctor charged, tended to "discourage the people by their example." He also sometimes looked down on the ministers because they lacked his level of professional education, referring to them as men of "very mediocre ability" who retained their influence through "psychological trickery." Particularly skeptical of the Adventist ministry's financial abilities, he accused them of wasting money in needless travel, using poor judgment in allocating the church's limited income, and being shortsighted because they promoted the publication of religious literature to a larger extent than they did medical missionary activities. John Harvey also complained that Adventist preachers were dictatorial and arbitrary. It would seem that his attitude toward the clergy, which even his friends admitted was frequently "arrogant and haughty," inevitably aroused antagonism in church circles, not only toward Kellogg, but also toward the causes he pushed so vigorously. Unfortunately the doctor never learned the truth of the old saying "You catch more flies with honey than with vinegar."

During the last decade of his church affiliation, Kellogg demonstrated particular criticism of the top Adventist leadership. He complained that they used their great influence with the Adventist rank and file to lure most of the promising youth into the ministry or the sale of denominational publications, while encouraging only the less talented to enter medical lines. Many of the preachers believed that the doctor was guilty of the same activity—only in reverse. They noted that he continually used all kinds of attractions to get the most talented Adventists, including energetic young ministers, to leave their work in order to become doctors or nurses. What he claimed was the Adventist leaders' attitude toward his food creations also irked Kellogg. He maintained that men ridiculed his products when he first introduced them, but after they became financially successful, the administrators were eager to appropriate the profits for use in activities that they controlled.

Toward the end of the nineteenth century, issues arising out of the new Battle Creek Sanitarium charter contributed to the increasing tensions between Kellogg and other denominational administrator. The proclaimed "undenominational and nonsectarian" character of the institution raised questions in the minds of many Adventists. Dr. Kellogg's position that the new articles of incorporation prohibited the sanitarium from sending any of its revenue outside the state of Michigan particularly disturbed Ellen White. She recalled that when she and James White had first solicited funds to help launch the sanitarium, they had promised that it would use its earnings to help other church institutions to get started. Now John Harvey claimed that the law prohibited the sanitarium from sending any funds to help launch a sanitarium in Australia.

By the turn of the century Dr. Kellogg's attitude toward Ellen White, her messages, and her role became critically important to most Adventist leaders. What disturbed them was, as George I. Butler put it, that John Harvey did not always talk the same way about Mrs. White. Butler remembered that in Kellogg's earlier days it had seemed that "the doctor believed the Testimonies (Mrs. White's writings) more than he did the Bible." Certainly the doctor had repeatedly assured Ellen White that he believed God's Spirit spoke through her. "I often used to make a test in my mind, saying nothing to anybody," Kellogg wrote. "I would say to myself, now here is an evident wrong. Sister White knows nothing about it, or if she knows anything about it, the circumstances are such as would produce a personal prejudice in favor of the wrong rather than against it. If the Lord leads her to denounce and correct this evil, I shall know that she is being specially led. In not a single instance did the test fail, and so my confidence grew. I mention these facts very often to those whom I find doubting."

The inherent danger in such a position was that Kellogg made his own ideas of right and wrong the yardstick for testing Ellen White's statements. He rather intimated so to W. C. White when he wrote, "My faith in your mother's teachings has been based on my belief in the fundamental correctness of the principles which she teaches rather than upon any natural disposition to trust in the supernatural." Yet in the doctor's campaign to convince Adventists to practice all aspects of biologic living, it certainly suited his purposes to point out that Mrs. White's teachings on healthful living were "words direct from the Lord."

During meetings with sanitarium employees Dr. Kellogg frequently read from Ellen White's writings "by the hours" as tears streamed down his face, and he commented on how wonderful the messages were as "God's gift to the church." The doctor could scarcely forget the motherly attitude she had taken toward him in his youth and young manhood. Nor could he forget that on numerous occasions she had both publicly and privately rebuked Adventist leaders who had been critical of Kellogg and who had not cooperated with him in fully promoting health reform principles. Repeatedly she assured him that God had made him chief of the Adventist medical fraternity for a definite purpose. To others, she expressed the belief that few physicians in all the world were Dr. Kellogg's equal.

About the turn of the century his attitude toward her began to undergo a noticeable change. As early as 1899 he started to complain that someone was misinforming her about him and his activities, and that others had made her believe "untrue and contemptible" statements. He professed the belief that W. C. White and others were attempting to influence her opinions. To some Adventist leaders it seemed that Kellogg was himself guilty of the same charge that he was lodging against others.

George I. Butler put his finger on probably the chief reason for Kellogg's changing attitude. "Most everybody believes the Testimonies very strongly as long as they favor them, and sustain them, and stand up for them, and fight their battles," Butler wrote from the vantage point of 40 years of observation. "The time when they become questionable about the Testimonies is when the Testimonies begin to reprove them, and present before them certain faults, and wrong courses, or methods, or motives of action."

Ever since the start of John Kellogg's career, Ellen White had counseled him to alter certain actions and personality traits. She had urged him to be more humble, to be more willing to take advice from others, to take better care of his personal health, to delegate authority, and to share the resources of the Battle Creek Sanitarium rather than using them to continually enlarge the institution's facilities. In general his attitude had been appreciative, and he regularly promised to follow her suggestions.

From 1898 onward, however, Ellen White's advice to him became more pointed and forceful. She reproved his tendency to cast doubt on fundamental Adventist doctrines through careless conversation, and she urged him both to stop undermining the influence of the ministry and to refrain from plans to separate the denomination's medical enterprises from church control. In addition she expressed the belief that the doctor was making his humanitarian endeavors too predominant, using in them funds needed for other aspects of the Adventist program. Ellen White frankly told him that he had gathered too much power into his own hands and that he was employing it in a selfish way.

Kellogg's initial reaction to her reproofs was to express pain and disbelief. For a time he considered resigning from all official denominational positions, but before long he convinced himself that the smoothness of the sanitarium reorganization indicated divine approval of his actions. He retreated to the explanation that Mrs. White had written in the way she did only because "some one has made you believe things of me that are utterly false." The doctor maintained that her comments about a large building in Chicago offered a perfect example of her receiving and using misinformation.

The dispute centered around a vision in which Mrs. White was shown a large and expensive building in Chicago to be used in connection with the Medical Mission. She wrote that Adventists should not spend their funds to erect such large buildings in support of an activity that, although good in itself, was never-ending. Since the Chicago Medical Mission did not own the type of building described, Kellogg professed to believe that her statements justified his suspicions of some of her counsels. What he failed to admit until several years later was that a committee had prepared plans for a large building in Chicago that would have included a hospital, dormitory, classrooms, and laboratories—plans drawn and approved when John Harvey was in Europe. Upon his return he had vetoed the idea, possibly because of Ellen White's earlier statements concerning the Chicago medical and social work. When others presented all the facts to her, she indicated that the vision and her counsel had been designed to prevent the construction of the building being considered, and that Dr. Kellogg should have realized this. The doctor agreed, but he continued to cite the instance to others as one in which she had been mistaken.

About this same time she rebuked him for his practice of requiring prospective medical and nursing students to sign contracts agreeing to work under the direction of the Medical Missionary and Benevolent Association for a certain time as a prerequisite to the student's acceptance into the American Medical Missionary College or the Battle Creek Sanitarium School of Nursing. Kellogg had also instituted similar contracts for an institution desiring to receive MMBA aid or permission to manufacture his food products. She considered such contracts to be monopolistic and against the divine pattern of organization. Although the doctor publicly acknowledged that his actions had been a mistake and would be discontinued, there seems little doubt but that he found the retreat humiliating.

Mrs. White's attitude toward the rebuilding of the Battle Creek Sanitarium following the great fire of 1902 further served to irritate Dr. Kellogg. Following the conflagration he discussed with other Adventist leaders where the sanitarium should be rebuilt. But he did not seek Ellen White's views on the matter, probably because he was convinced that the institution must remain in Battle Creek, while a dozen years before she had stated, "I sincerely wish that the sanitarium were miles away from Battle Creek. From the light given me of God, I know this would be better for its spirituality and usefulness." For some months following the fire, she refrained from any comment on the problem of rebuilding, evidently waiting to see if he would heed her past advice. Eventually, however, she commented that the new sanitarium in Battle Creek was too large and that it would have been better to have constructed smaller institutions in various places rather than concentrating everything in one mammoth structure. Dr. Kellogg replied that Mrs. White was being misinformed as to what was being done.

Although he had specifically pledged denominational leaders that he would "never go a dollar in debt to rebuild," he soon found that building costs ran much higher than expected. As a result he had to find some way of borrowing funds to complete the new edifice. To meet the emergency, church leaders approved a plan for the sanitarium to raise cash by selling bonds. John Harvey then appealed to W. C. White to issue a special plea to Adventists to buy the sanitarium securities since it was necessary "to raise several hundred thousand dollars right away." Several months later, however, Ellen White publicly stated that Adventists should not purchase sanitarium bonds lest their funds be unavailable for other church needs. Much to his exasperation, most Adventists followed her counsel, with the result that few of the bonds sold. A widespread impression that they were fraudulent even developed, and the doctor complained that church leaders did nothing to correct the belief, which he regarded as an implication against his good character.

The difference of opinion between Kellogg and other Adventist administrators concerning the amount of emphasis the church should place on humanitarian endeavors has already been alluded to. Also, disagreement arose over the relationship between Adventist medical activities and the church's formal organization. As early as 1890 Ellen White had suggested that doctors should work under the general direction of local Adventist conferences, an idea that John Harvey had opposed from the start. His resistance hardened as he became disenchanted with some of the decisions of the General Conference Foreign Mission Board. "Self-respecting medical men are willing to work on an equal footing with preachers even though they may be of inferior education and ability," Kellogg proclaimed, "but it is not human nature that they could be willing to be slaves to such men while doing their own professional work." He did not believe that a preacher had "any business in a medical institution," and he determined that none of the medical enterprises he had any association with should ever fall under the domination of a group of ministers.

On the other hand, he was quite willing for physicians to occupy the pulpit, although he himself refused ordination as a minister in 1901. Kellogg believed that "the doctor should be the best of all preachers" because he knew best how to live. His attitude, coupled with the fact that by 1901 more Adventists worked under the immediate supervision of his Medical Missionary and Benevolent Association than under the direction of the General Conference, caused some Adventist leaders to suspect that he was seeking to gain control of the entire denominational machinery. They determined to avoid such a possibility at all costs.

Dr. Kellogg seems to have reached about the height of his influence within Adventism in 1901. Before the General Conference of that year he had persuaded G. A. Irwin, General Conference president from 1897 to

1901, to agree to a larger representation for the church's medical institutions at the 1901 Conference. With the increased representation and also because many ministers desired to make another attempt to end their differences with the denominational medical contingent, John Kellogg managed to play a major role in the reorganization of the general church structure, the session's chief accomplishment. The doctor emerged as a member of both the 25-member General Conference Executive Committee and the denomination's Foreign Mission Board. Many believed at the close of the 1901 meetings that the breach between the medical and ecclesiastical leaders of the church had for all practical purposes healed.

The 1901 General Conference broke a 38-year-old precedent by giving the chief authority between biennial Conferences to an executive committee rather than to a president. Arthur G. Daniells, selected as chairman of the executive committee, at first appeared to get along well with Dr. Kellogg, but subsequently the two men disagreed sharply. In 1902 some of John Harvey's supporters made an unsuccessful attempt to make Alonzo T. Jones chairman of the executive committee in place of Daniells because they believed that Jones would work more harmoniously with Kellogg.

During the early weeks of 1903 Kellogg, Jones, and their allies endeavored to round up the support necessary to replace Daniells at the 1903 General Conference session. Not only were their efforts unsuccessful, but the 1903 Conference amended the constitution by reinstating the office of president, and elected Daniells to the post. Kellogg received another setback when the same session approved a resolution recommending that all denominationally operated institutions come under direct denominational ownership. Even before the adoption of the resolution, John Harvey announced that he did not "expect to be bound by it in anything" he had "anything to do with." He declared that the thought of sanitariums being controlled by persons not living in harmony with all the principles that the institutions taught was intolerable. When President Daniells expressed the opinion that ownership need not necessarily mean control, Kellogg snapped back that ownership always meant control and if Daniells said that it did not, he didn't know what he was talking about.

Dr. Kellogg's first major conflict with the new General Conference president developed in 1902 out of a disagreement over fiscal policies. Daniells had found the denomination plagued by a burden of debt

Review and Herald Collection

Arthur G. Daniells

incurred by many of its subsidiary institutions. In harmony with recent counsel from Ellen White, he decided to pay off the debts and to keep all future expansion on a cash basis. Although Kellogg frequently expressed regrets that the Battle Creek Sanitarium had fallen so heavily in debt, he greatly wanted to have an Adventist sanitarium opened in England, and he desired denominational leaders to approve the purchase of a site that he had discovered, even though they would need to borrow funds for it. When Daniells and his associates refused to agree to the purchase until after the necessary funds had been raised, Kellogg accused them of not wanting to see the Adventist medical program established in England. The doctor summarily announced that he could never work with them on the basis of their new cash policy.

Daniells was a man of forceful personality who arrived at decisions after much thought and prayer. Once he had made up his mind that a certain course of action was the right one, it was not easy to convince him to change. To Kellogg, the administrator seemed stubborn and unreasonable. Daniells particularly offended the doctor when he told a group of Adventist leaders that John Harvey had "an imperious will" that needed breaking. Kellogg also became convinced that Daniells was not a strict vegetarian, an unpardonable fault in the doctor's estimation. For his part, Daniells became increasingly concerned over what he felt was Dr. Kellogg's deteriorating attitude toward the messages the church received through Ellen White.

During the last two decades of the nineteenth century she issued increasingly urgent calls to Adventist believers to reverse their tendency to congregate in Battle Creek. She maintained that unless the process stopped, divinely ordained calamities would strike the denominational institutions in that city. Her warning played a large part in the decision to relocate Battle Creek College as Emmanuel Missionary College in Berrien Springs, Michigan, in 1901. Then, 10 months after the great sanitarium fire of 1902, the church's giant Battle Creek publishing house burned to the ground. Since most Adventist leaders saw the two calamities as divine judgments, the 1903 General Conference decided to remove both denominational headquarters and the Review and Herald Publishing Association from Battle Creek.

Although in earlier years Dr. Kellogg had professed to see the wisdom of decentralizing Adventist activities, his attitude underwent a rapid transformation once the Adventist exodus began. The doctor undoubtedly feared that if a large number of church members should leave the city, it would be difficult to operate the sanitarium successfully, since it was largely staffed by Adventists willing to work for minimum wages only because they believed they were furthering a vital part of the denomination's program. He began to ridicule Adventist leaders who, he maintained, were trying to persuade good church members to leave Battle Creek or be "burned up or destroyed by an earthquake or some other horrible catastrophe."

In the fall of 1903 Kellogg began some maneuvers aimed at reactivating Battle Creek College. He announced that he was simply trying to develop a way to give legal standing to the tutorial work students were receiving preparatory to their acceptance in the American Medical Missionary College. Medical licensing boards, he explained, were beginning to require new doctors to show evidence of high school graduation and some college work in addition to their medical training, and he claimed that the trend made it necessary to have a college in Battle Creek, where AMMC students could make up any educational deficiencies. Adventist leaders generally regarded his attempt to reopen Battle Creek College as undercutting their efforts to decentralize church activities. Their objections led Kellogg to abandon the idea of re-establishing the college, but the abortive attempt had increased the mistrust that each side felt for the other.

By then many Adventist ministers had become convinced that Battle Creek was a dangerous place for young Adventists. They believed that Dr. Kellogg's powerful influence caused many youth to lose faith in denominational teachings—particularly their faith in the inspiration of Ellen White. Also they felt concern because, although the church had taught for years that the tithe should go exclusively to pay the ministry, he maintained that individuals were free to devote it to any good cause that appealed to them. The denominational leadership had grown apprehensive of the doctor's tendency to regard large portions of the Bible as figurative, particularly those prophetic sections on which Adventist scholars built much of the church's theology. Most of all, however, they, and Ellen White as well, feared John Harvey's promotion of what they regarded as pantheistic heresies. On this point they decided to make a determined stand against the doctor.

Much of the controversy over Dr. Kellogg's pantheistic ideas centered around statements concerning the personality of God and the divine presence in all living things that appeared in the doctor's book *The Living Temple*. In it John Harvey specifically proclaimed his belief in a personal God, but he also included statements such as, "There is present in the tree a power which creates and maintains it, a tree-maker in the tree, a flower-maker in the flower." To many Adventist theologians, to say that "God is not behind nature nor above nature; he is in nature—nature is the visible expression of his power," seemed perilously close to nature worship. Individuals such as William A. Spicer, newly returned to the United States from mission service in India, saw in Kellogg's emphasis on the divine presence in human beings and animals similarities to the pantheistic aspects of Hinduism. Others, such as Stephen N. Haskell, believed that the doctor's ideas of God would destroy the basic and distinctive Adventist doctrine of the heavenly sanctuary.

Kellogg expressed surprise at the objections raised to *The Living Temple*. Almost plaintively he noted that he had taught similar things at three General Conference sessions without hearing any criticism. It is true that in the talks the doctor gave to the 1897 General Conference he made frequent references to God being in various natural phenomena. At the important 1901 Conference, Kellogg had dramatically stated that it was God in the sunflower that made it follow the sun and that in every brain cell dwelt "a divine presence." Now that he was under theological fire, he maintained that he had held the ideas being attacked for more than 20 years, and had developed them from studying certain of Ellen White's statements. He maintained that his views were really no different from those expressed by Mrs. White in the chapter "God in Nature" in her book *Education*.

If he hoped that the injection of her name into the pantheism controversy would help his cause, he was badly mistaken. Almost immediately she denied that her writings contained the same concepts that Kellogg expressed unless someone took her statements completely out of context, which she intimated that the doctor had done. Mrs. White recalled that, even before her husband's death in 1881, Dr. Kellogg had discussed with her some of the same erroneous views of God in nature that he was now teaching, and that she had strongly advised him not even to talk about such things.

Throughout the long dispute over the philosophy expressed in *The Living Temple,* Dr. Kellogg fervently maintained that he was not a pantheist and had not even known what the word meant until others accused him of teaching it. He argued that all he was doing was stating the biblical doctrine of God's omnipresence in such a way as to show its "practical significance," to show the "obligation it puts us under to live in harmony with God, . . . physically, mentally, and morally." Since the doctor was overwhelmingly dedicated to natural laws of living as being basic to the health reform doctrines he was constantly advocating, it is probable that he advanced such arguments to impress his readers to harmonize their will "with that of the divine occupant."

Most Adventist administrators seemed willing to believe that Kellogg had not deliberately set out to introduce pantheism among Adventists. Ellen White indicated that the doctor's theories, "carried to their logical conclusion, would destroy faith in the sanctuary question and in the atonement." But she added, "I do not think that Dr. Kellogg saw this clearly. I do not think that he realized that in laying his new foundation of faith, he was directing his steps toward infidelity."

What did sincerely trouble Adventist leaders was that although the doctor repeatedly said that he repudiated anything in *The Living Temple* not in harmony with what Ellen White had written, he also remarked candidly that he had not in any respect changed his mind on the views expressed in the book. As a matter of fact, several Adventist ministers who had heard Kellogg discuss these matters freely, felt that his statements in *The Living Temple* represented only a mild version of his real beliefs.

The pantheistic slant of Dr. Kellogg's teachings must have seemed to Adventist administrators but the capstone of a long campaign to discredit the ministry, utilize the resources of the denomination for his own purposes, and, in later years, to discredit the counsel of Ellen White. They feared that the denomination's actual existence would be in jeopardy unless Kellogg changed his beliefs and actions. Curbing a man with his dominant personality, however, was not an easy job. Inevitably the doctor resented the advice of those often younger than he, both physically and in their adherence to Adventism. He grew increasingly bitter toward the Adventist leadership who, he was convinced, were attempting only "to break me down."

As the church's top leaders, President Daniells and vice-president William W. Prescott necessarily assumed major responsibility for attempting to get him to harmonize his views and policies with those of mainstream Adventism. As a result, they encountered the doctor's wrath in full measure. Kellogg professed to believe that Daniells, Prescott, and their associates possessed a "thirst for power" and a "determination to rule or ruin." Such statements only added fuel to the controversy, that by 1903 seemed on the verge of splitting the Adventist Church in two.

In an effort to prevent such a disaster, two veteran Adventist leaders, G. I. Butler and S. N. Haskell, sought to reconcile the two factions. Nearly a quarter of a century earlier, Butler and Haskell had combined with Kellogg to curb the activities of James White. Now, while writing John Harvey letters of appreciation, sympathy, and encouragement, they also attempted to convince him to confess his past mistakes, renounce his pantheistic views, and, most particularly, to cease his criticisms of Ellen White. At the same time Butler and Haskell wrote favorably to Ellen White of Kellogg's work and contributions to the church. They also counseled the Daniells group to be temperate in what they said about the doctor.

Alonzo T. Jones

On at least three separate occasions it appeared as if a permanent reconciliation between Dr. Kellogg and the Adventist leadership might be achieved. During the meetings of the Medical Missionary and Benevolent Association in the spring of 1903, Alonzo T. Jones brought the opposing camps together. As a member of the General Conference Executive Committee, Jones read a number of past letters and statements from Ellen White that called for the unity of Adventist medical and evangelical personnel. After both sides had expressed a desire for such unity, Jones read to Kellogg a special letter in which Ellen White urged the doctor to make every effort to seek reconciliation to the church's leadership. John Harvey announced that he accepted the letter as "a message from the Lord." The following day he confessed his past mistakes before a session of the General Conference Executive Committee and asked forgiveness for his errors. Daniells and Prescott made similar confessions. From the meeting Kellogg and Daniells went to a public assembly in the Battle Creek Tabernacle, where they announced that they had settled all of their differences. Within a few weeks, however, the two sides were once more engaged in bitter disagreements. Ellen White placed the blame for the renewal of hostilities largely upon Kellogg, who she indicated had completely failed to reform his actions and beliefs.

The next major effort to restore harmony came at the annual Fall Council of Adventist leaders in Washington, D.C., in October 1903. At this time Professor Percy T. Magan, a close Kellogg friend, talked with the doctor about a recent visit with Ellen White. Magan told the doctor of her great concern for him. Deeply moved, John Harvey indicated that he could see his past mistakes and was determined in the future to give himself "wholly to the Lord in healing the sick and preaching the gospel" and leave the management of institutions to others. He promised the General Conference leaders that he would renounce his plans to control all Adventist medical work and would eliminate any theological references in The Living Temple. Also he admitted to having been wrong in occasionally speaking in too critical a fashion of some of Mrs. White's messages. Following his open confessions, Kellogg had long private talks with both Prescott and Daniells, during which the latter told the doctor, "We will pull together." Once more the denomination believed that it had achieved unity, but the differences proved too basic. In less than three months, deep division again split the church.

In May 1904, during an Adventist Lake Union Conference Session at Berrien Springs, Michigan, occurred the last substantial effort to effect a reconciliation between Kellogg and the Daniells group. Before the meeting began, the doctor determined that during its course he would resign from the presidency of the Medical Missionary and Benevolent

W. W. Prescott

Association. The Berrien Springs meeting differed in several respects from the two previous attempts to restore unity. This time Ellen White herself was present and worked actively to bring the two sides together. A more violent spirit of controversy was also evident. After sharp public exchange between the two sides, she renewed her pleas for unity, and a number of Kellogg's associates confessed to having maintained an incorrect attitude toward the Adventist leadership. John Harvey, however, refused to make such a retraction, and he declared that the confessions of the others were "a mere form intended to meet the emergency." He also boasted that although this time Prescott had made a public statement about his failures, he had not. Ellen White reproved his gloating attitude. In addition, she rebuked a number of the doctor's supporters, whom she accused of encouraging him to take an unyielding position. W. C. White later reported that his mother firmly believed that Dr. Kellogg would have been permanently saved for the Adventist cause if at Berrien Springs some of his associates had only encouraged him to humble himself and strive once more for harmony with the ministry.

Instead, some in the Kellogg camp expressed resentment because they believed that Daniells had not followed Mrs. White's advice to "reach out his hand" to Dr. Kellogg and make peace. For a short time Kellogg regarded the Berrien Springs meeting as a personal triumph, but when he found the opposition unwilling to help meet the grave financial problems facing the Battle Creek Sanitarium, he realized that he had won a poor victory, if indeed it was one at all.

The situation worsened when he learned that the General Conference officials were reluctant to assume responsibility for the Benevolent Association. Determined to force the issue, the doctor arranged for the Association to go into bankruptcy, with I. H. Evans, General Conference treasurer, being appointed receiver. Almost immediately a conflict developed over the disappearance of MMBA assets. The church leaders believed that before filing for bankruptcy, Kellogg and his fellow directors had deliberately transferred all the real property of the Association to other corporations that they controlled. Left with many notes for loans advanced by individual Adventists, Evans had no funds available to meet them.

Dr. Kellogg admitted that most of the funds which the MMBA had received as gifts or loans it had given away, but he maintained that since the denomination had received benefits to its sanitariums through the gifts, and had also had many of its young people trained as doctors and nurses at MMBA expense, it should now be willing to care for the Association's debts. He also reasoned that it was wise to place deeds to property in the hands of individual institutions so that "whatever happened to one institution, others would not be disturbed." In an obvious attempt to shift responsibility, the doctor claimed that if the General Conference had not allowed the diversion of Missionary Acre funds originally promised to the MMBA, it would have had no outstanding debts. Although he maintained that he had no moral or legal obligation to repay any loans made to the MMBA, Kellogg did repay some of them from his personal funds. The Battle Creek Sanitarium or a nonprofit charitable foundation Kellogg had established in 1906 repaid others.

Early in 1906 Dr. Kellogg became convinced that the local Adventist congregation in Battle Creek would soon expel him from its membership. Not until November 10, 1907, however, did the Tabernacle Church congregation formally consider in business session the continuation of his membership. A week earlier the doctor and several of his associates had received notification of the impending meeting. Although John Harvey had previously indicated his desire to receive a formal heresy trial, he did not appear at the Tabernacle on November 10. Instead, he sent his secretary, Dr. J. T. Case, to take notes on the proceedings.

The approximately 350 members present that November evening heard their pastor, M. N. Campbell, outline the main charges against Dr. Kellogg. Campbell pointed out that the doctor had not attended services at the Tabernacle for a number of years, and that he failed to pay a tithe or contribute to the expenses of the church in any other way. The pastor also stated that Kellogg was antagonistic "to the gifts now manifest in the church" and "was allied with those who were attempting to overthrow the work for which this church existed." A report from Augustin C. Bourdeau and George W. Amadon, veteran Adventist officials who had interviewed Kellogg as representatives of the local congregation a few days earlier, followed Campbell's statement. After they had indicated that the seven-hour meeting which they had held with Kellogg had convinced them that Campbell had presented a correct picture of the matter, Bourdeau officially moved Kellogg's expulsion from the church. The motion carried unanimously.

Dr. Kellogg's initial reaction was that he had no fault to find with the outcome of the November 10 meeting. But he declared that his religious beliefs were essentially what they had been for the preceding 30 years. He observed the seventh day as the Sabbath, believed in the Bible as God's Word, and was sure that Jesus was sinful humanity's only hope for salvation. Although he never regularly attended or joined any other church, he did encourage the few of his associates who discontinued their Adventist membership to do so, for he believed that "some church, any church, is better than no church."

By the 1920s considerable evidence had accumulated that Dr. Kellogg had seriously modified some of the religious beliefs in which his parents had reared him. For several years he had been sponsoring "quiet" Sabbath recreational activities for sanitarium guests. He also began with increasing frequency to cite evolutionary theories in support of his system of biologic living. Old Adventist associates reported that the doctor no longer professed belief in certain parts of the Bible, such as the stories of Jonah and Job; denied the virgin birth and divinity of Jesus and the need for an atonement; constantly joked about the personal appearance of God; and expressed the view that it was possible for human beings to work out their own salvation through a program of eugenics and biologic living.

A little more than a year after his dismissal from the Tabernacle Church, Kellogg retaliated by arranging to have a number of Adventist leaders deprived of membership in the Michigan Sanitarium and Benevolent Association, the organization that legally owned and operated the Battle Creek Sanitarium. An annual meeting of the Association, attended by only 28 of its nearly 700 members, expelled A. G. Daniells, W. C. White, and a number of other Adventist clergy as being antagonistic to the purposes for which the Association had been formed. The group stopped short of removing the name of Ellen White from its rolls.

In later years Dr. Kellogg estimated that the most harmful effect for him of his break with the Adventist church was that it deprived him of close association with many young doctors whom he had attracted to the profession of medicine, helped to train, and for whom he had high regard. Almost all of the young Adventist doctors who had gone out to supervise sanitariums in various parts of the nation and the world remained loyal to the denomination. They were willing to follow Dr. Kellogg in his emphasis upon biologic living and also in his belief that medical personnel rather than clergy should control medical institutions, but they refused to follow Kellogg's theology. Many of them eventually joined the faculty of the Adventist medical school begun at Loma Linda, California, in 1906.

At first Dr. Kellogg was bitterly antagonistic toward the new medical school, and he attempted to discourage Dr. George Thomason, a former secretary and one of his most brilliant students, from joining the Loma Linda faculty. "The future of the Loma Linda Medical School is absolutely hopeless," Kellogg wrote in 1916. "The medical profession will not tolerate such a thing as a medical college under sectarian control, . . . which has for its purpose the education of men to engage in sectarian propaganda." As the years progressed, Kellogg's attitude gradually mellowed. When many of his old associates became top administrators in the new institution, he expressed confidence that they would inspire their students with ideals that would "enable them to assist in the work of informing men and women about the evils and perversions of our modern world." Kellogg even condescended to visit Loma Linda, and he congratulated its administration upon receiving an A rating from the American Medical Association. He went so far as to suggest that he would like to have several Loma Linda graduates as interns at the Battle Creek Sanitarium. The Adventist leadership's continued fear of John Harvey's magnetic personal appeal and heretical theology prevented the completion of any such arrangement.

At the time that Dr. Kellogg's official Adventist connections ended, a third of his life still lay ahead of him. With his typical driving personality he attempted to engage in various activities to fill the void left by his church-related endeavors. Although he continued his busy schedule, the days of real creativity were past. The conflicts with church leaders were over—but those with his brother Will had just begun.

Chapter XVII

FOOD MANUFACTURING
AND FAMILY QUARRELS

EVEN BEFORE THE FORMAL severing of his Adventist ties, Dr. Kellogg had begun a perhaps unconscious search to find new outlets for his abundant energy and new means to encourage biologic living. In the manufacture and promotion of his food creations he managed, at least in part, to fill both drives.

Shortly after the production of Granola for patients at the Battle Creek Sanitarium began in 1877, Dr. Kellogg organized the Sanitarium Food Company as a subsidiary of the Battle Creek Sanitarium. Operated as an adjunct to the sanitarium bakery, for more than a decade it marketed a variety of oatmeal, graham, and fruit crackers and whole-grain cooked cereals—all originally devised to provide variety in the menu of sanitarium patients. Sanitarium Food Company products had three things in common: all were made from whole grains, carefully prepared to avoid the loss of natural elements; they were free from certain common baking materials of which Kellogg disapproved, such as soda, saleratus, and baking powder; and they all underwent prolonged high-temperature baking designed to dextrinize their starch content.

By 1889 the Sanitarium foods had become popular enough to warrant the establishment of a separate factory; Granola alone sold at the rate of two tons a week. The manufacture of Caramel Cereal Coffee and the sanitarium bread and cracker products required several additional factories. Twenty years after launching Granola, the Sanitarium Food Company offered 42 varied products, including special diabetic and infant foods, for sale to the general public.

In the early 1890s W. S. Sadler, then only an 18-year-old sanitarium employee, convinced Dr. Kellogg that a program of special demonstrations in retail stores could substantially increase the sales of Sanitarium

Foods. The doctor approved a plan for Sadler to conduct a sample campaign in Michigan City, Indiana. The results proved so gratifying that John Harvey decided that the time had come to expand the food manufacturing business. The other sanitarium directors were more skeptical. When they refused to vote the funds needed to develop new products, Dr. Kellogg decided to move ahead on his own initiative and at his own expense. Relying heavily on his younger brother, Will Keith, who had served as his personal accountant and business manager since 1880, he launched the Sanitas Food Company. The Sanitarium Food Company continued to produce Granola and the old line of biscuits, breads, and cereals, but John Harvey's new flaked cereals and vegetable meats became the property of the Sanitas Company.

Relations between the two food companies remained friendly, since the doctor considered the Sanitas Company to be "a part of the sanitarium." After all, a major portion of its earnings supported his various philanthropic endeavors.

During the last years of the nineteenth century, however, John Harvey was too busy with the Medical Missionary and Benevolent Association to give much supervision to the food business. His major contribution lay in devising new food formulas and in making suggestions for new experiments. He had just enough contact with the developing prepared cereal industry to become convinced that it had great financial possibilities. The flaking process could turn a 60-cent bushel of wheat into breakfast food that would retail for nearly $12. Small wonder that he wrote Ellen White that the new industry could conceivably "support the entire denominational work."

The multiplicity of the doctor's interests led him to delegate more and more responsibility for the Sanitas Company to Will Kellogg. He considered his brother to be "one of the most faithful, careful, painstaking persons" he had ever met, a man who carried a heavy load without complaining. Yet in spite of his high regard for Will's abilities, the doctor could not bring himself to accept his brother's suggestions for sponsoring a more extensive promotional campaign in order to increase Sanitas sales. John Harvey was also adamant in refusing to let his name be associated with the new foods in any advertising. Since the regular medical profession looked with suspicion on so many of his ideas, he wanted to avoid giving "any occasion for thinking

I was actuated by commercial or financial motives." Despite such attitudes, Sanitas business expanded, "almost in spite of itself."

Kellogg was not alone in sensing the potential financial rewards of the flaked cereal industry. The early years of the twentieth century saw Battle Creek engulfed in a "wheat-flake boom comparable to a Texas oil strike." In a matter of months the Sanitas Company found itself faced with more than two-dozen competitors in Battle Creek alone. Former Sanitas employees organized some of the new companies. Promoters who lured away Kellogg bakers and production staff with offers of higher salaries formed the others.

At first Dr. Kellogg seemed just a bit proud of all his imitators, and he hopefully proclaimed that the competition would lead to more business for the originators of flaked cereals. Within a year, however, the doctor realized that the intense rivalry hindered rather than helped Sanitas business. John Harvey's company received a hard blow in 1903 when courts declared the doctor's patent on flaked cereal foods invalid. Faced at the time with the financial strain of rebuilding the sanitarium, Kellogg began to believe that he might as well sell some of his food creations to others for a lump sum, because if he did not, "they will pirate them anyhow."

Since he had agreed that Will Kellogg should receive one fourth of the Sanitas profits as compensation for managing the company, it was quite natural for the younger man to push the development of a product that he believed would have wide appeal and which would also return substantial profits. He found such a product in cornflakes, although it took several years to develop a flaking process to produce flakes of a size that could be sold profitably. In spite of his brother's disapproval, Will Kellogg decided to try adding sugar to the malt and corn combination from which he made the flakes. The sugar greatly enhanced the cereal's taste appeal, and, as a result, the cornflakes business was booming by late 1905.

Will Kellogg was convinced that cornflakes could not really become profitable until the company freed itself from the parsimonious restraints John Harvey imposed on advertising and from his propensity to meddle in affairs in which he had only incomplete information. After convincing C. D. Bolin, a St. Louis insurance executive, that cornflakes might turn into an extremely profitable business, Will set out to persuade his brother to transfer the exclusive rights to produce them to an independent company. The time was auspicious for Will's proposal, because his brother just then had to meet a personal debt of $35,000 and had also cosigned $180,000 worth of sanitarium notes, which would soon fall due. Even so, John Harvey hesitated, and it took Will Kellogg nearly six months to persuade him to relinquish Sanitas' rights to cornflakes. Finally a separate Battle Creek Toasted Corn Flake Company, financed with Bolin's aid, incorporated early in 1906, with Will Kellogg as the company's president and chief executive. Even though litigation by others cast doubts as to the doctor's claim to the product, Will insisted that his brother receive generous compensation in the form of Toasted Corn Flake Company stock, but John Harvey had to agree not to take an active part in the new company's management.

Six months later John Harvey decided to change Sanitas' corporate name to the Kellogg Food Company. The doctor later claimed that he had never been enthusiastic about the Sanitas name but had used it because of its similarity to Sanitarium. Some years after organizing the Sanitas Company, the Kelloggs had discovered that a German firm with the same name sold disinfectants in the world market. Since the possibility of the public linking of foods and disinfectants was not likely to enhance the salability of the former, Will Kellogg and his assistants urged the doctor as early as the fall of 1907 to choose a new company name. But at that particular time John Harvey could not bring himself to give the family name to the food corporation.

The doctor later insisted he based his decision to use the name "Kellogg Food Company" upon information given to him by John L. Kellogg, Will's son, who was then serving his uncle as a Sanitas plant manager. The nephew reported that a patent-medicine promoter named "Professor" Frank J. Kellogg, who was then selling an "obesity cure" made in Battle Creek, was contemplating the establishment of a food company. John Harvey had suffered considerable inconvenience and embarrassment because many persons assumed that he was the one marketing the obesity cure. The doctor now envisioned similar confusion resulting from the sale of inferior food products bearing a Kellogg label. He considered such a situation, he later remembered, as "a little more than I could possibly bear," and he quickly decided that he must preempt the name Kellogg for his own company.

The new Kellogg Food Company began operating in July 1908 with

Dr. Kellogg owning all but two of its 15,000 thousand shares of stock. Not only did the new company absorb the old Sanitas Company, but it also leased the entire plant, machinery, goodwill, and business of the Battle Creek Sanitarium Food Company, thus bringing the manufacture and distribution of all Dr. Kellogg's food products into one organization. By then John Harvey had decided that it would be a good thing to put out all company products under the trade name "Kellogg's."

His attaching the family name to his food company and his plan to associate it with as many of his food products as possible filled his brother Will with anger and indignation. Will felt certain that "the sole purpose in the doctor's making this change is that he may be benefited somewhat by the several hundred thousand dollars the Toasted Corn Flake Company had expended in advertising to make the name Kellogg's of some value."

The younger brother referred to the fact that during the doctor's absence in Europe in 1907 the directors of the Toasted Corn Flake Company had decided to change their product's name from Sanitas to Kellogg's Toasted cornflakes, and they had advertised their product under the Kellogg name ever since. In order to meet any objections that the promotion compromised the doctor's professional reputation, Will Kellogg had arranged to have his own signature printed across the labels of all cornflakes boxes. In doing so he was simply following a practice he had employed at the Sanitas Company, apparently with the doctor's permission, as early as 1903. Both brothers had defended the use of Will's signature as simply a device to protect their trade rights to cereal and nut foods.

Even before John Harvey renamed his food company, relations with his younger brother had become strained. Less than a month after the doctor assumed active management of the Sanitas Company, Will protested what he believed to be his brother's role in initiating false rumors that the Corn Flake Company had defrauded Sanitas. "For twenty-two and one-half years, I had absolutely lost all my individuality in you," the younger brother wrote. "I tried to see things with your eyes and do things as you would do them. You know in your heart whether or not I am a rascal. You also know whether or not I would defraud anyone, under any circumstances. The fact that we worked together for so many years would seem to be a reply to the above inquiry." Several months later Will complained that the new statement printed on all Sanitas Wheat Flakes cartons indicating that "Sanitas Toasted Wheat Flakes is the only flaked product which has a legitimate pedigree" was unfair. His Corn Flakes had a "legitimate pedigree" too, he maintained.

When Will Kellogg learned of John Harvey's intent to use the family name for the doctor's food company and its products, he decided that if the Toasted Corn Flake Company gave his brother competition by bringing out a wheat flake, "the doctor will consider that he has been forced off and . . . will not continue to interfere." The Corn Flakes executive may well have been trying either to bluff or to buy out his brother when he asked John Harvey for the right to manufacture wheat and other toasted cereal flakes on a royalty basis. Dr. Kellogg turned down the request because, he said, the remuneration offered was "quite inadequate."

An ad for one of the Sanitas products

To Will it seemed that since John Harvey had not put his foods out under the Kellogg name during the 15 years that he had had an opportunity to do so, he should now leave the use of that name to those who had taken the initiative in popularizing it. And the younger brother felt that he had some rights to the family name, too. "I claim to have worked with you, nights and mornings, and overtime, without compensation, in the matter of developing the first Granose Flakes," he wrote. He also pointed out that the more than 50 million packages of Corn Flakes bearing his signature should have alerted the public to the fact that more than one Kellogg lived in Battle Creek.

Once he had renamed his company, John Harvey moved quickly. Within a few days his company had marketed "Kellogg's Toasted Wheat Flakes" in both New York and Chicago. However, he intimated that he might be willing to drop the word "Kellogg's" from the lead position on his cereal flakes since he did not wish to engage in conflict with his brother. Shortly afterward, Dr. Kellogg later testified, Will Kellogg called upon him late one evening and requested that the doctor should leave "Kellogg's" off of his products. After "having been importuned for many hours in a most strenuous manner," John Harvey agreed to the request "purely as a matter of brotherly regard." In return, Will Kellogg promised to pay John Harvey $50,000 for discontinuing use of the family name. A few days later, when someone presented a legal contract for his signature, John Harvey claimed that the agreement "contained conditions and obligations not previously spoken of" to such an extent that it was impossible for him "or anyone else" to accept them. He refused to sign the document, and all negotiations concerning the matter ended.

Some time later Dr. Kellogg decided, "as an evidence of goodwill," to drop the name "Kellogg's" from the packages of Toasted Rice Flakes that he was manufacturing and selling through a separate corporation organized for that purpose. He telephoned his decision to his brother only to learn the next day that Will Kellogg had lured the Kellogg's Toasted Rice Flake and Biscuit Company's sales manager into his employment with the offer of a higher salary. The new sales manager whom Dr. Kellogg hired refused to try to sell Toasted Rice Flakes without the Kellogg name attached, and, in all probability, the doctor was not too unhappy at having an excuse to renege on his recent promise to Will.

Throughout the next few months "voluminous letters and memoranda were fired back and forth between the brothers." Among other things, Will Kellogg claimed that the doctor's salesmen misrepresented themselves as agents of the Toasted Corn Flake Company. Finally, on August 11, 1910, the younger Kellogg filed suit in Calhoun County Circuit Court to have his brother enjoined "from using the name 'Kellogg' either in a corporate name or as a descriptive name of a food." The lengthy bill of particulars that Will Kellogg's lawyers filed to support their request for an injunction claimed that John Harvey was deliberately trying to reap the benefits of $2 million worth of Toasted Corn Flake Company advertising; that his sales representatives displayed cornflakes while demonstrating the doctor's rice flakes in order to give the impression that the same manufacturer produced the two cereals; that dealers had been falsely informed that if rice flakes did not sell, they could be replaced with cornflakes; and that the doctor's companies were deliberately copying the distinctive packaging of the Corn Flake Company. In addition to the permanent injunction requested, Will Kellogg asked for a judgment of $100,000 in damages.

During the litigation that followed Dr. Kellogg stated that the value of the Kellogg name in the advertising of food products was the result of his activities. If harm had come to anyone, he insisted, his brother had actually done it to him. The doctor's attorneys protested that the requested injunction would ruin the Kellogg Food Company's business and would cause their client to lose his entire investment in it. An out-of-court settlement prevented the dispute between the two brothers from reaching final adjudication. As part of the compromise, John Harvey and his companies agreed not to use the word "Kellogg" as a portion of the name of any flaked cereal food they manufactured. He could, however, employ the family name in his two companies, but he could not conspicuously display it on the boxes or cartons his foods came packaged in.

The 1911 peace treaty between the Kellogg brothers turned out to be only a brief armistice. After several preliminary skirmishes in New York and Canada, the last major legal encounter between the brothers got under way on August 13, 1916, and lasted until December 21, 1920. It began when Dr. Kellogg requested a restraining order to prevent Will Kellogg and his companies from shipping cornflakes outside the United States, attaching the name "Kellogg's" to the Toasted Bran Flakes that they were then producing, bringing harassing suits in other states, using the secret and confidential processes of making foods discovered by Dr. Kellogg, and manufacturing candy and surgical apparatus under the name "Kellogg's." The doctor also asked for an accounting of the profits of his brother's corporations and for appropriate financial remuneration for damages suffered.

It appears that a "Battle of Bran" between the two companies triggered Dr. Kellogg's decision to initiate legal action against his brother. John Harvey had long advocated the natural laxative qualities of bran. Early in 1908, at his suggestion, the old Sanitas Company had begun marketing a sterilized bran that could be mixed with other cereal foods. At first its sales were small, but they gradually increased until in 1914 alone more than 100,000 boxes sold, an amount more than 10 times the sales in 1909. Early in 1915 Dr. Kellogg decided to change the name of his bran product from "Battle Creek Diet System Sterilized Bran" to "Kellogg's Sterilized Bran." He claimed the name change did not violate his 1911 agreement since that document applied only to flaked foods. Furthermore, he declared that his action could not harm Will's interests because his brother's company did not market any bran product.

Shortly after adding the name "Kellogg's" to its sterilized bran, John Harvey's company began an extensive advertising campaign in periodicals such as *Good Housekeeping* and the *Ladies' Home Journal* and in some of the major New York City newspapers. Company demonstrators also called special attention to Kellogg's Sterilized Bran in displays at leading retail stores, including Chicago's Marshall Field's and the Fair Store. Kellogg's Bran sales subsequently showed a rapid increase. The public bought more than 250,000 packages in 1915, and more than 600,000 in 1916.

In the autumn of 1915 Will Kellogg's company began manufacturing Kellogg's Toasted Bran Flakes. Then early the next year it brought out Kellogg's Flaked Bran, and six months later, Kellogg's Bran in granular form. Will's products caused considerable confusion in the grocery trade and brought a protest from the doctor's company. He and his associates considered Will's invasion of the "bran" market as part of a vindictive plot to "get" the older brother.

Not until the spring of 1917 did Dr. Kellogg's suit actually come to trial. The arguments in the case were long, involved, and confusing. At one point Judge Walter North, who was hearing the case, complained that counsel for both sides had failed to define the real issues and that he had never previously been "confronted by such a situation." He professed that he was not sure whether the doctor was protesting against illegal appropriation of trade secrets or "wrongful use of the name 'Kellogg.'" Actually the doctor was concerned about both things and much more besides, but his complaints would prove futile. The case ended on May 15, 1917, after three weeks of testimony. Judge North did not make a ruling until 18 months later, and it went against the doctor on every major point.

John Harvey appealed the unfavorable decision to the Michigan State Supreme Court, which, on December 21, 1920, unanimously upheld judge North. The justices found that Will's Toasted Corn Flake Company had first made the trade name "Kellogg's" valuable. They reasoned that if Dr. Kellogg had wanted to protest the company's use of the name

"Kellogg's," he should have acted in 1907 when it first became a part of the product's name, for the doctor was at that time an officer and a large stockholder in the Corn Flake Company. In effect, the Michigan Supreme Court ruling gave Will Kellogg's company the exclusive right to the trade name "Kellogg's." It also awarded the Toasted Corn Flake Company the right to collect all profits that the doctor had received from the infringement of the Kellogg trade name and assessed John Harvey the costs of the litigation. At the doctor's request, Will Kellogg agreed to waive any right to damages provided his older brother paid all of the legal costs, amounting to nearly $225,000, incurred by both sides during the litigation. The long court battles brought about an estrangement between the Kellogg brothers that never completely healed.

In the spring of 1921, to avoid further difficulties with Will Kellogg's manufacturing interests, Dr. Kellogg changed his concern's name to the Battle Creek Food Company. Although he maintained that "the chief purpose and effort of the Battle Creek Food Company has been to meet . . . dietetic needs and to solve dietetic problems rather than to produce commercial products," the company enjoyed a good return on his relatively modest investment. It declared a 30 percent dividend on outstanding stock each year during 1926, 1927, and 1929. In 1928 the dividend was only 20 percent, but in 1931 it amounted to a substantial 40 percent.

The Battle Creek Food Company might have had much greater financial success if Dr. Kellogg had chosen a better general manager. During the 1920s Kellogg placed B. F. Kirkland, a former Battle Creek Sanitarium pharmacist who had married one of the girls raised in Dr. Kellogg's home, in charge of the company and turned over to him for safekeeping more than $500,000 of food company profits. Kirkland invested the money unwisely during the great bull market and lost the entire sum. For several years he managed to hide the loss from Kellogg, but during the early 1930s, when Chicago bankers threatened legal action against the Battle Creek Food Company for failure to pay its debts, the truth leaked out. Dr. Kellogg forgave Kirkland, but the latter did not mend his ways. He continued to siphon off legitimate food company profits through a dummy food brokerage firm that he and two other company officials had established in Chicago in 1928. When Dr. Kellogg, in 1936, finally found out what his employees were doing, he brought suit to recover nearly

$130,000, the profit the three men had made on their illegal operation. The doctor received a favorable judgment for the amount of loss claimed, but he never recovered more than a small portion of the money.

During the 1930s the Battle Creek Food Company experienced a decline in business and profits as a result of the general economic depression. Even so, the company was prosperous enough in 1939 to appear to an old hand in the food business to be a good investment. Ross Adams, former treasurer of brother Will's Kellogg Company, requested an option to buy the Battle Creek Food Company for $1,500,000 in cash. Dr. Kellogg rejected the offer because he considered the business "worth very much more," and he indicated that he "had already turned down much larger offers." The doctor confessed to Mr. Adams that he could hardly sell the food company, as it was in reality his experimental laboratory, a place where he tried out the stream of ideas that continually went through his mind.

Even after 1930, when his interest in the new Miami-Battle Creek Sanitarium diverted some of his attention from food manufacturing, Kellogg demanded weekly reports on the company's operation during the periods when he was not in Battle Creek. For many years he continued to write a large portion of the food company's advertising material himself, and he remained active in the development of foods and the formulation of company policies as late as 1939. Although the food manufacturing business consumed some of the energy that Dr. Kellogg had formerly channeled into church activities, it appears doubtful that it provided the deep personal satisfaction for which he had hoped.

CHAPTER XVIII

NEW OUTLETS FOR PROMOTING AN OLD PROGRAM

IN HIS LIFELONG HEALTH crusade John Harvey Kellogg was in many ways an anomaly. Although always something of a loner in his activities, he also knew how to multiply organizations and utilize existing institutions for his own purposes. In the fall of 1906 he organized the American Medical Missionary Board, endowed it with 5,000 shares of Toasted Corn Flake Company stock, and commissioned it to carry out in a completely nonsectarian way the activities formerly sponsored by the Seventh-day Adventist Medical Missionary and Benevolent Association. The board's early activities centered around providing aid in the form of loans and gifts to the Battle Creek Sanitarium and the American Medical Missionary College.

With the demise of the latter institution, the AMMB shifted its support to *Good Health,* always plagued by chronic deficits. Eventually the board contributed more than $100,000 to keep the Kellogg journal alive.

For several years the AMMB sponsored annual Medical Missionary Conferences at the Battle Creek Sanitarium in an effort to promote interest in foreign medical missions among America's evangelical denominations. It also contributed to the activities of Sir Wilfred Grenfell in Labrador, Dr. Clarence Ussher in Turkey, and groups organized to work for prohibition at the state and local levels. On July 22, 1914, the American Medical Missionary Board trustees sought to gain wider support for their activities, particularly among those Americans engaged in publicizing eugenics, by transforming the Board into the Race Betterment Foundation.

During the first two decades of the twentieth century the interest in eugenics had become almost a scientific fad for large numbers of Americans. The modern eugenics movement, founded by Charles Darwin's cousin, Sir Francis Galton, dedicated itself to improving human

Race Betterment Foundation display at the 1915 San Francisco Panama-Pacific Exposition

characteristics through the study of hereditary laws and attempting to apply the knowledge thus gained to more selective human propagation. Early twentieth-century America had a strong interest in a wide variety of social programs. Eugenics appealed to many as a "scientific" reform that deserved their support.

In the early years American eugenicists particularly concerned themselves with demonstrating that groups likely to become social charges, such as paupers, the insane, the feebleminded, and epileptics, were chiefly the product of their heredity. Dr. Kellogg had seized upon the interest in the subject to point out that public hygiene alone would lead to the deterioration of the human race by keeping alive larger numbers of the weak and feeble. Instead, he advocated deeper commitment to the principles of biologic living as a way to offset such an "unfavorable tendency."

One major point of disagreement between Galton and Kellogg centered around the possibility of inheriting acquired characteristics. Galton denied the possibility, but Kellogg initially felt certain that human beings could pass along genetically "good" acquired traits to subsequent generations. Even long after almost every American eugenicist with the exception of Luther Burbank had become convinced that Galton was correct, John Harvey continued to hope that evidence would demonstrate that the adoption of correct health habits would make such habits the natural way of life for future generations.

As better public statistics became available, American eugenicists decided that the "growing incidence of feeblemindedness, insanity, crime, and pauperism" demonstrated racial deterioration in America. Naturally Dr. Kellogg took advantage of their concern and pointed to what he considered to be the chief causes: the increased use of alcohol, tobacco, tea, coffee, improper methods of dress, and unhealthful foods. The Darwinian connotations of the eugenics movement, however, limited the interest Kellogg dared show in it during his years as an Adventist leader. Once freed from religious restraints, his addresses and writings picked up a heavier coloring of the conventional statistical examples of racial degeneracy.

The very name "Race Betterment Foundation" utilized terminology congenial to the progressive middle-class intellectuals who comprised the American eugenics movement. Through his foundation, Kellogg arranged to get his ideas before many important molders of public opinion whom it would otherwise have been nearly impossible for him to reach. The most successful of Foundation activities in this respect were the three nationally publicized conferences it held in 1914, 1915, and 1928.

Newell Dwight Hillis, pastor of Brooklyn's Plymouth Congregational Church (made famous by its former pastors Henry Ward Beecher and Lyman Abbott), suggested to Kellogg the idea of holding a Race Betterment Conference. Hillis shared Kellogg's interest in the challenges to social Christianity posed by the growing problems of large urban areas. After talking with him, the doctor enlisted the assistance of several old friends—Yale economist Irving Fisher, journalist Jacob Riis, and agronomist Sir Horace Plunkett—in planning the first conference.

More than 400 official delegates journeyed to Battle Creek to take part in the first Race Betterment Conference, held January 8-12, 1914. During the general sessions such dominant personalities in the eugenics movement as Charles B. Davenport, J. McKeen Cattell, editor of Popular Science Monthly, and others presented more than 50 papers. Other leading figures, such as judge Ben Lindsey and Jacob Riis, who stressed the need to improve environmental factors, also attended. In the matter of a few days' time John Harvey had established a link between the Battle Creek Sanitarium and its program of biologic living and those interested in improving America through eugenics.

Sufficient public attention resulted from the initial Race Betterment Conference to cause Dr. Kellogg and his associates to sponsor another such gathering the following year. They decided to hold it in connection with the great Panama-Pacific Exposition scheduled for San Francisco. Although the second conference had fewer delegates and formal papers, several of the participants were men of national prominence, including David Start Jordan, chancellor of Stanford University, botanist Luther

Burbank, and Paul Popenoe, editor of the *Journal of Heredity*.

Kellogg caused quite a sensation at the Second Race Betterment Conference by suggesting the establishment of a eugenics registry. He proposed a campaign to get persons to receive physical examinations that would determine their physical fitness and their hereditary traits and tendencies. Afterward the examiners would enroll the names of those who met certain standards in a type of "human pedigree" book. Although Kellogg denied that he was advocating that marriages be arranged solely on the basis of some biological formula, he expressed the hope that such a registry would encourage intelligent persons to consider more fully the importance of hereditary traits in planning their marriages.

It appears that Dr. Kellogg wanted to make the Race Betterment Conferences annual events, but American involvement in World War I and the doctor's own health problems prevented another one until January 1928. Although Kellogg's Foundation sponsored the third conference and held it at the Battle Creek Sanitarium, the doctor persuaded University of Michigan president C. C. Little to plan and preside over the program. Dr. Little clearly showed his academic orientation in the presentation of papers by scholars from Harvard, Wisconsin, the University of Chicago, Tulane, and Johns Hopkins.

The third Race Betterment Conference received wide publicity: more than 1,600 news stories related to it appeared in 574 different newspapers scattered throughout 47 states. It provided an excellent forum for the doctor, and he made the best possible use by extolling biologic living in a ringing address entitled "Habits in Relation to Health and Longevity." The success of the third conference apparently caused him to plan once more to make them annual affairs. Again the times were against him. The onset of the Great Depression and the resulting financial difficulties of the Battle Creek Sanitarium delayed arrangements for a fourth conference, which had advanced to the definite planning stage when World War II intervened. Before the war ended, Dr. Kellogg's death had deprived the Race Betterment Foundation of its major source of energy and initiative. The Foundation limited its subsequent activities to the sponsorship of a variety of public lectures on biologic living, publication of *Good Health* until 1955, and encouragement of Battle Creek Sanitarium and Miami-Battle Creek Sanitarium.

The gradual demise of the Race Betterment Foundation presents a striking contrast to the vigorous growth and multiple activities of the W. K. Kellogg Foundation established by John's brother Will. The difference in the two organizations probably derives from the two men's differing approach to philanthropy. As *Time* magazine noted years ago, John Harvey believed in spending the money he earned from his food creations as it came in, while W. K. "insisted on letting the business amass a fortune before giving the money away." His viewpoint was that commerce should be the "benefactor of society." The doctor believed that "business should be the servant of society."

Just as John Harvey believed in business serving society, so he considered such service to be the duty of the individual, a point he demonstrated clearly in his personal role in the Chicago Medical Mission. For much of his life he channeled that involvement through church agencies and activities, but for 18 years he also worked to improve the health conditions in his home state as a member of the Michigan State Board of Health. His first dozen years of service with the organization began when he was a young doctor, not four years out of medical school. Then after an interim of two decades during his most active Adventist phase and his period of conflict with church leaders, he once more found in the State Board of Health an avenue for the promotion of biologic living.

In all likelihood Dr. Henry Baker, the board's first secretary and the moving force in its creation by the state legislature, instigated Kellogg's appointment to the agency. Like Kellogg, Baker had graduated from Bellevue Hospital Medical College. As one of his first acts as board secretary, he arranged for the systematic collection of a variety of climatological data at various points throughout Michigan in order to test his theory that a direct relationship existed between climate and respiratory diseases. John Harvey had volunteered to record the necessary data for Battle Creek shortly after he finished medical school. Over the years his contacts with Baker increased, and the two men developed a real admiration for each other.

In spite of a multitude of other duties, Dr. Kellogg devoted himself to the work of the State Board of Health with all of his customary energy. At Dr. Baker's request, he prepared a paper on the problem of arousing public interest in sanitary matters for presentation at the second meeting of the board that he attended. Soon, at its request, John Harvey began a study of the relationship of health to an individual's occupation, recreation, and personal habits. Also he became active in persuading the state board to study the causes of diphtheria and typhoid fever, two major communicable diseases about which medicine then knew little. Kellogg's interest in biologic living received a golden opportunity for expression when the board commissioned him to prepare papers on exercise, the effects of alcohol and tobacco, and the necessity for preserving an uncontaminated supply of drinking water.

The routine responsibilities of the State Board of Health included inspecting the sanitary conditions in public buildings throughout the state. In discharging its duties, the board established a committee, which included Kellogg, to draw up plans for model schools. In the course of his assignment John Harvey became particularly concerned with the problem of proper ventilation in public buildings. Becoming the board's expert on the subject, he prepared an influential report on basic principles and methods for best supplying fresh air to crowded rooms. His report strayed into the area of correct methods of breathing and even took a passing swipe at the harmful effects of the feminine corset in inhibiting proper respiration.

It is highly probable that the activity growing out of his state board membership that Dr. Kellogg valued the most was the opportunity to participate in a number of sanitary conventions the board sponsored throughout the state. The idea for them originated with board president Dr. Robert Clarke Kedzie in the spring of 1878. Kedzie wanted to bring together local health officials and interested citizens in convocations in which they could discuss community health problems. Kellogg participated in the initial convention held in Detroit and spoke at more than a third of the others held during his membership on the organization.

Although he generally appeared at a sanitary convention to give expert advice on his specialties of proper ventilation and the avoidance of water contamination, he usually included at least passing reference to other aspects of biologic living in his speeches. "Pure air, pure water, and pure food are the three great desiderata of human existence in its highest estate," the doctor told the Flint Sanitary Convention. In the course of the same lecture he also discussed the dangers in eating diseased meats and found opportunity to condemn overeating and the use of condiments, tea, coffee, alcohol, and tobacco.

Kellogg repeatedly stressed in his sanitary convention lectures the need for cleanliness of person and premises. The germ theory of disease was still in its infancy, and the public was not only generally unaware that filth provided a perfect breeding area for harmful bacteria, but also found it difficult to comprehend the fact that such minute organisms could actually be dangerous. John Harvey frequently recalled that at one sanitary convention, during which he gave the audience an opportunity to examine a drop of contaminated water through a microscope, a woman asked him how large the bacteria she saw actually were. The doctor answered that 20,000 of them placed end to end would make a line an inch long. Giving him a disgusted look, the woman departed, saying, "That's nothing to get excited about! I ain't afraid of them little fellers."

During the germ theory's early days Kellogg himself was not altogether clear as to the way bacteria spread from place to place. "Don't kill the fly," he said on one occasion. "Let him live. He is one of our best friends. He is a sanitary sheriff with a commission from the Creator to arrest and devour these agents of disease and death when they get into our dwellings." Within three years, however, the doctor changed his mind and recognized that the common housefly was a major carrier of disease. He saw it as an evidence of filth that needed to be eliminated.

In 1910, after a 20-year absence from the State Board of Health, John Kellogg began to yearn for the opportunities which membership on the body would provide for stirring up public interest in better health. The time seemed propitious, for that autumn Michigan elected an acquaintance of many years, Chase Osborn, as governor. Shortly after the election, Kellogg began to lobby for reappointment to the board, which he believed was becoming moribund. Some of Osborn's political advisers believed that the new governor's first appointments to the State Board of Health should go to doctors from the Detroit area. One of them, Dr. Beverly Harrison, secretary of the State Board of Registration in Medicine, recognized, however, that Dr. Kellogg was "probably the best-qualified medical man in the state for appointment on the State Board of Health. He not only has a national reputation as an expert in preventive medicine, but an international." Although Harrison considered Kellogg an extremist in some areas, he felt certain that John Harvey would "put some life into the board." Governor Osborn apparently agreed with his estimate and named

Kellogg to the first vacancy, which developed in January 1911.

Dr. Kellogg began his new six-year term with his customary enthusiasm. Shortly after his appointment he conferred with the state Attorney General on legislation needed to increase the board's authority and efficiency. The press throughout Michigan considered Kellogg to be "in strong" with Osborn, and the doctor himself believed that he had a "special commission" from the governor to invigorate the State Board of Health.

Less than six months later Dr. Kellogg summarized the progress he believed had been made in that time: the board had prepared a traveling health exhibit to tour the state in a railroad car attached to an exhibition train sent out by the state agricultural service; had approved plans to promote healthful living in connection with the winter farmers' institutes sponsored by the Michigan State Agricultural College; had authorized the issuance of weekly press bulletins on matters vital to public health; had established a committee on health education, with Kellogg as chairman, and was planning to hold sanitary conventions in various cities; and had authorized an inspector to examine water, milk, and food supplies, public schools, and "other conditions affecting health" throughout the state, with wide publicity to be given to his findings. Obviously John Harvey believed that one of the most effective things the state board could do was to make the people of the state more health-conscious. A few months later he and the state board persuaded Governor Osborn to proclaim an official Health Day. The doctor saw it as a wonderful opportunity to supply teachers and clergy with outlines for health talks. Small wonder that in later years, Dr. R. L. Dixon, the state board's secretary, characterized the atmosphere of those years as "evangelical."

Dr. Kellogg's close personal relationships with Osborn continued throughout the governor's term. When he assumed office, Osborn found the state in a difficult financial situation, and he decided to cut food costs in state institutions as one means of reducing expenditures. Kellogg supplied the governor with literature on nutrition that convinced Osborn that he could reduce the daily institutional food ration from 5,000 to 2,000 calories without ill effects. An increase in the proportion of less expensive carbohydrates in the diet provided in state hospitals, as compared to proteins and fatty foods, would, John Harvey suggested, not only reduce costs but would actually improve the patients' health as well. Several years later Osborn remembered that although the dietary innovations he had instituted at Kellogg's suggestion had temporarily won him the title of the "Starvation Governor," he had saved the state money, and the program had increased the rate at which state hospitals could discharge patients as cured.

In the summer of 1912 the Board of Health established a committee that included Dr. Kellogg to consider needed health legislation. Among other things, it recommended increased board control over contagious diseases, the right to supervise sources of public water supply, authority to regulate sewage disposal throughout the state, power to initiate proceedings for the removal of local health officers, and authorization to study and control all types of disease and to manufacture antitoxin and vaccine for the people of the state.

The arguments that the state board marshaled in favor of its proposals gained their reward when the legislature in 1913 passed more public health legislation than it had enacted during any previous session in the preceding quarter of a century. Although the board did not get all the laws that it desired, it did receive power to supervise and control urban waterworks and sewage disposal systems. It also secured laws requiring organizations supplying public drinking water to provide either individual drinking utensils or sanitary fountains, laws penalizing the sale of adulterated sausage and meat derived from sick or diseased animals, regulations providing for more sanitary conditions in milk processing plants, and legislation defining adulterated ice cream.

The State Board of Health found the 1915 legislative session less satisfactory. The only major legislation sponsored by the board that the governmental body enacted was a grant of $100,000 to finance a survey of the incidence of tuberculosis in the state. It was Kellogg who, in the fall of 1914, had stimulated interest among board members in the project because he believed that such a survey would have great educational value and would result in publicity that would increase public interest in health matters. Some representatives of the press blamed the defeat of other measures sponsored by the board on personal opposition within the legislature to several of the board members.

Part of the hostility may have been directed against Dr. Kellogg, who was becoming increasingly critical of the legislature's failure to appropriate what he considered to be sufficient funds for public health work. As early as the spring of 1912 John Harvey had complained to Governor Osborn that the state board needed an increase of $25,000 annually "to really do things which would exercise a controlling influence upon the lives and health of the citizens of Michigan." In 1915 the state board had asked for an annual appropriation of $25,000, but it had received only $15,000. Kellogg issued a public blast at the legislature in which he characterized Michigan as "the most niggardly civilized community in the world when it comes to safeguarding public health and life and educating the people concerning certain diseases." Pointing out that while Pennsylvania provided 30 cents per capita for public health work each year, the Michigan legislature was satisfied to dole out one cent per capita. The doctor contended that the Board of Health should have been receiving an appropriation of $100,000 annually. He indicated that the money actually appropriated would not even pay the postage on the educational material that the board should have distributed.

In what was perhaps an effort to shame the legislature, John Harvey announced that he would launch a subscription drive to provide funds for a public health educational campaign, and would make a personal contribution of $1,000 to the cause. But the contributions for which he appealed failed to materialize. Rebuffed, the doctor assumed a more passive role in the state board's activities during the remainder of his term. He did not seek reappointment in 1917.

CHAPTER XIX

THE LAST BATTLES

THE GREAT DEPRESSION, which brought so many changes to American life in the decade following 1929, also affected John Harvey Kellogg's long association with the Battle Creek Sanitarium. By mid-1930 interest charges of $500 a day on an outstanding debt $3 million necessitated both a substantial cut in the sanitarium staff and a drastic reduction in the wages paid those who remained. Faced with the mounting crises, Dr. Stewart and a majority of the sanitarium trustees were prepared to override Dr. Kellogg's opposition and return the institution to the Seventh-day Adventist Church. But the church's finances were in no shape to assume the sanitarium debts, and denominational leaders refused to give any serious consideration to such a plan.

The sanitarium managed to limp along until the close of 1932, but by that time its financial position was desperate. On January 1, 1933, the institution could not meet the regular payment on its bonded indebtedness. Then, a little more than a month later, the sanitarium directors, in Dr. Kellogg's absence, unanimously agreed to support the petition of a bondholder asking the Federal District Court to place the institution in receivership. Two days later, judge Arthur J. Tuttle agreed to the establishment of an equity receivership and named Dr. Charles Stewart as receiver.

The receiver operated

Battle Creek Sanitarium during the 1930s

LLU Archives & Special Collections

(217)

Battle Creek Sanitarium for five years. The banking interests that held a major portion of the sanitarium bonds immediately established a Bondholders' Protective Association. It constantly pressed for changes at the sanitarium they believed would improve the institution's financial condition and thus enable them to collect on their investment.

Dr. Kellogg feared their proposals might jeopardize the principles of biologic living he had so long championed. During the early part of 1936, in an effort to make sure that the facility would continue to uphold the old health reform practices, he attempted to persuade his former Adventist colleague and student, Dr. George Thomason, to leave his teaching position as head of the surgical department of the Adventists' College of Medical Evangelists and assume active direction of the Battle Creek Sanitarium. Although Kellogg promised to back his old friend in whatever changes he desired to make, Thomason decided after a trip to Battle Creek that the situation at the sanitarium was chaotic, and he therefore refused John Harvey's offer.

By early 1937 Kellogg, the sanitarium directors in Battle Creek, and the Bondholders' Protective Association had agreed that the receivership should end. The various interests could not agree, however, upon a plan of reorganization. The bondholders demanded majority representation on a reorganized board of directors, but both Kellogg and the Stewart group firmly opposed such a plan. The doctor was no more willing to have bankers dictate sanitarium policies than he had been to have it placed under the control of preachers 30 years earlier. He continued to maintain that if outside interests came into control of the sanitarium, they would probably force the abandonment of its distinctive health principles, and this, he held, would end the institution's reason for existence.

While Dr. Kellogg and the sanitarium directors worked to raise sufficient cash to make the bondholders an attractive offer, new complications arose when some of the institution's creditors attempted to force it into involuntary bankruptcy. Faced with the threat, the various factions finally agreed early in 1938 to terminate the receivership. Under a compromise plan of reorganization, the bondholders and underwriters received four positions on a newly elected 10-person board of directors. Dr. Kellogg was one of the six representatives of the existing sanitarium management elected to the new board. The new board also named him the institution's medical director. Neither the bondholders nor the Stewart group, however, apparently intended to allow him to regain a position of dominance. They entrusted the major responsibility for the institution's management to two newly designated officials, a superintendent and a chief of staff. Although under the new plan Kellogg was little more than a figurehead, he continued to hope that he could eventually reestablish his old leadership in Battle Creek.

The reorganized board showed little desire to let Dr. Kellogg's suggestions guide them. They flatly rejected his plan to sponsor a sanitarium exhibit at the New York World's Fair of 1939. More disturbing to the doctor was the increasing tendency at the sanitarium to disregard important aspects of biologic living. Some members of the sanitarium medical staff, as early as the late 1920s, had begun to use tobacco and to advocate the abandonment of a strict vegetarian diet. Additional departures from Kellogg's principles took place during the 1930s, and when the bondholders' representatives on the reconstituted board insisted upon bringing in new medical personnel, many of whom were unfamiliar and unsympathetic with the distinctive health program that had always been an integral part of the sanitarium, the move further antagonized the doctor.

He regarded the reorganization of the sanitarium management in 1938 as altogether unsatisfactory. There is every reason to believe that he would have attempted to reestablish his position of dominance in 1939 had not ill health intervened and caused him to spend most of the year in Florida. His absence from Battle Creek allowed the two major groups on the sanitarium board to reach an accommodation at his expense, and for the next several years the doctor continued to be only an ornament in the sanitarium's program.

By 1941 Dr. Kellogg had sufficiently recovered his health to make several attempts at "rescuing" the sanitarium from the control of those he believed were flagrantly violating the institution's basic principles. Early that year he again approached Dr. Thomason and stated that he would be willing to have a majority of the sanitarium board include Thomason and his Adventist associates. John Harvey even suggested that he might commit a portion of his Battle Creek Food Company's profits to support the Adventist medical school. Undoubtedly he assumed that such an arrangement would ensure the revival of the old health program in Battle Creek.

When his proposal came to nought, he resorted to a tactic that had served him well in earlier days—he told the annual meeting of the sanitarium's governing Association in March 1941 that unless they found administrators who would practice biologic living, he would have nothing more to do with the sanitarium and would retire to Florida.

Next he suggested that he personally lease the Battle Creek Sanitarium, but he failed to devise a proposal that satisfied the rest of the board members. During the summer of 1941 the relationship between Dr. Kellogg and the other sanitarium directors deteriorated rapidly. Those in active control of the sanitarium were disturbed because he reportedly advised some patients at the Battle Creek institution to transfer to Miami-Battle Creek. For his part, John Harvey was understandably piqued when the Battle Creek group refused to furnish him with office space in which to consult with patients in an institution of which he was the nominal head.

Since, in a certain sense, his hold on the Battle Creek Sanitarium had first begun to slip as a result of events growing out of American involvement in World War I, one could perhaps regard it as poetic justice that the nation's entry into a second great global conflict made it possible for him once more to assume leadership of a truncated but "purged" institution. In the early part of 1942 officials of B. C. Ziegler and Company, the firm that had underwritten the refunding of the defaulted sanitarium bond issues, suggested the sale of the main sanitarium building to the United States government for use as an army general hospital. After some negotiation, the government agreed in May 1942 to pay $2,250,000 for the main sanitarium building and certain subsidiary properties.

The proceeds from the sale enabled the sanitarium management to retire the entire institutional indebtedness then standing at $1,519,525, and still retain nearly $750,000 in cash, plus several farms and other buildings, including an 87-bed hospital. Shortly thereafter, the local county circuit court approved the dissolution of the Battle Creek Sanitarium Health Food Company and the transfer of its cash holdings of more than $275,000 to the Battle Creek Sanitarium and Benevolent Association. Thus by the summer of 1942 the Association had approximately a million dollars in cash on hand, and Dr. Kellogg enthusiastically began to plan to restore the sanitarium to its old "purity"—free from debt and from the meddling interference of creditors.

The agreement with the government required that the sanitarium evacuate the main building by July 31, 1942, which meant that if the sanitarium was to continue without interruption, it had to immediately find a place in which to house the patients then occupying beds in the institution. Dr. Kellogg proposed that it move them several blocks down the street to the old cobblestone Phelps Sanatorium, built as a competitive institution 40 years earlier. Neither Phelps nor physical culturist Bernarr MacFadden had been able to make it a success, and Dr. Kellogg's Race Betterment Foundation had long since acquired it to operate as an apartment house. John Harvey offered it to the sanitarium rent-free. In an atmosphere of good feeling, or perhaps in desperation lest anything jeopardize the sale to the government, the board members agreed to Kellogg's proposal, and they also elected him as superintendent. He was to assume the latter post, created in 1938 as the chief executive position in the sanitarium management, upon the withdrawal of the bondholders' representatives from the board of directors.

Back in command once more, Dr. Kellogg began to operate with his old-time vigor. As head of the sanitarium he concluded an agreement with the Race Betterment Foundation, of which he was the president, that committed the sanitarium to "sustain all expenses of upkeep, maintenance, improvements, repairs, taxes, special assessments, governmental charges, and insurance" during the period of its occupancy of the Foundation's property.

It soon became evident that it would take a good deal of money to transform the old Phelps building and the former Battle Creek College library, which adjoined it, into quarters suitable for sanitarium purposes. When some board members began to doubt the wisdom of spending so much money on property the institution did not own, Kellogg countered by offering to sell both buildings to the sanitarium for $500,000. After an independent appraisal by a committee of realtors had valued the buildings at only $283,000, Kellogg withdrew his offer, but meanwhile the process of remodeling had continued as rapidly as possible because of the July 31 deadline.

With the war on and priorities for many essential building materials difficult to obtain, the remodeling of the Phelps and college library buildings proved to be no easy task. Dr. Kellogg had understood that the contract of sale to the government would ensure that the sanitarium could obtain the necessary priorities for the materials to convert the two buildings into suitable quarters, but he found that official red tape and wartime confusion prevented the delivery of needed supplies. To expedite matters, he went to Washington, only to find himself shunted from office to office and eventually told to close up the sanitarium and send the remaining patients to local hospitals. Whoever told him to shut down the institution did not know John Harvey Kellogg, for he immediately took his case to some old sanitarium patients and friends high in Washington circles. After intervention on the part of United States Treasurer W. A. Julian and Secretary of the Navy Frank Knox, Kellogg returned to Battle Creek with orders for the necessary materials.

The withdrawal of the bondholders' representatives from the board of trustees necessitated a further reorganization of that body, and so the board created a committee consisting of Dr. Kellogg and two friendly trustees to draw up a reorganization plan. The sweeping reorganization it proposed became known as the "merger agreement," and it quickly became an issue that sharply divided him and a number of his old associates.

The proposed agreement called for the joining of the Battle Creek Sanitarium and Benevolent Association and the Race Betterment Foundation into a new corporation entitled the Battle Creek Sanitarium. Absolute control of the new corporation would rest in the hands of a self-perpetuating seven-person board of trustees, whose membership the agreement specified. The board would consist of Dr. Kellogg, one of his adopted sons (Dr. Richard Kellogg), and five Kellogg confidants. The effect of the merger would have been to place the future of the Battle Creek Sanitarium firmly in John Harvey's hands. At 90 years of age he, understandably, had no desire to do battle once again with recalcitrant board members.

Since he and his advisers apparently realized that, in order to counter any charge that the doctor was stealing the assets of the sanitarium, the merger agreement would need approval by a substantial number of the legal constituency of the Battle Creek Sanitarium and Benevolent Association, the agreement provided that at least two thirds of the Association's members must consent to it before the merger could become effective. The Association, which in the early years of the century had numbered nearly 700 members, had shrank by the time of its reorganization in 1938 to only 100 members, almost all of whom still were, or at one time had been, Seventh-day Adventists.

It was at this point that the provision that "no member shall be entitled to vote at any meeting except in person," which Dr. Kellogg had so carefully inserted into the original sanitarium articles of incorporation and which had served him so well during his struggle with the Adventist Church in the first decade of the century, proved to be his undoing. The Association's constituency had become widely scattered geographically, with the result that only 19 members appeared at a special meeting called for July 21, 1942, to consider the merger agreement. Since 19 did not even approach the required two thirds, the merger could not be accomplished. The constituency meeting twice recessed, first to August 18 and later to September 8, in an unsuccessful attempt to secure a large enough attendance to ratify the proposal.

After the July 21 meeting, Dr. R. H. Harris and Mr. George E. Judd, two longtime sanitarium board members who opposed the merger, circulated a letter to a number of the sanitarium Association members pointing out their objections to the centralization of power called for by the merger agreement. Among other things, they noted that the agreement gave the seven named trustees the only voting rights in the future operations of the Battle Creek Sanitarium. Harris and Judd argued that such action showed that "the contributions of money and of services which the members have made would be forgotten or not appreciated." The two dissident directors also objected because the new document specifically forbade the establishment of a pension fund for faithful sanitarium employees, something that had been "under consideration for many years." Thirty-five Association members who replied to the letter sent out by Harris and Judd indicated their disapproval of the merger plan. Since the Association's membership by then had dropped to 84, the negative vote of 35 persons would more than block the adoption of the agreement.

Dr. Kellogg was, naturally, much concerned about the two men's activities. He became convinced that they, with some other members of the Association, were simply trying to get their hands on the money from the sale of the main building and that their efforts were part of a widespread plot to wreck the Battle Creek Sanitarium and end its existence.

At this juncture John Harvey's brother Will tried to persuade the doctor that because of his advanced age he should not attempt to manage the sanitarium. Although Will had not been a member of the Adventist

Church for 35 years, he suggested that if the doctor really wanted to ensure the continued practice of the principles of biologic living at the sanitarium, he should again approach Adventist physicians such as Drs. George Thomason and P. T. Magan and try to secure their help in the institution's future development and management. Will Kellogg indicated that he had strong reasons to believe that they would rally to the doctor's aid if he approached them properly. Skeptically, John Harvey replied that he was "always glad to welcome help from any source that seems likely to be real help, but unfortunately most of the offers come from people who are, in fact, seeking help for themselves."

Kellogg may have rejected any thought of appealing to Thomason or Magan because Thomason had also expressed opposition to the merger agreement, or he may have discovered that Harris and Judd had appealed to the top leadership of the General Conference of Seventh-day Adventists for aid in blocking the merger. The two dissident directors were convinced that to effect his merger plans Dr. Kellogg would attempt to enlarge the membership of the sanitarium Association at the next annual constituency meeting by proposing the addition of a number of new Association members favorable to him. Under the rules, those in attendance at the annual meeting could, by a two-thirds vote, admit new members who had signed the declaration of principles and had made a small stated financial contribution to the Association. A sufficient number of friendly new members might then provide the two-thirds vote necessary to accept the merger. Harris and Judd believed that to thwart Kellogg's scheme, they needed the help of the top Adventist leadership to secure a sufficient attendance at the annual meeting of Adventists opposed to the merger.

Before deciding whether or not the church should once more involve itself to any extent in matters relating to the Battle Creek Sanitarium, Adventist leaders carried on an extensive correspondence with the church members of the sanitarium constituency and found that a "great majority" of them opposed Kellogg's merger plan and favored, instead, the continuation of the sanitarium under its old form of organization. Several Adventist leaders also conferred with W. K. Kellogg and received from him a pledge to help finance any efforts they might make to keep the sanitarium's assets from coming under the tight permanent control of seven individuals.

In October 1942, at about the same time that he met with Adventist leaders, W. K. Kellogg had his last personal encounter with his brother. They talked for more than five hours, and Will later recalled that their discussion had been "the most rambling conversation I ever had with anybody in my life." Will believed that some of the ideas Dr. Kellogg had advanced were "unheard of, unreasonable, and nonsensical," and that they demonstrated that the doctor was slipping mentally. The younger man, who evidently believed that some of the doctor's personal associates were trying to gain possession of the sanitarium's cash for their own selfish purposes, again tried to persuade John Harvey to request some of his old Adventist colleagues to help him to continue the operation of the sanitarium in its original manner. The doctor refused to consider the suggestion and began a long tirade against the Adventists, whereupon Will, who believed that the quarter of a century in which he had served the sanitarium as unofficial business manager gave him some interest in the institution, proceeded to give his brother a "tongue-chastisement" such as he had never before given anyone "during my rather long life." Later Will commented that the fact "that the doctor did not resent some of the cutting things I said to him indicated very plainly to me that he, in a way, admitted the truthfulness of my remarks."

For both sides in the developing controversy, the annual sanitarium constituency meeting scheduled for March 31, 1943, became crucial. Some six weeks prior to it, William H. Branson, vice-president of the General Conference of Seventh-day Adventists, after being assured by W. K. Kellogg of financial support of at least $5,000, addressed a letter to the Adventist members of the sanitarium Association urging them to be present in Battle Creek in person on March 31, since only in that way could they stop the proposed merger of the sanitarium and the Race Betterment Foundation. Branson indicated that traveling expenses of members opposed to the merger plan would be paid, and they would also receive an allowance for meals and for time lost from their regular employment.

From 400 to 500 persons assembled on March 31 to seek admission as new members of the sanitarium Association. Dr. Kellogg proposed approximately one third of the group for membership. His opposition, who had determined to beat the doctor at his own game, sponsored the others. The decision as to which of the applicants to admit to membership rested with the old members present. For the first time at an annual meeting an anti-Kellogg majority dominated the proceedings and rejected all the doctor's nominees. In spite of the delaying tactics employed by Dr. Kellogg as the meeting's chairman, the Association members then proceeded to accept 241 new members recruited by the anti-Kellogg forces.

The proceedings of the annual meeting continued the next day. Kellogg secured an injunction from local circuit court judge Blain W. Hatch that, according to him, automatically adjourned the meeting. When the deputy sheriff arrived and presented the injunction, Kellogg and his supporters immediately left the room. Upon reading the injunction, however, the legal counsel of the opposition expressed the opinion that it merely prohibited the General Conference Corporation of Seventh-day Adventists and W. H. Branson from participating in the proceedings. At the attorney's suggestion, the remaining members agreed upon a temporary recess, after which they reconvened and continued to transact business.

The April 1 meeting elected a nominating committee to bring in recommendations for a new 10-person board of directors for the sanitarium in conformity with the reorganization agreement made in 1938 when the sanitarium bankruptcy trusteeship had been terminated. The members present speedily approved the recommendations of the nominating committee, which included Dr. Harris and Dr. Daniel H. Kress, an old Adventist friend of Kellogg's. Although six of the members of the new board, including Dr. Kellogg, were not Adventists, the doctor refused to accept the decision. He claimed that an illegal "rump" session had elected the new board, and that the members who had done so were acting not as free moral agents but as paid representatives of the General Conference of Seventh-day Adventists. Kellogg obtained a second injunction from judge Hatch that forbade the new board to meet or to transact business.

Both sides now prepared for an extended legal battle, while a temporary board appointed by Judge Hatch and composed of members of both factions operated the sanitarium. Dr. George Thomason attempted to convince Kellogg that he would be able to work in harmony with the board elected on April 1, but the doctor refused to compromise. He maintained that Adventists had never been able to run a successful sanitarium and that "he couldn't either under their authority."

Before the court could rule on the legality of the proceedings of March

31 and April 1, John Harvey Kellogg died. His associates thereupon arranged a court-approved compromise with the Adventist Church. In return for $550,000 in cash and three farms valued at $75,000, which were turned over to a newly formed and Adventist-controlled Michigan Sanitarium Corporation for use in the promotion of medical activities within the state of Michigan, the Adventist members of the sanitarium constituency agreed to allow Dr. James Case and his associates a free hand in running the old Battle Creek Sanitarium.

The strenuous task of providing for new quarters, followed by the struggle to assure complete control of the Battle Creek Sanitarium, had placed a heavy strain on Dr. Kellogg's physical resources. During the last months of his life his hearing and eyesight both deteriorated in a marked way. Shortly before his death he began to suffer from Bell's palsy, and his pride led him to remain secluded in his home so that his condition might not become generally known. The doctor had not yet departed for Florida for the winter when, on the evening of December 11, shortly after a chat with his adopted son Richard, John Harvey suffered an acute attack of bronchitis. To his associate of 20 years, Dr. James Jeffrey, whom the family and friends called to attend him, Kellogg remarked, "Well, maybe this is the last time, doctor." In spite of expert medical attention, Kellogg developed pneumonia and, although he felt so well on December 13 that only Dr. Jeffrey's orders restrained him from making several appointments, he slipped into a coma that night from which he never awakened. Death came to the 91-year-old doctor at 11:30 p.m. on December 14, 1943. Three days later, after a eulogy by Carleton Brooks Miller, pastor of the First Congregational Church of Battle Creek, and prayers by E. L. Pingenot, pastor of the Tabernacle Church of Seventh-day Adventists, and Henry Jordan, sanitarium chaplain, Kellogg was buried by the side of his wife in Battle Creek's Oak Hill Cemetery.

His death brought a host of tributes from people in all walks of life, ranging from political boss Ed Crump, of Memphis, Tennessee, to singing evangelist Homer Rodeheaver and University of Wisconsin sociologist Edward A. Ross. Secretary of the Navy Frank Knox summarized them when he said, "The sudden passing of Dr. Kellogg robs the country of one of its greatest individualists and leaders in medicine. His contribution to national health and well-being was very great and will be long remembered."

AN EPILOGUE

ONE MAY APPROPRIATELY ASK just what John Harvey Kellogg's 70-year campaign to revolutionize American health habits had accomplished. Did the doctor make a permanent contribution to the manner in which Americans think and act, or was he simply a colorful personality, adept at making headlines in his day but properly forgotten after his death?

Among the most significant of his teachings was his insistence upon the interrelationship of health and personal habits. When John Harvey began medical practice, many persons still considered sickness and disease to be either divine judgments or the result of chance, the breathing of the night air, or of a "weak constitution." At the same time the introduction of the germ theory of disease threatened to divert progressive members of the medical profession into a search for the specific microorganisms responsible for all of humanity's physical ills in the hope that by finding a way to combat bacteria, they would solve all of medicine's problems.

Kellogg quickly accepted the germ theory of disease and used it to support his demands for personal and home cleanliness and for uncontaminated supplies of water, milk, and dairy products. At the same time, however, he stressed that improper diet, unhealthful clothing, insufficient rest and recreation, and mental and emotional strain could also cause illness. Furthermore, he recognized that neither the public nor the medical profession would accept the "natural" remedies for sickness that earlier health reformers had suggested unless scientific evidence demonstrated the usefulness of such agents. With this in mind, he not only conducted a number of experiments designed to justify his health teachings, but also regularly perused a wide range of professional literature to find support for his theories in the research activities of others.

Although it would be incorrect to suggest that he alone convinced both professional medical personnel and the average American of the interrelationship of diet, recreation, fresh air, and health, the doctor, by zealously promoting his ideas through lectures, a host of both popular and technical books and articles, and a variety of organizations, did make a major contribution in this area. It must also be noted that the hundreds of doctors, nurses, dietitians, health lecturers, and physical education instructors who had come to accept all or some of his ideas while attending the various schools and training courses he established in connection with the Battle Creek Sanitarium augmented his personal influence.

Dr. Kellogg made an impact on American eating habits that is perhaps even more apparent than his work in publicizing the relationship between common habits and good health. His search for a convenient way to utilize fully the best nutritional components of the cereal grains revolutionized the American breakfast. Not only did the flaking process he discovered open the way to the wider utilization of America's abundant grain harvests, but it also presented the American housewife with one of the first convenience foods. Packaged, ready-to-eat breakfast foods both greatly enlarged the variety of the morning menu and also made it possible to prepare the main ingredient of the meal in a matter of seconds.

His introduction of peanut butter added another widely accepted item to the American diet, and it probably did more to provide a market for peanuts than did the efforts of any other person, with the possible exception of George Washington Carver. John Harvey's development of meatlike products from nuts and legumes combined with wheat gluten has not only helped to enrich the dietary of thousands of persons who for ethical, health, or religious reasons choose to be vegetarians, but

Dr. Kellogg with a feathered friend

LLU Archives & Special Collections

such high-protein foods also hold possibilities for supplementing the diet in countries where the supply of meat is insufficient to provide enough protein for a rapidly expanding population. In addition to his food creations, Dr. Kellogg probably also helped to diversify American eating habits by his repeated emphasis on the desirability of including a wider variety of fruits, vegetables, and nuts in the diet.

John Harvey was among the first to become concerned about the problem of obesity resulting from overeating. He regarded obesity as not just a mere inconvenience or a deterrent to physical attractiveness but a definite health hazard. His repeated calls for moderation in eating, particularly by the growing number of sedentary workers, undoubtedly played a part in initiating the continuing investigation into the relationship between proper weight and good health.

Dr. Kellogg's scientific medical training led him to investigate and to demonstrate the physiological and psychological effects of "natural remedies," such as heat, electricity, hydrotherapy, and corrective exer-

cise. To a large extent he and his colleagues at the Battle Creek Sanitarium gave professional respectability to the wide variety of therapeutic measures employed by today's specialists in physical therapy.

Although he spent the last third of his life outside the Adventist church, Kellogg's personal contributions to that denomination's growth were great. Most Adventists accepted the church's teachings on healthful living largely because Mrs. White introduced them, but Dr. Kellogg's scientific justification of her principles undoubtedly reassured all Adventists, and it probably helped to persuade

Dr. Kellogg in later years

many of them to accept fully those parts of the health reform doctrines that they found strange or uncongenial. With the exception of Ellen White, no other person approached his contribution to the establishment of the large number of Adventist sanitariums founded after 1890. Even those started after the doctor's expulsion from the church had as their pattern the model he had developed at Battle Creek. By precept and example Kellogg helped to direct Adventists into a wide variety of social service activities. Although many of them went into a decline during the period when the doctor found himself in conflict with church leaders, they later reappeared in somewhat altered form and have since continued to be an important part of the Adventist idea of Christian witness.

John Harvey Kellogg was never satisfied with his accomplishments—he always saw much more that he believed needed to be done. For this reason, in all probability, he would have discounted the changes in American life traceable to his lifelong endeavor to promote biologic living. It seems clear, however, that he was a man who changed many of America's eating habits, who contributed to an awareness of the relationship between many "common" and "simple" habits and personal health and physical well-being, who was an early proponent of what today is called "preventive medicine," and who helped to establish a tradition of health doctrines and social service among Seventh-day Adventists. If Kellogg did not succeed in converting all Americans to a vegetarian diet and in persuading them to discard coffee, tea, alcoholic beverages, and tobacco, it was not because he did not make a major effort in that direction.

INDEX

A

Acidophilus bacteria, 58, 121
Adams, Ross, 206
Addams, Jane, 169
Aerobics, 54
Akeley, Carl, 77
Alcohol, 23, 40, 48, 59, 85, 91, 94, 106, 172,
    173, 208, 212, 231
Alcott, William, 24, 25
Amadon, George W., 193
American Association for the Advancement of
    Science, 39
American Association of Medical Milk
    Commissions, 88
American Book Company, 91
American College of Surgeons, 111
American Health and Temperance Association,
    107
American Home Economics Association, 161
American Medical Association, 38, 39, 194
American Medical Missionary Board, 207
American Medical Missionary College, 104-106,
    172, 173, 175, 187
American Medical Missionary College
    Settlement House, 172. 173
American Medical Temperance Quarterly, The, 94
American Public Health Association, 34, 39
American Soybean Association, 88
American Vegetarian Society, 23
Amundsen, Roald, 77
"And He Ate Meat," 42
Aristocracy of Health, The, 86
Association of American Medical Colleges, 105
Atlantic City, New Jersey, 73, 76
Austin, Dr. Harriet, 27
Autointoxication, 57, 58, 110

B

Babson, Roger, 78
Bacteria, 213
Bacteriological World and Modern Medicine, 93
Bailey, John, 76
Baker, Henry, 211
Barron, C. W., 78, 151
Barton, Clara, 119
Bates, Joseph, 16, 20
Battle Creek Breakfast Food Company, The,
    Quincy, Illinois, 118
Battle Creek College (Kellogg's), 100-104, 187,
    221
Battle Creek College (SDA), 64, 95-98, 155,
    186, 221
Battle Creek Diet System Sterilized Bran, 204
Battle Creek Food Company, 102, 103, 170,
    205, 206, 219
Battle Creek Food Idea, The, 94
Battle Creek Idea, The, 93
Battle Creek, Michigan, and Sanitarium, 73-76
Battle Creek Sanitarium, 30, 37-39, 41, 44, 50,
    54, 56, 62-84, 87-89, 92, 93, 98-100,
    103, 104, 106, 109, 110, 113-118,
    120, 121, 123, 134, 135, 138, 139,
    141, 145-151, 154-157, 160, 161,
    169-172, 174, 180, 181, 186, 187,
    193-199, 205, 207, 209, 210, 217-227
    and depression, 81, 209, 217, 218
    court settlement, 227
    expansion of, 68, 67
    fire, 72, 73, 75, 105, 113, 183
    golden anniversary, 79, 88
    government buys building, 220, 221
    Kellogg's final struggle for, 217-227
    merger agreement, 222-227
    1927 expansion, 80, 81
    Normal School of Physical Education, 100
    put into receivership, 217, 218
    rebuilding of, 73, 74, 183, 184
    rechartering of, 69-71
    School of Domestic Economy, 99, 100
    School of Health and Home Economics,
        100, 161
    School of Hygiene, 98, 99, 155
    taxing of, 75, 76
    Training School for Medical Missionaries,
        99
    Training School for Nurses, 98-100
    transferred to Phelps Building, 221, 222
Battle Creek Sanitarium and Benevolent
    Association, 220, 222
Battle Creek Skallops, 120
Battle Creek Steaks, 120
Battle Creek Tabernacle, 193, 227
Battle Creek Toasted Corn Flake Company,
    199-205
Beard, George M., 36
Bell, Goodloe Harper, 18, 96
Bellevue Hospital Medical School, 33-36, 39,
    108, 211
Benton Harbor, Michigan, 73
Berlin, 37, 110
Berrien Springs, Michigan, meeting, 191, 192
Bible and meat-eating, 41
Biddle, A. P., 79
Billroth, Anton, 37
Billroth, Theodore, 109
Biologic living, 40-61, 111, 212, 213, 219
Bird, John, 76
Blanket, electric, 124, 133
Bolin, C. D., 198

Bondholders' Protective Association, 218, 222
Bourdeau, Augustin C., 193, 194
Bowery Mission, 168
Bradford, Edward N., 77
Branson, William H., 225, 226
Breakfast foods, 94, 196-206
     competition in, 166, 198
     development of, 114-118
     J. H. Kellogg's first idea for, 35
Brisbane, Arthur, 76
Bromose, 119
Brownsberger, Sidney, 64, 96
Bryan, William Jennings, 57, 77, 79
*Bulletin of the Battle Creek Sanitarium and
     Hospital Clinic,* 93
Burbank, Luther, 208, 209
Burroughs, John, 78, 107
Butler, Clara, 153
Butler, George I., 65, 85, 153, 180, 181, 190
Butler, Hiland, 153
Byington, Fletcher, 18

C

Caffeine, 59
Calhoun County Medical Association, 38
Calomel, 22
Campbell, M. N., 193, 194
Candy, health, 121
Cannon, Joseph, 78
Cantor, Eddie, 77
Caramel Cereal Coffee, 120, 196
Carver, George Washington, 229
Case, James T., 80, 147, 193
Cattell, J. McKeen, 209
Cereals, see Breakfast foods
Chair, vibrating, 121, 127
Chautauquas, 77, 83, 85, 86, 107
Cheese, 44
Cheyne, Dr. George, 23
Chicago Branch Sanitarium, 169
Chicago Loop, 169, 170
Chicago Medical Mission, 104, 168-176, 182,
     211
     meals offered, 171, 172
     Visiting Nurse Service, 171-173
     Workingmen's Home, 171, 172
Chicago Women's Club, 173
Chicago World's Fair, 123, 169, 171
Chittenden, R. H., 48
Chocolate, 40, 59
Christian Help Bands, 176
Christian Science, 61
Clark, Francis, 78
Clarke, George R., 168, 169
Clothing, white, 147

Coffee, 40
Cola drinks, 59
Coles, Dr. L. B., 26, 27
College of Medical Evangelists, see Loma Linda
          Medical School
Columbia Gramaphone Company, 54
Columbian Exhibition, 87
Combe, Andrew, 23
Committee of Fifty to Study the Tobacco
          Problem, 107
Condiments, 45
Cornaro, Luigi, 24
Cornell, M. E., 16
Cornflakes, see Breakfast foods
Corsets, 60
Country Club Hotel, 81, 82
Crump, Ed, 227
Currie, James, 34
Curtiss, Glenn, 81, 82

D

Dabney, Charles W., 119, 120
Dafoe, A. R., 121
Daniells, Arthur G., 185, 186, 190, 191, 194
d'Arsonval, Jacques-Arsine, 122
Davenport, Charles B., 209
Dewey, John, 97
Dickinson, Lansing, 13
Diet, 40-50
     natural, 46
Digestive disorders, 40, 49
Dionne, Marie, 121
Dixon, R. L., 214
Dowkontt, George, 168
Dress, 60, 61
Drugs, 58
Dunster, Edward S., 33, 108
DuPont, Alfred, 78
Durant, Will, 78, 90
Dynamometer, muscle, 122, 123

E

Earhart, Amelia, 141
Eaton, Ella, see Kellogg, Ella
Eddy, Mary Baker, 61
Education, 188
Edwards, S.P.S., 104, 105
Eggs, 44, 45, 48
Electric light bath, 123
Electrotherapeutics, 36, 60, 111, 170
Emmanuel Missionary College, 186
Emmet, Thomas, 109
Estell, Angie, 82
Estell, Gertrude, 82
Eugenics, 194, 207-211

Eugenics Registry, 210
Evans, I. H., 192, 193
Exercise, 54, 111
Exercising machines, 54, 121-123

F

Fairfield, W. J., 38, 39
Federal Trade Commission, 44
Federation of Women's Clubs, 161
Ferris, Woodbridge, 79, 90
Finck, Henry T., 90
First Book in Physiology and Hygiene, 91
Fischer, Louis, 88
Fisher, Irving, 54, 55, 78, 79, 107, 207
Flaked cereals, see Breakfast foods
Fletcher, Horace, 49, 50, 107, 147
Fletcherizing, 49, 50
Flies, 213
Flint, Austin, 34
Folk, Joseph, 77
Ford, Henry, 107
French, Theresa, 18
Fresh air, 56, 57, 125, 212
Froebel, Friedrich, 29, 96
Fruit, 46, 47
Fuller, Margaret, 29, 30, 96
Funk, F. W., 50

G

Galton, Sir Francis, 207, 208
Gandhi, Mohandas, 88
Garcia, Alberto, 159
Geisel, Carolyn, 148
General Conference Executive Committee, 184,
    190, 191
General Conference Fall Council of 1903, 190
General Conference Foreign Missions Board,
    184
God and health, 61
Good Health, 50, 66, 88, 91-93, 150, 155, 160,
    207, 210; see also Health Reformer
Good Health Publishing Company, 89, 90
Good Housekeeping, 204
Gorgas, William, 107
Gove, Mrs. Mary, 25
Graham, Sylvester, 24-28, 32, 46
Grainger, Percy, 77
Grains, 46, 47
Granola, 115, 118, 196
Granose Flakes, 117, 118, 166, 201
Granula, 27, 114, 115
Granville, J. Mortimer, 37
Grenfell, Sir Wilfred, 207

H

Hall, James, 22
Halliburton, Richard, 77
Hamilton, Frank, 108
Hanks, Horace T., 109
Hanly, J. Frank, 149
Harper and Brothers, 91
Harriman, Karl, 150
Harris, R. H., 223-225
Harrison, Beverly, 213
Hartelius, T. J., 37
Haskell, Mrs. Caroline, 163, 164
Haskell, Stephen N., 65, 188, 190
Haskell Home for Orphans, 164, 165
Hatch, Blain W., 226
Health and Efficiency League of America, 107
Health and the mind, 61
Health, or How to Live, 27, 28
Health Reform Institute, See Battle Creek
    Sanitarium
Health reform movement, 22-28
Health Reformer, 28, 30, 36, 38, 57, 64, 66, 91,
    92; see also Good Health
Health Series of Physiology and Hygiene, 91
Henderson, Mrs. Mary B., 100
Henderson, Mary F., 86
Henry, David I., 102
Herald of Health, see Water Cure Journal
"Hildah's kid," 157, 159, 160
Hillis, Newell Dwight, 79, 209
Hitchcock, Edward, 23
Holstein-Friesian Association of America, 88
Home Handbook of Domestic Hygiene and Rational
    Medicine, The, 90
Hydropathy and hydrotherapy, 25-27, 51-53,
    60, 170
Hypnotism, 61

I

Illinois, University of, Medical School, 106
Illinois State Board of Health, 106
International Health and Temperance
    Association, 93
Irwin, George A., 71, 184, 185
Iturbi, José, 77

J

Jackson, J. C., 21, 26, 27, 114
James White Memorial Home, 163-165
Janeway, Edward G., 34
Jeffrey, James, 227
Johnson, Martin, 77
Jones, Alonzo T., 185, 190, 191
Jones, Samuel M., 86

Jordan, David Start, 209
Jordan, Henry, 227
Journal of Inebriety, 94
Judd, George E., 223, 224
Julian, W. A., 78, 222
Jungle, The, 42

K

Kedzie, Robert Clarke, 212
Kellogg, Ann, 14-19, 152, 153; and hydrother-
    apy, 15, 16
Kellogg, Clara, see Butler, Clara
Kellogg, Ella, 36, 60, 61, 85, 99, 134, 138,
    154-161, 227
Kellogg, Emma, 15, 16
Kellogg, Frank J., 199
Kellogg, John Harvey,
    ability as publicist, 77-79, 87
    activities in Chicago, 104, 168-176
    addressed General Conference, 84, 91-107
    aged, home for, 163-165
    ambition, 143, 144
    American Medical Missionary College,
        104-107
    as educator, 87, 95
    as lecturer, 83-88
    as surgeon, 108-113
    as writer, 88-94
    assisted father at San, 63
    associates, 148
    attempt to reconcile with SDAs, 185-192
    attempts San reform, 67, 68
    attends Bellevue Hospital Medical School,
        33-36
    attends Michigan State Normal College,
        30
    attends Trall's health school, 30-32
    attitude toward ministers, 84, 178-180,
        184
    Battle Creek College (SDA), 95-98
    B.C. San falls under dominance of, 65, 66
    becomes San's physician in chief, 62-64
    Berrien Springs meeting, 191, 192
    birth, 16
    break with Adventist church, 178-195
    business trips, 135, 136, 142
    charitable gifts, 150, 151
    charity operations, 113, 162
    Chicago Medical Mission, 168-176
    child-raising, theory of, 157-160
    children, attitude toward, 152-160
    children of relatives, 152-154
    Christian Help Bands, 176
    city missions, concept of, 174
    coins name "Sanitarium," 65

    conflict with Daniells, 186-191
    conflict with SDA Church, 70-72, 74, 91,
        106, 153, 165, 175, 176, 178-195,
        223-227
    continuing medical education, 35-38,
        109, 110
    could work long periods, 134-137
    covenant with God, 64
    creates meat substitutes, 120
    critical attitude, 178, 179
    criticism, attitude toward, 144, 145
    death, 227
    debts, 151
    decides to study medicine, 32
    develops breakfast cereals, 114-118
    dictation, 135, 136
    diet theories, 40-50
    disliked surgery, 108, 109, 112
    dominate, need to, 144, 145
    dream of teaching, 19
    dress, style of, 146, 147
    dropped from SDA Church, 74, 91, 193-
        195
    drugs, attitude toward, 58, 59
    E. G. White, attitude toward, 180-183, 191
    E. G. White points out failings, 143-145
    early education, 18
    education, helped others get, 162, 163
    educational philosophy, 97
    enrolls at U. of Michigan, 32, 33
    eugenics, 194, 207-211
    Eugenics Registry, 209, 210
    exhaustion, 137-140
    expands San, 68, 69
    expels SDAs from San board, 194
    family moves to Battle Creek, 17
    faults, recognized some, 146
    final struggle to control San, 218-227
    financial income, 150, 151
    Florida projects, 81, 82
    food creations, 114-121
    food industry, turns to, 196-206
    foster children, 116, 152-160
    gave surgery fees to S.D.A. hospitals, 113
    gives up meat, 28
    golf, 142
    graduation from Bellevue, 35, 36
    graduation thesis, 35
    headstrong in youth, 143
    health ideas, 36-61
    health reform among SDAs, 84, 85, 178,
        179
    height, 28, 64, 143
    helped edit *Health Reformer,* 64, 91, 92,
        150
    humanitarian activities, 162-177

hypnotic influence, 148
ignores own health, 139
in Berlin, 37, 110
in London, 37 109, 110
in Mexico, 142
in St. Petersburg, 37
in Stockholm, 37
in Vienna, 37, 109-111
influence of, 228-231
inventions, didn't profit from, 133
inventor, 114-125
J. White treated him like son, 28
kindness of, 147
lack of rest, 56, 134-136, 138, 139
legal battles with brother, 120, 198-205
loses control of San, 76, 79, 80
loses lawsuits with brother, 203, 204
marriage of, 154, 155
Mary Kelsey, 154
meals, 134, 140
meat packers, 41-44
medical professional meetings, 87
membership, church, dropped, 193, 194
Michigan health legislation, 215, 216
Michigan State Board of Health, 211-216
miserliness, 149
nearly dies, 139, 140
1903 GC Fall Council, 191
opposes 1927 San expansion, 80, 81
orphanage, 163-165
pantheism, 188-190
patience, lack of, 146
persecution complex, 145
personal habits, 134-142
personal health reform, 28
personality, 143-149
physical collapse, 138-140
physical health, 137-140
politics, attitude toward, 148, 149
prayed before surgery, 112, 113
pushes J. White off San board, 65
racial issue, 176
reaction to E. White's criticism, 182, 183
recharters San, 69-72, 180
recreation, 141, 142
relationship with brothers and sisters, 153, 154
religious faith, 178-180, 194
"Residence, The," 156, 177
responsibility, failure to change, 141-145
revives Battle Creek College, 100-103
salary, 150
San merger agreement, 222-227
sarcasm, 145
secretary, several as, 28
set type for Health Reformer, 28, 91

significance of, 228-231
social consciousness, 162-177
social legislation, 177
spoke at camp meetings, 85
suggested as SDA medical secretary, 164
takes over editorship of Health Reformer, 92
talkativeness, 145, 146
teaches chemistry, 31, 95
teaches school, 29, 95
temperance lectures, 85, 106, 107
theological beliefs, 91, 178, 187, 188, 194
took care of parents, 152, 153
travels to Europe, 36, 37, 66, 108
trial before Calhoun County Medical
    Association, 38, 39
tuberculosis, 29, 137, 139
tutored medical students, 97, 98, 103
vegetarian, decides to become, 28
warned about health, 139
wealth, philosophy of, 151, 162, 211
wife, relationship with, 155, 156, 161
worked at Review and Herald, 20, 28, 30
worked in broom shop, 19
working habits, 134-139
"yes-men," 148
Kellogg, John L., 199
Kellogg, John Preston, 13-19, 30, 62, 63, 143,
    148, 152, 153
Kellogg, Mary, 13, 14
Kellogg, Merritt, 17, 30, 31, 144, 153, 154
Kellogg, Richard, 159, 222, 227
Kellogg, Smith, 13
Kellogg, Will Keith, 67, 116-118, 120, 141,
    149, 150, 153, 194, 197-206, 211,
    223-225
Kellogg Food Company, 199-206
Kellogg, W. K., Foundation, 211
Kellogg's Sterilized Bran, 204
Kellogg's Toasted Bran Flakes, 203
Kellogg's Toasted Rice Flake and Biscuit
    Company, 202
Kellogg's Toasted Rice Flakes, 202
Kellogg's Toasted Wheat Flakes, 201
Kelly, Howard A., 112
Kelsey, Mary, see White, Mary Kelsey
Keynes, E. L., 108
Kirkland, B. F., 205
Knox, Frank, 222, 227
Kresge, S. S., 78
Kress, Daniel H., 226

L

L. D. Lax, 121
Lactose, 112
Ladies' Home Journal, 204

Lakewood, New Jersey, 76
Lamson, Mary, 158
Landon, Alfred M., 148
Lane, Sir Arbuthnot, 57, 110
Laxa, 121
Laxative foods, 49, 58, 121
Lay, H. S., 27, 62, 63, 68
Leffler, Emil, 102
Legumes, 45, 47, 118, 119
Lewis, Dio, 27
Life Boat Magazine, 175
Life Boat Mission, 173, 174
Life Extension Institute, 107
Lindsay, Kate, 99, 154, 155
Lindsey, Ben, 77, 209
Lines, O. T., 35
Lister, Joseph, 34, 110
Literary Digest, 92
Little, C. C., 210
Littlejohn, W. H., 28
Living Temple, The, 74, 91, 188, 189, 191, 218
Loma Linda Medical School, 195
London, 37, 109, 110
London Medical Council, 105
Loughborough, John Norton, 62, 179

M

McAuley, Jerry, 168
McClure, S. S., 77
McCoy, Lycurgus, 154
MacFadden, Bernarr, 221
Mackey, Tom, 174
Maclean, Donald, 33, 108
McLearn, Alexander, 96
Macmillan Company, 91
Magan, Percy T., 148, 191, 224
Malted Nuts, 119
Manure experiment, 41, 44
Mayo, Charles, 110
Mayo, Will, 107, 110, 161
Meals, number of, 49
Meat and meat-eating, 40-44
Meat packers, conflict with, 42-44
Meat substitutes, 119, 120, 197, 230
Medical education, 19th century, 21, 22, 30-32
Medical Missionary, 93, 94
Medical Missionary and Benevolent Association,
    103-105, 164-168, 172, 177, 183,
    184, 190, 192, 193, 197, 207
Medical Missionary Conferences, 207
Medicine, early American, 21-27, 32
Metcalfe, William, 23, 24
Metchnikoff, Elie, 57, 58
"Methuselah's Meat," 42, 43
Miami-Battle Creek Sanitarium, 81, 82, 102,

206, 210, 220
Michigan, health legislation, 215
Michigan, University of, 32, 33, 103
Michigan Anti-Cigarette Society, 107
Michigan Medical Association, 38, 39
Michigan Sanitarium and Benevolent
    Association, 70, 71, 194
Michigan State Agricultural College, 214
Michigan State Board of Health, 211-216
Michigan State Medical Society, 32
Michigan State Normal College, Ypsilanti, 30
Michigan Supreme Court, 204
Michigan Women's Press Association, 161
Milk, 44, 45, 48
Miller, Carleton Brooks, 227
Millerite Movement, 16
Mind and health, 61
Minneapolis General Conference of 1888, 168,
    178
Missionary Acre Fund, 167, 168, 193
Mississippi Valley Medical Association, 87
Mitchell, Helen S., 102
Modern Medicine Publishing Company, 90
Monroe, Henry, 170
Moody Bible Institute, 174
Moral Reformer, The, 24
Mormons, 86
Mussey, Reuben D., 23, 24

N

National Association of Life Underwriters, 88
National Congress of Mothers, 161
National Microscopical Congress, 39
National Milk Congress, 44, 88
National Restaurant Association, 88
Natural Method of Curing the Diseases of the Body,
    The, 23
Negroes, 176
New Dietetics, The, 90
New York Academy of Medicine, 87
New York World's Fair (1939), 219
Niblack, A. P., 78, 123
Niles, Michigan, 73
North, Walter, 204
North Central Association of Colleges and
    Secondary Schools, 100
Northern Nut Growers Association, 88
Nut Butter, 118
Nut meal, 119
Nuts, 47
Nuttose, 120

O

Obesity, 48, 49, 54
Olsen, Ole A., 169, 176

Osborn, Chase, 79, 213-216
O'Shea, M. V., 91
Otsego, Michigan, 20, 21
"Our Home on the Hillside," 26, 27
Owen, Robert, 77

P

Pacific Garden Mission, 168, 171, 174
Pain, 59, 60
Palmer, Alonzo, 32
Pan-American Medical Congress, 87
Panama-Pacific Exposition, 209
Pantheism, 188-190
Paramels, 121
Parkinson, James A., 76
Patterson, Joseph H., 78
Paulson, David, 147
Pavlov, 37
Peabody, George, 107
Peanut butter, 118, 119
Peaslee, Edmund, 34, 108
Peddicord, Edward S., 173
Penney, J. C., 78
Pep, 149
Perky, Henry D., 115, 116
Phelps Sanatorium, 221
Philosophy of Health, 26
Pinchot, Amos, 77
Pinchot, Gifford, 77
Pingenot, E. L., 227
Plain Facts About Sexual Life, 89, 155
Plunkett, Sir Horace, 77, 209
Pneumograph, 124
Popenoe, Paul, 209
Post, C. W., 73, 120
Post Tavern, Battle Creek, 41
Posture, 55, 56
Potato Association of America, 88
Prescott, William W., 190-192
Priessnitz, Vincent, 25, 37
Primitive Physic, 21
Principles of Physiology Applied to the Preservation of Health, 23
Proper Diet for Man, 89, 155
Prostitutes, 173
Protein, 47, 48
Protose, 120

R

Race Betterment Conferences, 209, 210
Race Betterment Foundation, 101-103, 151, 207, 209, 221, 222, 225
Racial issue, 176
Rational Hydrotherapy, 90, 91
Rauschenbusch, Walter, 162

Republican Party, 148, 149
"Residence, The," 156
Rest, 56
Review and Herald Publishing Association, 17, 20, 30, 89, 92, 186, 187
Riis, Jacob, 209
Robinson, J. E., 79
Rockefeller, John D., Jr., 78
Rodeheaver, Homer, 227
Roosevelt, Theodore, 86
Ross, Edward A., 227
Russell, William, 65

S

Sadler, W. S., 147, 174, 175, 196, 197
Salt, 45
St. Louis World's Fair, 87
St. Petersburg, 37
Sanitarium Equipment Company, 122
Sanitarium Food Company, 74, 196-201, 220
Sanitariums, growth of, 165, 166, 231
Sanitas Food Company, 197-201
Sanitas Wheat Flakes, 201
Sanitation, 212, 213
Sayre, Lewis, 34, 108
Science and religion, 91
Science in the Kitchen, 160
Second Book in Physiology and Hygiene, 91
Seventh-day Adventist Church, Kellogg's conflicts with, 70-74, 94, 96, 106, 153, 174-176, 178-195, 222-227
Seventh-day Adventist Educational Society, 95
Seventh-day Adventist Medical Missionary and Benevolent Association, see Medical Missionary and Benevolent Association
Seventh-day Adventist Publishing Association, see Review and Herald Publishing Association
Sheldon, Charles, 78
Sherin, S. S., 174
Sherman, H. C., 48
Shew, Dr. Joel, 15, 25, 26
Shredded Wheat, 115, 116
"Simple Life, The," 88
Sinclair, Harry F., 78
Sinclair, Upton, 41
Sinusoidal current, 111, 122
Smith, Stephen, 34, 35, 79
Smith, Uriah, 64
Société d'Hygiène, 37
Soy milk, 121
Soybeans, 47, 229
Spicer, William A., 188
Spiritual Gifts, 20
Stagg, Alonzo, 107

Stanley, Ann, see Kellogg, Ann
Star of Hope Mission, 174
Starr, Floyd, 160
Starr Commonwealth for Boys, 160
Steele, Mrs. A. S., 177
Stefánsson, Vilhjálmur, 77
Stewart, Anna, 99
Stewart, Charles, 79-81, 217-219
Stockholm, 37
Straus, Nathan, 76
Studies in Character Building, 160
Sugar, 45
Sunlight, 56, 57
Surgical instruments, 121
Surgical recovery, 111, 112
Sutherland, E. A., 97

T

Tabernacle Church, 193, 194
Taft, William Howard, 77
Tait, Lawson, 110
Talks With Girls, 160
Tea, 40, 59, 107, 163, 208, 231
Thomas, Lowell, 77
Thomason, George, 147, 218, 219, 224, 226
Thomson, Samuel, 23
Time, 211
Tissier, 58
Tobacco, 40, 59, 91
Townsend, Charles, 77
Trall, R. T., 21, 26, 27, 92
Trall's Hygieo-Therapeutic College, 30-32, 63, 91
Tranquilizer, water as, 52, 53
Trembley, Jennie, 30
Trudeau Society, 140
Tuttle, Arthur J., 217

U

United States, health in early, 21-23
U.S. Air Force, 54
U.S. Department of Agriculture, 43
U.S. Naval Academy, 78, 123
Unwed mothers, 173
Uses of Water in Health and Disease, The, 89, 90
Ussher, Clarence, 207

V

Vaccination, 59
Van Buren, William, 108
Vegetables, 45, 46
Vegetarianism, 23-25, 40-48
Vienna, 37, 109-111
Vienna Polyclinic, 37, 111
Visiting Nurses Association, 171

Vocational education, 96
Voelker, Paul F., 101, 102

W

Waggoner, E. J., 97
Ward, Montgomery, 78
Water as tranquilizer, 52, 53
Water cure, see Hydropathy and hydrotherapy
Water Cure Journal, 15, 16, 26
Water filter, 133
Water Street Mission, 168
Welch, Edgar, 78
Wesley, John, 21
Wessels, Francis, 169
Wessels, Henry, 169
West, Luther, 102
West Point, 123
Western Health Reform Institute, see Battle
    Creek Sanitarium
"What Is Disease?" 35
Wheat Flakes, see Breakfast Foods
White, Edson, 30, 176
White, Ellen G., 20, 21, 27, 28, 30, 57, 62-65,
    68, 72, 73, 84, 107, 113, 138, 139,
    143, 146, 148, 163, 175-184, 188-
    192, 194, 197, 230, 231
    counsels Kellogg, 143-145, 180-183
    pleads for unity between JHK, Daniells, 192
    warns Kellogg about health, 139
White, James, 20, 27, 28, 30-33, 62-64, 68, 69,
    92, 107, 145, 163, 164, 165, 180, 190
White, Mary Kelsey, 154
White, W. C., 30, 154, 180, 181, 183, 192, 194
Wickersham, George W., 77
Willard, Frances, 161
Winternitz, Wilhelm, 37, 123
Wölfler, Anton, 109, 110
Women's Christian Temperance Union, 85, 161
Women's League, 161
Wood, C. E., 76
Wood, James, 108
Woodruff, Wilford, 86
Workingmen's Home, 171, 172

Y

Yogurt, 45, 58
Young Women's Christian Association, 161

Z

Zander, Gustaf, 37, 121, 122, 133
Ziegler (B. C.) and Company, 220